# COMMONSENSE CONSTRUCTIVISM

# International Relations in a Constructed World

# COMMONSENSE CONSTRUCTIVISM
## or the making of world affairs

**RALPH PETTMAN**

*M.E.Sharpe*
Armonk, New York
London, England

**Library of Congress Cataloging-in-Publication Data**

Pettman, Ralph.
    Commonsense constructivism, or, The making of world affairs / by Ralph Pettman.
        p. cm. — (International relations in a constructed world)
    Includes bibliographical references and index.
    ISBN 0-7656-0577-5 (cloth : alk. paper)
        1. International relations. 2. Constructivism (Philosophy) I. Title: Commonsense
constructivism. II. Title: Making of world affairs. III. Title. IV. Series

JZ 1308.P48 2000
327.1′01—dc21                                                                99-087793

Printed in the United States of America

The paper used in this publication meets the minimum requirements of
American National Standard for Information Sciences
Permanence of Paper for Printed Library Materials,
ANSI Z 39.48-1984.

∞

BM (c)   10    9    8    7    6    5    4    3    2    1

# Contents

# Acknowledgments

This book has been thirty years in the making and I'm grateful indeed to all those who helped. They are many by now—far too many to name here. That said, I would like to thank three people in particular.

For the last few years Jim Rolfe has been my closest critic. As I inched toward the obvious, it was he who did most to keep me honest. It was a task he performed with all the aplomb of the professional soldier he once was. Thanks, Jim.

Vendulka Kubálková pointed out my proclivity for "commonsense constructivism." It is her term and it could not be more apt. She also helped me to recast the manuscript so that my radical affinity with the Miami Group might be made more apparent. Thanks, VK.

Nick Onuf went through it one last time with a fine-toothed comb. We still disagree, but not by much. Thanks, Nick.

# COMMONSENSE CONSTRUCTIVISM

# Introduction

# Commonsense Constructivism

## In the Beginning . . .

I first encountered International Relations (IR) as an undergraduate student in Adelaide, South Australia. The course I took then discussed contemporary states, the national interest, the balance of power, causes of wars, alliance structures, and the United Nations. It did so in an historically discursive way, and our textbook was Hans Morgenthau's analysis of power and political "realism," *Politics Among Nations*.

International Relations in Australia at that time was very much a hand-me-down version of what was taught in the imperial mother country, Britain. Morgenthau's American textbook marked a transition, therefore. What had been a discipline with a strong British accent (and literally so, since our lecturer was from the London School of Economics and Political Science) was beginning to lose its characteristic cadence. International Relations at that time was becoming more American, and the choice of text symbolized that change. Thus, while we were given the works of British analysts to admire, and in particular E.H. Carr's *The Twenty Years' Crisis*, the text was *Politics Among Nations*, and the approved approach was U.S.-style *realpolitik.*

## The Behavioralist Turn

Following a well-trodden path, I went to Britain and did my postgraduate work at the above-mentioned London School of Economics and Political Science (LSE). There I was introduced to an even more notable American approach, namely, behavioralism. The Americans had emerged from World War II top dogs of the democratic world. They had emerged to face a well-organized ideological antagonist, however, and American state-makers felt the need to foster the study of world affairs as a consequence. A confrontation of the Cold War kind required a discipline with the power to explain and predict. The power to control world affairs presupposes such a capacity, and the most reliable knowledge—the kind that best allows of prediction and control—is scientific knowledge. It is no accident therefore that the American discipline of world affairs became at this time a self-consciously scientizing one.

I learned at the LSE that scientizing meant giving human rationality primary cultural status and that this was a European cause that dated from the seventeenth century or thereabouts, and arguably from the ancient Greeks. Eminent Europeans have promoted it globally ever since, though they have had to contend with copious evidence of human irrationality in the process, much of that on their own continent.

I also learned that, by the eighteenth and nineteenth centuries, rationalism had come into its own as a way of getting not only to God or wealth or honor, but to ends defined in rationalistic terms alone. In its broadest sense, rationalism means the commitment to reason, the willingness to follow the use of the reasoning mind wherever it might lead (Cottingham 1984). Having made this mind-move in general, however, one can double or square it, as it were, and use reason in ways specifically designed to provide reliable knowledge. The "social sciences" were one outcome of this doubling process, with thinkers like Auguste Comte expressing the hope that the study of society could be made to match the study of nature in scientific terms. Comte saw the natural and social realms as being fundamentally the same. He saw the power of reason as capable of describing and explaining social realities as natural ones, not only in general terms, but in particular terms as well. He sought as a consequence to apply scientific methods to the study of human society—conceptualize! hypothesize! test! He sought, as he saw it, a "positivist" approach that could be applied to human beings and nature alike (Comte 1875).

Wars, deep ideological conflicts, rampant ethnic passions, and other expressions of "man's inhumanity to man" undermine rationalism's basic promise of boundless human progress. Rationalism in general (and scientific methods in particular) now seems less destined to deliver all good into all of our lives.

The cause has never been abandoned, however, and in the new world of the United States it still finds a congenial home. The inhabitants of the United States have never become as pessimistic as their European counterparts about what social scientizing can achieve. They remain happy to follow Comte's lead, trying to replicate the quantitative rigor of disciplines like physics and chemistry. They still take the behavioralist turn, using exacting research methodologies in the hope that they can get more reliable conclusions, more predictability, and hence greater policy control. The original behavioralists also rummaged through divers disciplines looking for anything they thought might help them describe and explain world affairs, though this more eclectic approach has few adherents now.

The scientizing study of human behavior that has come to characterize the American discipline of world affairs is arguably most notable for the desire it fosters to discriminate between "facts" and "nonfacts," appearance and reality. Anything characterized nonfact is designated nonknowledge in scientific terms. It is "ideological." Anything characterized as a fact is praised as reliable knowledge. It is nonideological. The realm of the real and the meaningful is narrowed down, in other words, to those questions that can be "asked and answered . . . in falsificationist terms [that is, terms amenable to disproof]. Accordingly, statements about political judgment, moral activity, and social justice . . . [are] deemed meaningful only if couched in the language and logic of the value-free analyst responding to . . . data" (George 1994, 59).

To behavioralists, this remains the best way, even perhaps the only way, to get the reliable knowledge that analysts want and state-makers need. To others, however, it is entirely predictable that from the mountains of scientific scholarship should come, in terms of reliable results, an emaciated mouse.

Most British analysts, for example, piqued in part at the loss of British power, write off the attempt to scientize the discipline. Led first by a colonial ally (Bull 1966), they still tend to dismiss behavioralism in all its forms. For a subject like world affairs, they say, the more precise the methodology is, the more trifling the result is likely to be. Thus they argue that if we confine ourselves to "strict standards of verification and proof," there is "very little of significance that can be said about international relations" (Bull 1966, 361). Bull, as a consequence, cites history, philosophy, and law as the most relevant cognate disciplines, not the natural sciences, and he says that intuition, wisdom, and understanding are the most important methodological tools.

To most U.S. analysts, there is really not a debate worth having here. They consider the British, when they bother to consider them at all, irrelevant and quaint. They see no reason whatsoever why the attempt to emulate the success of the physical sciences should not be given a fair go (Kaplan 1966).

British analysts of world affairs are mostly not positivists, in other words, though they are all rationalists in that they all believe the study of international relations should be built upon the "philosophical foundations" of modern science (Bull 1966, 375). Bull himself is self-professedly so.

When Descartes, at the very beginning of the European Enlightenment, demanded that we no longer rely on "unfounded opinions, prejudices, tradition, or external authority, but only upon the authority of reason itself" (Bernstein 1983, 17), we get the first clear statement of these foundations. The British do not reject them. They valorize the use of human reason as an end in itself. They do not, however, valorize the use of reason in ways more systematic than those the subject matter allows, they say.

What I am calling here the British approach (though it is not confined to only British analysts) suggests that a belief in rationalism, both general and particular, has limits. More especially, it suggests that human behavior, including the behavior that characterizes world affairs, may not be explicable in the way that natural scientists explain natural affairs. It argues that there is no radical unity to the sciences and no "hard" science of world affairs, only, perhaps, a "soft" one (Neufeld 1993, 43). Research into the subject, therefore, can reveal only *a* reality, not *the* reality. It cannot provide a very objective description of world affairs. It can try to do so, but we have no way to know if the trying is working or not. We have no way of showing whether this or that version of reality is conclusively true. Decisive experiments able to demonstrate as much are not possible in world affairs. The nature of the subject matter precludes them.

A belief in rationalism, therefore, while it can be used to further our explanatory powers, does not produce "truth" as this is known in the natural sciences. Descartes put his faith in his mental capacities by declaring: "I think, therefore I am." He could find no more fundamental ground to stand upon. He was not to know what such a faith would lead to, though we know now that Descartes' faith brings with it some very mixed blessings indeed. Early thinkers guessed as much. In the eighteenth century, Vico, for example, said in effect "I am, therefore I think," and though it was Descartes whose approach historically prevailed, it was the writings of analysts like Vico that warned us not to expect more as a consequence than the human ego writ large (Descartes [1637] 1912; Vico [1744] 1984).

## International Political Economy

I am getting ahead of myself, however. On my return home from London, I lectured in IR myself. I also watched as nearby countries, like the Solomon Islands, gained their independence. As they went from being colonies to being something much more ambiguous, namely, sovereign nation-states, it was clear that they were in very great danger. Mining transnationals and the like were gearing up to explore and exploit them. A few canny members of the local elites were trying to hold the line. Others, however, were queuing up to do the bidding of these big, highly organized commercial concerns.

I began to read books on dependency theory and neoimperialism. I discovered International Political Economy (IPE).

International Political Economy was a subject-area considerably older than my own, with a longer history and arguably a greater grasp. It clearly had a lot to do with IR, but the Cold War standoff with the Soviets and the communist Chinese seemed to have largely precluded a meaningful account of it within the IR discipline.

The more I read, the more intrigued I became, however. I began talking about IPE in classes on international relations, and when I subsequently went to teach in the United States, I took my interest in IPE with me. Once in class, it quickly became apparent that U.S. students, inhabitants of one of the great historical homes of world liberalism, knew a lot about their own point of view, but notably less about anything else. Karl Marx was not in local curricula, and since Marx was the intellectual mentor of the United States's Cold War enemies, this was no surprise. But Friedrich List was absent too. Alexander Hamilton wasn't read. It was apparent, in fact, that IPE was a kind of lost analytic world and that any attempt to explore that world was distinctly unfashionable.

When I came back to Australia for the second time, I could not get an academic job. As it turned out, this was not because of my interest in nineteenth-century German radicals, but in part at least because I taught IPE as if it were an integral aspect of IR. I got paradigm policed, as it were, and once this became clear, I went to work for the government instead.

The sea change did finally come, since it ultimately proved too difficult to keep politico-economic issues out of the purview of international relations. This was particularly so in those countries like Australia where ministries of foreign affairs were busily renaming themselves "Foreign Affairs *and Trade*" (my emphasis). The discipline's most authoritative arbiters were ultimately obliged to affirm the central importance of its material dimension. My old colleagues were no longer able to say, as one of the most eminent of them did, "I must look at that economics one weekend." Those IR specialists who had heretofore rejected IPE began accommodating and co-opting it, and it was deemed legitimate at last to talk about "international relations" and "international political economy" as two dimensions of the same subject. The field of IR—belatedly but irrevocably—became IR/IPE.

## Postmodernism

Years later I trickled back into academe from government service only to find that the postmodernists had struck. Now, while postmodernism in art and architecture refers to the reaction against the banality of *modernism* (a style of painting and building that arose in the late nineteenth century, exalting function over form), postmodernism in IR/IPE is a term with a somewhat different meaning. It refers here, as it refers in the study of society more generally, to the reaction against the limits of modernity (a style of research that arose in the mid-seventeenth century that exalts rationality, or the use of reason as an end in itself). As indicated above, postwar American IR/IPE was built largely along modernist lines. It prioritized scientizing research. In the 1960s and 1970s, however, a handful of American scholars, under the influence of contemporary—and not so contemporary—European ones, began reexamining the first premises of the scientizing study of world affairs. This opened the door to the postmodernist approach. Through that door came analysts looking for ways to transcend the frame that the scientizers had put around knowing in IR/IPE, and the study of world affairs seemed poised to take another, even more dramatic turn.

As the label suggests, postmodernists want the "Western," modernist mindset put in the past. They want modernist thinking, with all that it entails, superseded.

Western cultures—the cultures of those societies that define themselves as being "Western," that is, because of their Euro-American locale with respect to the "East" and because of their penchant for the rationalist use of reason—place a high value upon the sovereign model of the state. They also place a high value upon liberal capitalism and upon an acute sense of the individualistic self. Transcending all this promises to be a dramatic turn indeed.

The postmodernists undermine the foundations upon which Western culture constructs the "modernist project," though by using the word "project" I do not mean to suggest that this process is deliberately designed and executed. While modernity does have to be made and remade (or it reverts to premodernity or becomes something else), it is a contingent and emergent set of practices. It is not one that was preplanned. No one ever sat down, collectively or alone, and said: let this be the basis upon which world affairs will be built in several hundred years' time. Nonetheless, for the last three or four hundred years, the protagonists of the "modernist project" have been making the world over into tightly governed, territorially bounded entities, embedded in a world market, where individualistic selves prevail and where the objectifying use of reason is the politico-cultural norm. These assumptions come from the European Enlightenment and most political thinkers in the United States are its direct heirs, being culturally committed to knowing about "truth" by rational means and to the kind of world affairs that "modernization" entails.

There is an important proviso to be made at this point. Many analysts in the United States are also committed to knowing about "truth" by revelation too, and not just rationalism. How can this be, however? Rationalism emphasizes reason, not revelation. It is a secularizing doctrine that ought to make religions redundant. It ought to make secular humanism prevail. Why is it, therefore, that we find so many rationalists in the world, in general, and in the United States, in particular, who are religious believers? Shouldn't modernization (in terms of the growing acceptance of rationalism) result in atheism, or at least agnosticism, instead? Doesn't the concept of the cosmos as a vast machine, which rationalism has reinforced for much of its history, militate against religious faith? And if that is the case, how come we have so much religious faith still manifest in ostensibly rationalistic societies like the United States?

The answer lies in the failure of rationalism to detach its proponents from their social milieus. As we shall see in Chapter 2, a commitment to reason makes for a sense of self mentally removed from the world. Those who use reason to follow arguments wherever they lead become removed in this way and begin communicating with each other in the metasocial realm that objectifying opens up. In that realm they create abstract doctrines of human rights, democracy, and the like. This metasocial realm is a public one, however, and as such stands apart from people's private, socially embedded lives.

Despite their public detachment, rationalists remain private/social persons too. As such they are able to highlight nonrational ways of knowing (like religious belief) at the same time as rationalistic ways of knowing (like science). Standing back mentally to look at the world allows people to argue rationally about what they "see" there. They still remain in that world and of that world, however, and in their capacity as socially embedded beings they can and do hold nonrational beliefs. Indeed, the alienating effects of standing back mentally to look at the world can be the direct cause of compensatory behavior, of which religious fervor can be a notable example. The discovery (by rational means) of the nonmechanistic nature of reality lends additional support to the conclusion that religious feeling, while nonrational, may in fact be a feeling worth having and promoting too.

Social scientists, who spend a lot of time studying private (subjectifying, social, nonrational) feelings in a public (objectifying, individuated, rational) way, tend to find it harder to keep the two realms apart in their minds. They succumb more easily to secular humanism. Natural scientists, doctors and the like, who have learned to treat the world like a machine, have learned to keep the public and private realms apart in their minds. As a consequence, they find it easier to be rationalist and nonrationalist at the same time.

With this proviso in mind, we also find that rationalism, turned back on itself, can be used to find reasons for not accepting the assumption that truth is singular: "Why one truth? Why not many truths?" It can also be used to question the primacy of rationalism itself as the only way, or at least as the most important way, to know what is true: "Why not use nonrational, extra-rational means as well?" Turned back on itself, rationalism allows us to look beyond the limits that rationalism sets. This is paradoxical, but turning reason back on itself does in fact let us see the significance of a wide range of worldviews of a nonrationalistic kind.

The postmodernist turn is not a new one. Heraclitus, for example, put its implications to the ancient Greek world. He argued that no true thing can ever be said, and ever since the advent of European rationalism, there are analysts who have argued likewise.

The war in Vietnam was instrumental in shaking disciplinary confidence in this regard. So was the collapse of the Soviet Union—a monumental series of events mirrored by an equally monumental failure in the capacity to predict and control world affairs. Standing back to look at the world from an analytic distance and to predictive effect had conspicuously failed. Faith in rationalist principles seemed compromised as a consequence, and a new approach, more sensitive to the way we interpret as well as represent what it is we want to know in world affairs, seemed a distinct and necessary possibility.

International Relations and International Political Economy is not the postmodernists' primary concern. They are not interested in extending the scope of IR further. Rather, they are interested in how we understand the world, how we "world" this world, how we live in it and how it lives in us. More particularly, they claim to see reality in terms of relationships, not in terms of reified entities like the "state" or the "market." They portray these relationships as dynamic, contingent, subjective, emergent, and relativistic, too.

Their main target is the modernist conception of reality. To them the modernist mind-set requires a mechanistic conception of the world that makes it much easier to study objectively, but which deprives the people in it—whether individuals, groups, or sovereign states—of free will. Indeed, the world most suited to the modernist/rationalist/positivist mind-set is one where people's behavior has material consequences that then determine what they do. This denotes, postmodernists say, a concept of reality as static, predictable, objective, given, and true. And while this conception might help those who do social science, it is still an assertion, an argument. It is not fact.

I had long harbored an intuitive mistrust of the rationalist/positivist conception of reality. I found all this, therefore, extremely interesting. I found the writings of the postmodernists very helpful in articulating my own misgivings. The fact that those doing this writing were considered somewhat of a lunatic fringe at the time seemed to matter much less than the chance they offered to talk in terms other than those condoned by the proponents of IR/IPE (Waever 1998).

The conclusions that the postmodernists helped me articulate were quickly confirmed by my reading of the work of feminist scholars as well. This was writing that was just then starting to get a serious disciplinary hearing, and it had radical implications for all analytic thought about world affairs.

My conclusions were also confirmed by what I later learned at a university in a nonmodernist culture (Japan), where the key cultural assumptions that underpin a "modernist" country like the United States simply do not obtain. They received more support again from what I subsequently came to learn in a country that has a large minority of indigenous people in it (Aotearoa/New Zealand). Some of the Maori of Aotearoa/New Zealand are extremely articulate critics of IR/IPE, and I gained very valuable insights listening to what they had to say.

## Constructivism

Most recently I have been exploring these conclusions in constructivist terms. That is where they seem to lead—for the moment at any rate.

Very generally, constructivism can be defined, much as Berger and Luckmann did a generation ago, in terms of the reality we make, not find. "Man is biologically predestined," these analysts argue, "to construct and to inhabit a world with others. This world becomes for him [sic] the dominant and definite reality. Its limits are set by nature, but, once constructed, this world acts back upon nature. In the dialectic between nature and the socially constructed world the human organism itself is transformed. In this same dialectic man produces reality and thereby produces himself" (Berger and Luckmann 1966, 204). The dialectic is not only between society and nature, however. The "socially constructed" world is dialectic, too. It takes place between "man" and "man," as well as between "nature" and "man." We are biologically predestined to construct and inhabit a world that is real in social as well as natural terms.

In practice, constructivism means different things to different people. Analysts disagree radically, that is, about who is "constructing" the world, how much it is constructed, and in what ways.

There are those, for example, who see "states" playing a much greater role than heretofore in "constructing" their interrelationships (and who would bring the idea of interstate society back in to the discussion as well). There are those who highlight how the beneficiaries of the modernist project use their power, wealth, and knowledge to "construct" the kinds of world they are able to dominate. And there are those who focus on individuals, in particular on our inherent capacity for language, and who highlight how we use this capacity to "construct" our worlds and all of their affairs.

There are some, that is, who want to continue to focus on IR/IPE, but to place more of a sociological "construction" upon it, thereby propping up the discipline's core concerns and preserving them largely unchallenged. There are others who want to emancipate us from the inequities implicit in contemporary IR/IPE. And there are others again who would sweep IR/IPE aside in favor of social theorizing of a much more comprehensive kind; in favor, that is, of a different discipline, or even a different world.

Given the many connotations attributed to "constructivism," I find it useful to look for ways in which those who use the concept can be grouped (Adler 1997; Checkel 1998; Hopf 1998). Taking my lead from the rise of scientific reasoning discussed above and from the work of those who are most authoritative in the discipline in terms of scientific reasoning, I see three main categories of constructivism at the moment. I call these categories *conservative, social theory,* and *commonsense.*

### Conservative Constructivism

The first category—the conservative constructivists—consists of those who see their key task as the defense of their core concern—the primacy of strict scientific reasoning—against what they construe as peripheral denial. This defense, to be sure, may and usually does involve offense too. It may require advocating adaptation and change, for example, and most conservative constructivists do, in practice, advocate adaptation and change. None of these changes are meant to undermine the disciplinary commitment to the use of strict scientific reasoning, however. Indeed, they are meant to conserve this commitment—hence the name I have given this group. They are meant to perpetuate the attempt to provide cumulative knowledge of an empirically tested kind.

There are two main groups of conservative constructivist. The first one (hard-line "co-constitution") confronts the postmodernist challenge head-on, with the explicit intention of co-opting it. The second one (soft-line "social constructivism") is more oblique, seeking to extend the core study of IR/IPE to bring "people" and "social relationships" back in, though always in a social scientizing way.

### Hard-Line "Co-constitution"

The first group is conservative constructivism at its paradigm-policing best. Here we find scholars declaring constructivism *the* way to come to terms with postmodernist critiques of IR/IPE's scientific aspirations and defining constructivism in such a fashion as to make this possible (Katzenstein, Keohane and Krasner 1998).

This group began by dismissing postmodernist critiques out of hand. They were the part of the profession that found it too difficult to listen to arguments that rejected outright any chance of studying world affairs in social scientific terms. To postmodernists, no explanation tells "the truth." Explanation involves not only representation but also interpretation, and since interpretations differ, so too do truths. To postmodernists, the assumptions upon which social scientism are based are untenable. To social scientizers, this makes postmodernism utterly unacceptable in turn.

The criticisms that postmodernists were making proved too compelling to ignore, however. At first it was not the scientizers themselves who started listening. It was their students. Indeed, so many students started listening that an attempt clearly had to be made to accommodate, and if possible to co-opt, the alternative view that postmodernism presented. Faced with the possibility of a shrinking client base, the scientizers moved to domesticate the postmodernist threat.

Enter "constructivism." Enter also its definition in terms of "co-constitution." Constructivism was the concept the scientizers chose with which to stem the postmodernist tide. And co-constitution was the way they defined constructivism to achieve this purpose.

"Agents" and "structures," for example, were said to be constructs and to co-constitute each other. This allowed the scientizers to talk about the competing interpretations agents and structures construct of each other. This, in turn, brought the whole postmodernist critique within the compass of their core concerns. No wonder they began urging all and sundry to start including constructivism and co-constitution in their analyses of world affairs— the proviso being that we continue to cast our hypotheses in falsifiable form, so that competing claims to the "truth" might be made amenable to empirical test.

What does constructivism mean here, however? And more particularly, what does it mean in terms of co-constitution? Co-constitution can be defined in more than one way, though, not incidentally, the scientizers chose a definition that served the scientizing cause.

The problem with co-constitution is that it can be used, in principle, in such a way as to make social scientizing harder to do. It can be used, for example, to replace tangible, objectified "things" such as states and state-systems (which are relatively concrete and more amenable as such to scientific analysis) with intangible, mercurial, highly dynamic processes (which are harder to objectify and harder, as a consequence, to study in a scientific way).

The scientizers used co-constitution in practice as if it were a methodological fence, not a holistic field. Furthermore, they construed this fence as none too steady, forcing analysts to come down on one side or the other. Analysts were obliged to choose either "agent" or "structure." They were discouraged from seeing agents in terms of "agenting," for example, or structures in terms of "structuring." They were not invited to consider the conceptualizing and dichotomizing of the agent-and-structure problematic as a case of misplaced concreteness, as an attempt to reify a world in train.

By getting analysts to jump between agent and structure, the scientizers made it possible to remain modernist, and to do strict science, while talking about interpretation too. Wittingly or unwittingly, however, they thereby obscured the extent to which agenting and structuring are parts of a complex field of ongoing human practice, that is, the extent to which they are a process.

The point was never constructivism, however. Nor was it co-constitution. The point was to conserve the social scientific agenda. It was to continue to make possible, "in the final analysis," a "productive" research program— one where the analyst operationalizes key variables, casts key propositions in a falsifiable form, and does empirical tests (Katzenstein, Keohane and Krasner 1998: 648–649).

## Soft-Line "Social Constructivism"

The second approach that conservative constructivists take is more oblique— and subtler as a consequence. Thus, while it seems to address new questions and suggest new approaches, it remains a deep defense of the strictly conceived scientific worldview as well.

John Ruggie, for example, represents himself as a reformist, not as a conservative, with the task of bringing "society" back into the debate (Ruggie 1998). He calls his approach "social" (or "ideational") constructivism because he wants to highlight the fact that the state system is an international society too and that ideational factors have causative force in world affairs. (This is very different from the "social theory" constructivism I discuss below, which is much more radical than Ruggie's).

Like his hard-line compatriots, Ruggie does not question the possibility of a "naturalistic" social science, however. He does, it is true, suggest the need for concepts that do not represent "a priori types derived from some universalizing theory-sketch." He notes, too, some of the limits of "normal science" in studying IR/IPE, such as the failure of "normal science" to grasp "truly" the force of intersubjectivity. He remains convinced of the power of scientism, nonetheless. His reforms are not meant to negate his core commitment to studying world affairs in strict scientific ways. What matters most, he believes, is how the competing conceptions of constructivism relate to the "possibility of a social science" (880–881).

It is no surprise, therefore, to find Ruggie concluding by telling constructivists to strive for "greater analytical rigor and specification" and by declaring the benefits of rigor and specificity, which, as far as he is concerned, are "self-evident" to all (882). He may want a broader church for social science, that is. He may even see the point of more diverse forms of worship. But he is not about to repudiate the faith or make any recommendations of a non- or postpositivist kind (885).

So Ruggie sees the state system as being constructed of shared "cognitive practices." These practices invest our world with social meaning. They provide world affairs with a social dimension, and in the process they make human consciousness an active factor in configuring those affairs.

Ruggie defines "cognitive practices" to include ideas, beliefs, aspirations, identities, and norms, a definition that would include, for example, the international norms that govern diplomacy, treaties, and balances of power (Bull and Watson 1984). By including these practices in his analysis of world affairs, he is able to include people's common knowledge, their sense of collective purpose, how they define others and themselves, and what it is they might believe they want. This makes the conventional study of IR/IPE more comprehensive, since it lifts the constraints on the need to consider only interests, for example, or preferences, or rational choices. It allows us to consider what world affairs mean to people. It lets us talk about how people interpret global events, how they understand them, and how these meanings and interpretations and understandings help to fabricate the world affairs they have.

Ruggie exhorts us as consequence to include "culture" and "identity" in the study of world affairs. "Culture" and "identity" can be defined in many different ways, of course, but the key to their definition here is the concept of "intersubjectivity." In practice this means no more than the cognitive practices listed above. The "culture" of international society includes the norm of nonintervention, for example, and it is adherence to that norm by statemakers that gives "state sovereignty" cognitive substance. The "international society" is constructed in the same way.

But regardless of how sociological the discipline becomes, Ruggie, as a good conservative constructivist, remains committed to "theory development." Bringing society back into the debate is not meant to disqualify the analyst from formulating cause-and-effect hypotheses about how, when, and why intersubjectivities ("cognitive practices") matter. Quite to the contrary, since incorporating shared beliefs and meanings does not, Ruggie says, preclude the positivistic appreciation of who is doing what and under what circumstances.

The key point of conservative constructivism, in both its hard- and soft-line forms, remains the defense of social scientizing. Bringing society back into the debate, and adding "mental" causes to "material" ones are supposed to make that protection easier. They are not supposed to contradict it. The description and explanation of world affairs are still supposed to proceed in a social scientific way.

Another example of the Ruggie-style, sociological, approach to soft-line constructivism is provided by Peter Katzenstein. As the editor of, and as an author in, a comprehensive study on "national security" Katzenstein argues the case for bringing society (and "culture" and "norms" and "identity") back into the strategic thinking field. He also wants to specify the key concepts as clearly as possible, however. And that is because he wants to develop a "theoretically coherent, empirically oriented research program" (Katzenstein 1996, 5). While he asks, therefore, how state interests are constructed in terms of people's social interactions, he is concerned at the same time to defend the primary status of "theory and evidence" and the importance of adhering to the "conventions" of an "empirically oriented social science." Indeed, he decrees that it is on these grounds alone that our "best chance" of engaging other points of view actually lies (2, 22, 30).

To define his perspective, Katzenstein has to describe security studies in terms of the dominance of two other perspectives, namely, "structural neorealism" and "neoliberal institutionalism." It is the limits these approaches set that he sees himself transcending.

To those who always considered the dominance of these two points of view a mere fact of academic practice, however, not one of academic principle, this is a very straw man. To those for whom the other analytic languages used in the study of security have always been just as important as these particular two—languages like globalist suprastatism or moderate neomercantilism or reformist neo-Marxism or essentialist nationalism or radical individualism—Katzenstein is no pioneer.

Those who have heretofore confined themselves to neorealism and neoliberalism, in other words, may be deciding now to look further afield. But those who never accepted the primacy of these doctrines in the first place are apt to wonder why they did not do so before. Those outside the limits that neorealism and neoliberalism set have long labored in much broader and deeper intellectual domains. From British or European or Antipodean perspectives, for example, it is hard to know quite what to make of social constructivists who discover what is already self-evident. Having written a book twenty years ago on state security that was subtitled "the sociology of international affairs," the first section of which was on culture and consciousness, I count myself among the bemused.

Katzenstein's purpose is not only to go beyond neorealism and neoliberalism, though he does, it is clear, want to problematize the assumptions made about state interests by leading analysts of both approaches. His statement maintaining as much appears on the very first page. This statement is preceded, however, by one about the need to make "intellectual progress," by which he means "the diminishing of sloppy logic, flabby prose, circularity in reasoning, and vacuousness of insight" (Katzenstein 1996, 1).

Katzenstein's primary purpose is to meet the challenge that nonrationalist modes of analysis present and to domesticate them. It is to ensure that the world remains safe for scientizing scholars. "Parisian" concerns are to be avoided, he says. So is historical work or anything else that holds out limited prospects of the possibility of moving toward a "deductive style of 'theory' anytime soon." Katzenstein's hopes for the future are clearly pinned upon scholarship that makes "[c]ontrasting analytical claims . . . articulated in the form of specific hypotheses that are applied in particular empirical domains" (Katzenstein 1996, 26, 29–30). This is the heartland that he sees put at risk by loose contemporary talk about culture and identity and norms. It is our ability to do strict social science that he specifically wants to conserve.

## Social Theory Constructivism

The second main category of constructivists—the "social theory" constructivists—consists of those who see their main task as formulating systematic social theory, not furthering a strictly conceived social science. This harks back to the beginnings of the scientific turn in the discipline in the 1960s. At that time behavioralist scholars began not only applying the methods of the physical sciences to world affairs, but also formulating general theories comprehensive enough to replace the discipline with something else (Banks 1966). The behavioralist turn, in other words, was always *both* more focused *and* broader than the discursive approaches that preceded it. In its more focused form, it looked for regularities. Of what general principle, its proponents were wont to ask, is this world affair a particular instance? In its broader form, however, behavioralism pursued the vision of a social theory encompassing all. The most extreme example of such a vision was General Systems Theory (GST), which in its transdisciplinary exuberance completely ignored the existence of the disciplines of sociology, anthropology, psychology, economics, history, politics, and international politics, and tried to build a general social theory that would include everything. Though GST, and the holistic approach it exemplified, did not ultimately prevail, the allure of the approach it represented has proved perennial. It is clearly at work in the attempt by some constructivists, for example, to reconstitute our understanding of social relationships from first principles like "language" and from the "cognitive acts" or "speech acts" that language makes possible.

There is a potential confusion here, since conservative constructivists see themselves formulating and confirming social scientific "theories" too. Doesn't this make them social theory constructivists, therefore? Aren't they doing the same thing?

The short answer is: no. Conservative constructivists want world affairs analysts to do "social science," strictly conceived. They want conclusions that are cast in falsifiable terms that they can empirically test. "Social theory" constructivists, on the other hand, want to arrive at conclusions about social relationships, of which international relationships are only one particular case. Thus, while conservative constructivists seek to conserve their scientific approach to world affairs, social theory constructivists seek to do away with world affairs as a separate subject of social enquiry.

Social theory constructivists are social scientists, too, I hasten to add, though they are not as strict as the conservative constructivists are about how social science should be done. They do not, for example, try to formulate falsifiable hypotheses and then subject them to empirical tests. On the other hand, they do not reject the rationalistic use of reason. They arrive at their conclusions systematically, using reason in a rationalistic way, and emphasizing in the process the use of reason as the best way to know.

Why do social theory constructivists eschew strict scientizing? For the simple reason that, when narrowly conceived, it delimits what can be talked about as world affairs. This is why social theory constructivists see the conservative constructivists (who favor strict scientizing) as walling IR/IPE off by methodological means. Within these walls, social theory constructivists see conservative constructivists talking about states, for example, as if they were all the same, despite the manifest differences between them in terms of their "identities," for example. They see conservative constructivists trying to determine no more than if this proposition is objectively true.

They prefer themselves to start with social relationships. And they prefer to talk about these relationships (which include international relationships) without regard to preexisting disciplinary delimitations.

Is it possible, as social theory constructivists claim, to make the discipline part of a much more comprehensive one? The answer is far from clear. Conservative constructivists find the prospect very threatening, since if and when social theory constructivists succeed, conservative constructivists will be out of business. Not surprisingly, conservative constructivists respond by marginalizing their social theory rivals. They reinforce the current disciplinary boundaries, and they reduce the chance for social theory constructivists to get a serious disciplinary hearing. All this aside, making the discipline part of a much more comprehensive one encounters problems of its own, however, and to understand why we must look more closely at what social theory constructivism involves.

The most prominent school of social theory constructivists articulates an analytic language about the use of language itself. This analytic language can be used, as a conservative constructivist might do, simply to highlight the way "co-constitution" works. It can also be used, however, to show that language is not passive and that to speak is to act, since in speaking we make declarations, demands, and promises that assert and commit us and seek to direct others.

This language can be used to show that language itself is never neutral and that relationships between people and their societies are therefore never neutral either. This is why, in the co-constituting process, rules get made that determine what is to be done and who is to be in control. This is also why, in one notable variant of this kind of constructivism, we are enjoined to give particular regard to the rules that assert, direct, and commit us. These are the rules that constitute any society, it is said, and all social institutions, including the societies and institutions that constitute world affairs. These are the rules that make in turn for rule (Onuf 1998).

At this point, language has clearly ceased to be a window on the world, representing that world to us in ways we can trust not to shape what we see. If language is active like this, then we are always implicated in what we say and do. It is not an untainted medium, providing an untainted account of reality "out there."

At this point, what we know is clearly also "in here." As such, it is always an interpretation of reality as well as a representation of it. It is part of reality, though which part we cannot know, since in knowing we are speaking, and our language is not a window on the world. We are therefore implicated in what we say and do. And so on.

This is not a circle we can break. We can always choose not to speak at all, but this is not a very practical alternative. We can also social scientize, but social scientizing uses language, and language is an active, not a passive, tool and cannot be used, therefore, to account for Reality (with a capital "R") without our becoming implicated in the knowing process. This makes Reality subjective in turn, which makes objective hypothesizing impossible to do.

Reenter social theory constructivism. While social theory constructivists do not subscribe to the idea of a strict social science, they do think that social science is possible if it is done in a less strict way. Objectifying the world and thinking about it rationally, they believe, will provide a systematic account of it. In this sense, social theory constructivism is part of the rationalist/modernist project. Because social theory constructivists do not subscribe to the strict tenets of social science positivism, however, they are much more likely to be methodological eclectics (Onuf 1999). They are much more likely to be aware of the excesses of modernity. They may even be postmodernists, particularly if they construe "truth" as predominantly a question of power and a function of "discourse and discipline."

The reference point for social theory constructivism remains "modernity," and this is the problem with it. For all their comprehensiveness, social theory constructivists still look in toward the scientific project, and not out toward other ways of knowing. They still want to know what "the truth" might be, even if that truth can only be provisional, even if it can never be absolute. As a consequence, there is only one potential comprehensive discipline for world affairs to be subsumed by, despite the fact that for those prepared to use nonrationalist research methods, this is patently not the case.

Social theory constructivists do not require the truth to be eternal, universal, or necessary. The sun doesn't always have to shine, for example, for them to know that the sun does shine. They accept a degree of contingency that a conservative constructivist would not.

They do not do nonrationalistic research, though. They would not, for example, seek to know if the sun shines by holding their minds' hands toward the morning sky. They trust the evidence of their minds' eyes alone. On the evidence of their minds' eyes alone, furthermore, there is only one comprehensive theory possible. There is not a plurality of theories.

### Commonsense Constructivism

It is because of the limits that reason sets when used in rationalistic ways—more and less strictly; more and less positivistically—that I want to highlight another kind of constructivism, called here "commonsense" constructivism. This approach goes beyond the limits that rationalism sets, and it does so, moreover, by bringing people back in, not as "societies," not as the bearers of norms and ideas, not as individual "agents," but as holistic, world-knowing, social selves.

I take my lead again from Berger and Luckmann (1966). More than thirty years ago, these authors pointed out that "[t]heoretical thought, 'ideas,' *Weltanschauungen* are not *that* important in society. . . . [They] do not exhaust what is 'real' for the members of a society" (26–27). I would concur, for what I consider four important reasons.

Nonspecialist knowledge of world affairs is significant, I believe, because of what it reveals in terms of scope, process, structure, and understanding. First, it reveals the full scope of what making world affairs involves. Second, it reveals the highly dynamic nature of the making process. Third, it shows how the making process results in global structures that put some people in the core and other people on the margins. And fourth, it suggests that all the above can only be understood accurately and comprehensively if we use nonrationalistic as well as rationalistic means.

If we are prepared to concern ourselves with "what people 'know' as 'reality' in their everyday, non- or pre-theoretical lives"; if we are prepared to recognize "precisely this [commonsense] 'knowledge'" as constituting the "fabric of meanings without which no society could exist" (Berger and Luckmann 1966, 27); then we have a better chance of finding out what constitutes world affairs today. If the commonsense constructivist case is a plausible one, in other words, we need to understand how world affairs feel to ordinary people and not only elites.

## World Affairs as a Whole

On the first issue, that is, the range of what making world affairs involves, I would say that wanting to know what is "real" for the ordinary people who constitute world affairs, wanting to understand what world affairs mean to them, wanting to explain what their nonspecialist, nontheoretical sense is of how the world works, leads directly to an awareness of the limits that specialist knowing sets and of what might lie beyond them. It led me from IR to IPE, for example. And it led me subsequently to an awareness of the significance of international political society (IPS), of world political culture (WPC), of the margins that the world culture of modernity creates, and of those who try and speak from those margins to those who make modernist world affairs.

There is, of course, no one common sense of world affairs. One person's common sense can be another person's nonsense. To those ordinary people imbued with IR realism, for example, it is common sense to talk in terms of power politics and a competitive sovereign-state system. To those imbued with IPE liberalism, it is common sense to talk of free markets and the free flow of international capital. To those who are masculinist, it is common sense to have a gender-based division of labor. And to those who are environmentalists, it is common sense to want an ecologically sustainable future.

It should also be made clear at the outset that I am not suggesting people are not rational. The capacity to reason is part of the human condition and is self-evident in practically every person.

People are not, on the whole, rationalistic, however. World affairs do, it is true, mean highly rationalized ways of living for most of us, ways that are statist, capitalist, and individuated. The scale of these ways of living is not usually apparent, though, unless we ask what modernist world affairs mean to ordinary people and unless we ask in nonrationalistic ways.

It is the mark of Western cultures that they privilege the rationalistic use of reason. Even in the West, however, rationalism is few people's primary passion, and while most people there are coached in its use and do as a consequence appreciate its power, it is not how they usually engage the world. Only scholars and administrators do that as a matter of course, and then only part of the time. Most people mostly know the world in nonrationalistic ways.

And while the rationalistic research that abounds in the West lets us talk about nonrationalistic meanings, it does not account for these meanings in their own terms. For this we require nonrationalistic research techniques, which give us access to these meanings in a more appropriate way. Techniques like these do not turn meanings into something else in the process of knowing them. They allow us to know how world affairs feel, not only how they look.

### World Affairs as a Process

On the second issue, that is, the highly dynamic nature of the making process, it is clear that conservative constructivists and social theory constructivists alike paint a relatively static picture of world affairs. They talk of agents and structures, for example, or social relationships and rules, and, as a consequence, they both render our understanding of world affairs less dynamic than it otherwise might be.

Commonsense constructivism suggests that concepts like "agenting" and "structuring," "social relating" and "ruling," are more meaningful than their reified equivalents. As a consequence, they suggest a view of world affairs that is significantly more vivid and arguably more "real."

The commonsense image of world affairs, in other words, is one of a world in train. If we carry this thought through so that the reified concepts and categories we use for our convenience in talking about world affairs all become verbs, not nouns, seemingly solid structures suddenly become repeated patterns of human practice whose stability, furthermore, suddenly seems highly contrived. They are repeated patterns: therefore we can and do make sense of them (though the complex character of what they involve will largely preclude prediction and control.) They are repeated *practices* and therefore we do stand back to look at and to label them, to hypothesize about and to systematize them. And they are repeated *human* practices, which is why we are only able to explain and understand them by standing close to listen to those involved and by taking part ourselves.

Everyday world affairs look radically different, in other words, in what are Heraclitean terms. They appear to be in a continuous state of flux. They appear practiced and incomplete, contingent and emergent, contrived and constructed. Whatever is found in a seemingly finished fashion in the world is, on closer inspection, revealed to have been made before. It is also in the process of being made again. Indeed, if it isn't being made again, it isn't likely to be found again. If it isn't being made again, that is, it is likely simply to cease to be—at least in the form it currently presents.

In that all human meaning is constituted like this, it too is in train. To know world affairs in terms of its meaning to ordinary human beings is to know this flow.

No one makes world affairs as they please, of course, since others make world affairs in ways we cannot avoid. We cannot avoid being coached to know world affairs in particular ways as we grow up, for example. We cannot ignore how other people think the world should be made, especially if what they do directly impinges upon what we do too. This gives a predetermined feel to most of what we do.

If we get into the habit of asking what people think and feel who are not specialists in world affairs, however, we find that world affairs are being made all the time, and at the grass-roots level too. If we get ourselves into the habit of talking of "state-making" instead of "the state," for example, we remind ourselves that making states means taking people and turning them into citizens who respond reliably in statist terms. And we remind ourselves that markets, or individuation, or rationalism itself entails such repeated patterns of human practice as wealth-making (marketeering), self-making (individuating), and mind-making (rationalist enculturation).

*World Affairs as Producing Peripheries*

The same applies to modernity's peripheries. The modernist project involves gendering practices, for example, and ethno-centering practices, and ecologically damaging practices, and spiritually alienating practices, and all these make margins to what modernists do.

The point is that "the state," for example, is never "done;" nor is "the market" or "the individual" or the priority accorded rationalism. Nor is the priority *not* accorded women, indigenous peoples, or environmental activists, however. The making of modernist world affairs means the making of patriarchy as well, or western hegemony, or environmental degradation. State-makers can never assume that the state has already been "made" and that all they have to do now is more of the same to keep it in good repair. Their "doing" is "making" too, and the same applies to markets, the individuated, the rationalistic, the gendered, and the ethnically hegemonic.

World affairs looks very different as a result. Our awareness of the extent to which world affairs involves constructing the consciousness of ordinary people extends not only to how extensive that consciousness can be but also to how hierarchic it can be. The commonsense world gets made not only so that "things" like states, markets, autonomous selves, and the rationalistic use of reason can continue to prevail, but also so that "things" like males and Westerners can also continue to prevail. The process of making world affairs is not neutral. It favors some and in the process disadvantages others. That is, world affairs are made with centers and cores, and margins and peripheries. Women, for example, are systematically sent to the periphery of world affairs by the modernist construction of it, and world affairs are radically patriarchist as an (ongoing) consequence. Similar observations can also be made about environmentalists, ethnics, postcolonials, indigenes, and the poor.

## World Affairs as Known Nonrationally

On the fourth issue, that is, the ability of nonrationalistic research to access ordinary experience, commonsense constructivism differs notably from social theory constructivism and conservative constructivism. To commonsense constructivists, rationalist research is not enough. It must be complemented by nonrationalist research if we are to know what world affairs mean to most of the people who live in this world and, therefore, what are world affairs. To commonsense constructivists, rationalism confines as well as informs. It obscures as well as explains. It fosters confusion as well as furthers our understanding. It is extremely useful as a way for us to know, but it is only one way for us to know, and as such, it is not necessarily the best way for us to know, at least when it is used on its own.

To ordinary people, who must deal with the feelings that world affairs involve all of the time, this is self-evident. To those engaged in the rationalistic explanation of world affairs, it is less so. They are insulated to some extent from how world affairs feel by the objectifying nature of their own research methods. This allows them to assess the patterns of human practice involved with relative clarity and detachment. It inhibits them, however, from knowing how they feel and what world affairs mean to those taking part, including even themselves.

Commonsense constructivists, in sum, highlight the everyday aspect of people's knowledge of world affairs. In doing so, they highlight the full reach of the global construction project, the process nature of this project, its peripheralizing propensities, and alternative ways to know how this project works. They highlight the ordinary experience of world affairs, the construction of this experience in every aspect of human life, the ongoing nature of that construction, and the significance of doing research by experientially proximal means.

None of this is as simple as it might sound. Doing experientially proximal research, for example, "even in a limited domain for a short period, requires thousands of pages of reading, months of interviews and archival research, and a host of less conventional activities, such as riding public transportation, standing in lines, and going to bars and cafes to participate in local practices. . . . [Commonsense c]onstructivism is no short cut" (Hopf 1998, 198). Experientially proximal research is the long cut, in fact. The result is not only different knowledge, however. It can be said to be better knowledge, too—more comprehensive, more accurate, simply better informed.

Commonsense constructivism is not a simple approach because it requires not only due cognizance of the analytical languages that rationalists use, but also due recognition of the limits that every such language sets. Ordinary people use these languages in a refracted form. From the everyday use of these languages we distill rationalistic versions of them by objectifying and abstracting them. If we stop there, however, we risk misrepresenting the world since the world is neither abstracted nor objectified. It is concrete and subjectified, and nonrationalistic research methods are needed to explain the nature of this concreteness and this subjectivity. We need both rationalistic and nonrationalistic research, in other words, to do the discipline justice, and that is not an easy need to meet. Rationalistic analysts of world affairs see nonrationalistic research as too subjective to be reliable. Nonrationalistic researchers see rationalist research as too objective to be meaningful. Too much regard to one risks alienating the other. Too much regard to both risks winning the credence of neither. It is, as I said, a difficult position to sustain, especially in the rationalistic world of Western academe.

## Making the History of the Study of World Affairs

So here we are. Or, at least, here am I.

I provide this autobiographical introduction with some hesitation. I do so because I want to show how much my working life has been bound up with the history of the study of world affairs. For me, the discipline has not just been a place to go to, where I labor and learn. It has shaped me. It has been an experience or, rather, a series of experiences that have made me aware, not just intellectually but experientially too, of how the discipline works, what it has most to say, and what it typically does not say as well.

As a result, I still see world affairs, as I was first taught to do, as being about ordering, about governance, about state-making, that is, and the making of an interstate system. It was about these things in 1919, when the discipline was founded as "international relations," though then it was about "states," not state-making. Ordinary people can confirm, from everyday experience, the way state-making works. That state-making is a process is not so apparent to the analysts who study it professionally, however. To them, abstracted "states" are easier to see, even though abstracted states are not what constitute world affairs. States are in a constant state of construction and so are world affairs.

I see world affairs now as being about producing and consuming too—that is, about sustenance, market-making, and market-making systems. It was about these things in 1919, though "international political economy" was not the initial focus of the discipline. It is certainly a key focus today, and the commonsense meaning that world affairs has for ordinary people confirms not only the significance of this dimension but its process nature as well. Capitalist markets, that is, are also in a constant state of construction.

I also now see world affairs as being about socializing, about social coherence, and therefore about self-making. World affairs was about these things in 1919, though the "international political society" that individualism makes (including, but not exclusively, the society of states that state-makers make) was not the initial focus of the discipline. Nor is it a core focus today, though the meaning that "society" has for ordinary people suggests that it certainly should be one. The meaning that society has for ordinary people also suggests that we are dealing here with what society *makes*, not with completed selves. Any particular self, and any particular self-making system, is in a constant state of construction, like the states and markets cited above.

I see world affairs as being about the making of a "modernist" world culture, too, with the making at the same time of margins to this culture—feminist, indigenist, ethnicized, environmentalist, spiritualist, post-colonialist, and impoverished. The proponents of modernist culture promote rationalism, or the ideology of reason. The attempt to establish a belief in reason as an end in itself I see as the most significant human project of our day. Historically it has set the scene for all of the above, and its implications for world affairs are immense. The study of world affairs was about this project in 1919, though world affairs as a discipline was not usually thought of in terms of the making of a "world political culture" then. These terms are not the way world affairs are usually thought of now, either. That said, there are scholars both on the periphery of the discipline and in its core who do appreciate the subject in these terms (as there were in 1919). There are also those who appreciate the limits that rationalism sets, and how and why we might transcend them, while the experiences of ordinary people, and the meanings that world affairs have for them, confirm the need to do so.

None of these are "natural" categories. Regardless of our biological propensities, there is nothing in our genes that says we ought to live in what is currently a state-made, marketeering, individuated world, where rationalism gets privileged as the predominant cultural value and belief and where women, indigenous peoples, ethnics, environmentalists, post-colonialists, the religious, and the poor get put on the periphery. The experience of ordinary people, however, confirms that these are the categories that dominate modernist world affairs, and the making of world affairs is the making, at the moment at least, of world affairs in this form.

## Skewing the History of the Study of World Affairs

Contemporary world affairs are couched by conventional proponents of the discipline in very particular terms. They stress, as will be pointed out in the next chapter, particular *dimensions* of the subject and particular *analytical languages*.

What I want to highlight here is that other dimensions to these world affairs are made harder (if not impossible) to see in the process and that other analytical languages are made harder (if not impossible) to hear as well. What we mostly get in the name of the study of world affairs, therefore, while it may be highly cogent and may sound truly comprehensive, is usually neither. What we usually find, for example, is that those who talk about state-making do not talk about market-making. And if they do talk about market-making, then they are likely to neglect nation-making and the significance of international societies. And if they manage to include these too, then they are still likely not to acknowledge the margins that get made by constructing a world on the basis of scientific reason. Or highlight the constructive nature of all of these processes. Or appreciate the limits to rationalism itself as a research technique, and how we might transcend them.

## Why "World Affairs"?

As an addendum to this Introduction, I would also like to note the use throughout this book of the term "world affairs" in preference to the term "world politics" or "international affairs" or "international relations." While "international relations" is a time-honored way of referring to the discipline, it really only refers to one dimension of the discipline—the politico-strategic one. If we think about the word "international," it has statist and ethnic connotations that are problematic too. This limits the capacity of "international relations" to account for the scope of the study of world affairs. It also limits the scope of the term "international affairs." As to "world politics," the word "politics" is too often employed, particularly by liberals, to exclude matters of political economy and political society. If we want to avoid this liberalist bias, we are left with "world affairs," which does not discriminate in this regard. Thus, while "world affairs" is a very general term, it is not so general as to cease to make sense when referring to the subject as a whole—hence, its use here.

## What Next?

In the next chapter, I look at the fundamentals of the making of world affairs. I look first at the importance of language, both in itself and as used by the media. I then discuss the making of modernity in terms of the attempt to make a global culture that places its highest priority upon the use of reason (and that creates in the process premodernist and postmodernist alternatives, whose proponents do not privilege the use of reason to the same extent). Historically, modernist culture, this particular way of life, did not spring into the world fully formed. It was and is a social process, involving the development and the dissemination of the appropriate forms of mental speech. Analytically, however, its full significance can only be appreciated if we distinguish it from society and if we talk about the construction of the politico-cultural context within which modernist world affairs get made.

I look next at world affairs from the three main perspectives that this rationalistic/modernizing culture prioritizes, and that ordinary experience shows to be predominant as well. I highlight in the process the main practices involved, namely, state-making, market-making, and self-making. And I conclude by arguing for experiential research techniques that take us beyond the limits that rationalism sets.

Having sketched in brief how I see modernist world affairs being made, I go on to look at the making process in more detail. I do so mindful as well of the need to use subjectifying as well as objectifying research methods (which is why I array subjectifying readings throughout).

Chapter 2 is the first of two chapters, each of which discusses an aspect of the making of world affairs that is still largely missing from the current discipline. Ordinary people know about it. Modernist analysts, in the main, do not. Thus, Chapter 2 discusses in detail the politico-cultural process that makes for global modernity in general and for modernist world affairs in particular. Chapter 3 focuses on one dimension of modernist world affairs, namely, the politico-social one. As indicated already, this is a relatively neglected dimension, not as far as ordinary people are concerned, but by modernist analysts of world affairs, who neglect all three of its most characteristic languages, namely, individualism, nationalism, and collectivism.

Chapter 4 brings us to two other key dimensions of modernist world affairs, namely, the politico-strategic and the politico-economic ones. These are well-established areas of study in the contemporary discipline of world affairs, though the study of politico-strategic world affairs is of much longer standing, at least in the United States, than the study of politico-economic ones. Because these dimensions are so well-established, they tend to dominate the current analytic accounts of the subject. This is witnessed by the familiar character of the conceptual languages involved, namely, realism (including neorealism), mercantilism, internationalism (including neoliberalist institutionalism), liberalism itself, globalism, and Marxism.

I should say at the outset that all the chapters that follow, describing not only the politico-cultural context of modernist world affairs but also the three key dimensions of them (politico-strategic, -economic, and -social), are highly compressed. The account I give of modernity and its major alternatives, and of the analytical languages that characterize each dimension of modernist world affairs, introduces only the main terms and how they are defined.

The staccato effect of having to be succinct is hard to avoid, even perhaps inevitable, given the huge size of the literature in each case and the impossibility of providing any more than the most abbreviated account of it. I hope, however, that the perils of condensation do not obscure the point of the enterprise. This, I repeat, is not the adequacy or otherwise of my summary of the complex arguments waged over every aspect of what follows. My account is doubtless sketchy, telegraphic, uneven, simplistic, and whatever else offends. I am working to a particular purpose, however, and I hope that some sense of this purpose survives, despite the vast scope of the terrain that I must traverse in order to make my case.

The purpose of this book is to show, by accounting for world affairs as ordinary people live them, that most contemporary analysts neglect key dimensions of their own discipline. They also neglect the process nature of every aspect of world affairs, the way these world affairs privilege some and peripheralize others, and the way important knowledge about world affairs is made available to us only by nonrationalist means.

International Relations and International Political Economy are the most familiar ways of talking about world affairs. What I attempt to do here is to put these aspects of world affairs in context, first, by adding a social dimension to the political and economic ones (that are the heart of the art so far); second, by showing that all three of these dimensions embody a belief in rationalism and as such can be seen as modernistic, that is, they put a high value on the use of reason as an end in itself (and what this entails); third, by demonstrating that this is a project in train, in all respects (exalting some people and marginalizing others); and fourth, by showing that rationalism puts limits on our capacity to know (and how these limits might be transcended).

The need to pursue such a purpose is immediately apparent when we ask how world affairs are constructed and, more particularly, when we ask what world affairs mean to the ordinary people who take part in them. In the light of these questions, and the answers they elicit, it appears that the study of world affairs in its current form is inadequate. How inadequate should be apparent once we finally reach the discussion of IR/IPE below. It should also be apparent from the inclusion throughout of a process perspective and of examples of experientially participative research. We can do better, it seems, and what follows tries to show how.

My choice of readings in this regard is not dictated by the desire to provide the voice of an "authority." I merely seek to provide representative voices, ones that I think are worth heeding as accounts of what it is like to take part in world affairs.

The readings provided vary enormously in fact. Some are the voices of recognized authorities. Some are the voices of ordinary people. They range from the refined prose of St. Augustine to a brief documentary account of the life of an Indian sandal-maker. In providing such readings I am trying to give the reader a sense of how the particular kind of world at issue actually feels, before returning to a more rationalistic distance in the conclusion.

The readings show, however vicariously, what the world is like from other perspectives. They represent ideas in such a way as to compensate for what rationalist analysis cannot do, complementing it and seeking to transcend the limits it sets.

# 1

# Making World Affairs

As a species, we have a unique capacity for language. As far as we can tell, no other animal on earth is able to share information with other members of its species in as much detail as we do. This capacity is largely reliant upon speech, or speech surrogates like signing, and so important is it that we cannot exaggerate its significance for the study of world affairs. I start with language because I start with words. With these words I will make an account of world affairs and of how they have been crafted, and this account in turn will help to make a particular kind of world affairs.

In biological terms, the acquisition of language and the expansion of the neocortex occurred together. Which one caused the other, or whether both were the consequence of something else, is much debated. Suffice to note that it did happen, and the result is a species-specific skill that never ceases to astound. Sitting in a public place where we do not know the language, we hear people making sounds in complex sequences. They read from papers and books that have marks on them in intricate columns and rows. Having learned, while they grew up, the same sounds and marks, and the same rules of sequence and meaning, they are able to share what they speak and read. They are able to store it in written form, too, vastly increasing the potential audience for what they have to say, both in space ("writing for the world") and in time ("writing for posterity").

The power of language, and the power to think in words that is the necessary condition for speech and written speech, is a power indeed. It makes possible both memory and imagination—the capacity to recall the past and to anticipate the future. It also allows us to make and change our most taken-for-granted ideas about the world (which is why those not vigilant in this regard find the words in their heads doing much of their thinking for them, as it were).

## Making the Words for World Affairs

With such a power at our command, it is no wonder that when people study world affairs they do so largely linguistically. They do so mostly in words. The great debates in the discipline have rarely been made into ballets or movies. The main analytical languages used to articulate world affairs have rarely inspired paintings or plays. World affairs are spoken about and written about, as part of the word-made world. The words are the signs that denote the symbols that denote world affairs practices, and when the words are the words of those competent to make world affairs, they *are* world affairs.

This does not mean that a war between state-makers or a trade dispute between wealth-makers is nothing but a linguistic artifact. These practices take place regardless of what we say about them. They also take place through speech, however. A wordless world is inconceivable. It is speakers who discuss strategies, deploy resources, and give commands. Who speaks to whom, for whom, through whom, and about what are all crucial questions. They are world affairs.

### *Making "the News"*

Take three of the Western reading world's main organs of instruction: the weekly magazine *The Economist*, the daily newspaper the *New York Times*, and the nonstop television channel CNN. In describing and explaining world affairs, news organs like these (in descending order of generality) use language *per se*, the English language, sexist and ethnocentric language, models, technical language, and specific metaphors. On every level, world affairs get made in particular ways. Each has its own effects, then, on accounts of world affairs.

### *Language*

All language places very specific limits on global concerns. Written or spoken news, for example, is just that—written or spoken. It is not experienced. Words do not know pain, for example, however eloquently they may express it. Nor do they know such feelings as loyalty, fairness, freedom, honor, or equity. They can be used to talk about feelings like these, but the description of a particular feeling is not the same as having that feeling itself. Talking about the cause of a war is not the same as taking part in the war-causing process.

### *The English Language*

English, like all other languages, has its own way of representing the world (Sapir 1921; Whorf 1956). This can clash, sometimes radically, with the world as perceived by other language users, who because of the language they use render the world in other ways. Every language is its own thought-world.

As Whorf puts it: "every language is a vast pattern-system, different from others, in which are culturally ordained the forms and categories by which the personality not only communicates, but also analyzes, notices or neglects types of relationship and phenomena, channels his reasoning, and builds the house of his consciousness" (252). Whorf's unconscious use of the male pronoun helps make his case: "It is the 'plainest' English," as he says, "which contains the greatest number of unconscious assumptions" (244).

The fact that people experience the same world does not mean that they understand and represent that world the same way, either to themselves or to others, since to do that they must think and speak in the same language at least. In this respect, the world is not the same world to those who think and speak different languages. English, for example, objectifies. It says: "this is bread" or "that is a tree." Imagine a language, however, that says instead: "I feel this to be bread" or "there is treeing." To speak in such a language—Amerindian Wintu, for example—is to know "reality" in other than English ways. It is to imply the world, not objectify it. It is to express experience in noncategorical terms (Boas 1938, 218–221).

While an objectifying language like English has its uses, it also places limits on what we know. In this case, for example, it helps obscure a sense of reality as contingent and contrived. It obscures the sense of "the United States," for example, as a place and a people in process, as one where change is possible, including changes in the practices that constitute "the United States" itself.

What could this possibly matter to a local primary producer losing out on the world market, or to a state-maker having to decide whether to send troops abroad, or to a Welsh speaker watching his or her language disappear as English takes over? Everything, since all these are practices that are mediated linguistically. We think, speak, and act in language, and in particular languages, too, and this in turn affects—some would say determines—what we know and do. Surely we need to take account of these effects in trying to know world affairs. Since languages compete in this regard, the language that gets to prevail has an advantage. It gets to describe and explain the world, and to prescribe for it, too, in ways the speaker wants. Speakers of nondominant tongues have to wear the consequences, which can be notable and even dire.

## Sexism and Ethnocentricity

Media language is sexist and ethnocentric. Though major English-language news providers have made a concerted effort in recent years to use a more gender-neutral vocabulary, their success is still mixed. Subjects still get "mastered" rather than "mistressed." Masculine language still prevails. Ethnocentricity is a more complex issue since international English now comes in various forms. As well as the particular domestic vernacular that represents British English, there is also American English, Australasian English, Caribbean English, African English, and Indian English. The major news providers (CNN and the BBC for example) police their own preferred usage in this regard and in so doing are able to present their own cultural choices as global norms.

*Metaphorical Models*

Media language uses many metaphorical models. These are more elaborate than metaphors *per se*, which I shall discuss in a moment. We are often, for example, invited to "look at" an aspect of world affairs. What do we "see" there? This is a visual model. It suggests that we animate some kind of inner eye whenever we speak or read and that there are "things" out there to be "looked at" or "seen" once this inner eye is focused upon them. It promotes distance between us as observers and whatever it is that we are invited to observe. It denotes world affairs as detached and relatively remote from us. And it does all this ostensibly the better to describe and explain what world affairs involve. With this one metaphorical model, however, we would seem to have chosen a whole way of thinking and feeling about the world, a choice that eschews participation, subjectivity, or direct experience. Did we mean to make that choice? Was it an informed choice? Or did the habits of language make the choice for us, without our having considered their full implications first?

Metaphorical models are more common than we might suppose. Some consider the whole of our "ordinary conceptual system, in terms of which we both think and act" as "fundamentally metaphorical" (Lakoff and Johnson 1980, 3). They see much of the world as perceivable only in terms of metaphors and metaphorical models. Consider, they say, how common it is to depict hierarchies of global military power, or productive wealth, or social influence in terms of a pyramid. Consider how fixed, immovable, and difficult to invert this makes such hierarchies seem; how obvious it becomes that they should have a tapering superstructure with a small, remote, and exalted summit and a wide, load-bearing base.

Consider how common models of mechanism are in analyses of world affairs. Here the parts are "never significantly modified by each other, nor by their own past." Here "each part once placed into its appropriate position, with its appropriate momentum . . . remain[s] in place and continue[s] to fulfill its completely and uniquely determined function." Here, too, all sense of "irreversible change . . . growth . . . evolution . . . novelty . . . and . . . purpose" is taken away (Deutsch 1963, 27).

The "balance of power" is one such mechanistic image. In these terms sovereign states supposedly interact as solid, hard-shelled entities, impervious to each other and with a past perennially summed up by a competitive present. The system of states is supposed as a consequence to follow an objectified, machine-like logic of diplomacy and alliance, peace and war. That they follow this logic only in part shows the limits of such a model, a limit that obscures the capacity for whole-system change.

An organic image (like the one sometimes applied to the global system of states) seems to be more purposive and experiential than its mechanistic counterpart. Even so, an organic image "[leaves] no room for consciousness or will." It assumes no power to change the rules (Deutsch 1963, 38). Applied to world affairs, an image of organism makes for a highly deterministic ideology, too. The limits it sets are the same as those that the image of mechanism implies.

### Technical Language

Media language includes many specialized terms. Though mass-circulation news weeklies and newspapers are supposed to eschew jargon of any sort, this prohibition does not stop technical terms leaking through into their pages and thence into common parlance. Labels like "nuclear proliferation" or "underdevelopment" are obvious examples, but there are very many more.

Take nukespeak, that is, the jargon used by the practitioners and analysts of nuclear strategy. This is a vivid case in point, providing a good example of a specialized language that is used to distance its speakers from those who use ordinary words and to legitimate their expertise.

Nukespeak is not singular. There is a range of nukespeaks. The English version of it is different from the Russian, Mandarin, and Hindi versions of it. All nuclear strategists abstract from the welter of world events those aspects pertaining to themselves, however, developing in the process specialized concepts and expressions with which to talk about these events.

Nukespeak works not only to describe and explain nuclear weapons, but also to justify their existence. This is one reason why nukespeakers use euphemisms. These not only facilitate professional discussion, they also prevent the transfer of meaning from the nontechnical, highly subjective, and emotive experience of death and mass suffering that the "theater" use of nuclear weapons involves across to the technical, objectifying, and rationalistic experience of nuclear analysis.

At its most extreme, nukespeak policy is not a matter of protecting human beings from such weapons, but of protecting such weapons from human beings. For example, a colleague of mine once made a detailed postgraduate study of cruise missiles. He was a pleasant person, with a loving family. Yet the only decorations in his office were pictures of the missiles whose potential use he was trying to understand. They hung on all the walls, and each had a pet name. Any idea of what a cruise missile might do to people if it were ever actually launched seemed very far away. Some years later, as Director of the Nuclear Testing Section of a national Department of Foreign Affairs and Trade, this same colleague gave a public speech, in the course of which he said the following: "The endeavor to control and reduce nuclear weapons through negotiations is now 20 years old. If you can imagine yourself to be a nuclear weapon—the sort of thing we do for kicks in the Public Service—you would feel pretty pleased with yourself as the pre-eminent weapon, instrumental in keeping the central peace for what is now a record 44 years." Continuing to speak as if he were a bomb, this (by now) quite senior official said that the "harsh reality of the INF agreement signed in December 1987 and ratified in May 1988" means that for the "first time in over 40 years the future is uncertain—you [as a bomb] have a real sense of insecurity" (Huisken 1989, 70). Who is being defended here? The people? Or the bombs?

International political economists use copious amounts of jargon too. Adam Smith's "invisible hand," for example, arranges—seemingly automatically—all that we do as market self-maximizers (Adam. Smith [1776] 1892, 345). The whole concept is so discreet, in fact, that we are inclined to accept its touch without protest—unless the hidden hand becomes a hidden boot. Or take a concept like the "aggregate production function." This summarizes manufacturing and services provision in one mathematical expression (McCloskey 1986, 84). The whole jumble of responsibilities, habits, conflicts, ambitions, intrigues, and ceremonies that is the working life of the material world is supposed to be represented by a single geometric curve. "Economists" learn these figures of speech as part of their education, to the point where they cease to see them imposing any limits at all on what they supposedly know. Noneconomists find such habituation bizarre.

*Specific Metaphors*

Media language is "peppered" not only with jargon but with particular metaphors too. Here a literal account of what is meant is given a gloss that makes it more graphic and therefore more persuasive. One aspect of what is said is made easier to see. Other aspects are cast in the corresponding "shade."

Thus, while metaphors can make the world seem easier to understand, they are always highly partial, and they explain nothing of themselves.

Metaphors have a number of close relatives, which are all more explicit in how they go about transferring meaning. Similes, for example, directly equate one thing with another. Equating "the state" to a billiard ball, or state borders to "colanders" as opposed to "canopies," are examples in point. Synecdoche uses part of something to stand for the whole of it, the way "raising the flag" gets used as a way of describing "rallying a nation." And metonymy takes one name for another, the way "the White House" is used to denote the office of the President of the United States (Hawkes 1972, 3–4).

All metaphors have the virtue of making prose less prosaic. They make what we say more evocative, transferring meaning from one mental realm over to another. Thus, "your name is a bell that hangs in my heart" works as a specific metaphor despite the fact that there is no bell in my heart, nor could there be without its killing me. Likewise, the "power vacuum" that commonly occurs in world affairs could not exist without there being severe physical consequences. A particular metaphor can be literal nonsense. And yet it is not nonsense. We know it means something. The question is: what?

In making prose less prosaic, metaphors like these not only enrich news language, they also make it possible to achieve both wider and more precise meanings than those available to those who use only literal prose. This is where the trouble begins. On the one hand, we have Aristotle saying, quite categorically, "the greatest thing by far is to be a master of metaphor. It is the one thing that cannot be learnt from others; and it is also a sign of genius, since a good metaphor implies an intuitive perception of the similarity in dissimilars" (1946, 1458b). On the other hand, we have John Locke arguing, equally categorically, that "if we would speak of things as they are, we must allow that all the art of rhetoric . . . all the artificial and figurative application of words eloquence has invented, are for nothing else but to insinuate wrong ideas, move the passions, and thereby mislead the judgment; and so indeed are perfect cheats: and therefore, however laudable or allowable oratory may render them in harangues and popular addresses, they are certainly, in all discourses that pretend to inform or instruct, wholly to be avoided; and where truth and knowledge are concerned, cannot but be thought a great fault, either of the language or person that makes use of them" ([1690] 1894, 2:146).

Do metaphors say anything that cannot be said in plain English? Or should they be avoided "like the plague"?

Locke sees metaphors as a detachable tool, as a device to be used, quite rationally, to clarify meaning or otherwise to help the language-user achieve a purpose. As ways of representing the reality of the world, he sees them as being entirely dispensable, however, and he would dispense with them entirely in his rationalistic bid to tell the Truth.

Aristotle, by contrast, sees metaphor as inseparable from language. In articulating world affairs, he would find the allusive and evocative capacities that metaphors confer providing a distinct linguistic advantage.

While we might render our use of language less picturesque by deliberately eschewing all specific metaphors, we cannot, as Locke believes, escape from metaphor altogether. In one sense language itself is a metaphor. There is no reality without language, and in making the meaning of reality we cannot escape the "role" words "play" as interpreters and, therefore, as creators of world affairs (Onuf 1989).

This argument can lead to a particularly virulent relativism, since unless we impose one language on the world, and we cannot, then the meaning of that world is always going to be contested. This sort of argument also means that the world will never be fixed, however. It will be perennially in flux, inviting us to deconstruct and reconstruct it in pluralistic ways.

### *Making "the News" on TV*

Television presents particular limits of its own. What are we to make of the two-dimensional, twenty-one-inch images of war, famine, mayhem, disaster, political intrigue, consumer durables, social drama, the natural world, and even the cosmos presented to us in our rooms on little screens with loudspeakers attached? How are we to respond to TV's capacity to present profound human phenomena like war or famine or mass emigration in a discrete frame where the people do not stink, they do not make a mess, and they cannot threaten us, except in vicarious ways?

Some argue that, as the television medium expands, it actually closes people's awareness down. Postman, for example, says that TV transforms the world by giving people what they want, namely, entertainment. This is why, he says, when newscasters show us images and give us oral accounts of tragedy and barbarism, they can still urge us to watch and listen tomorrow. And we do (Postman 1985).

The spectator is provided with only hints of world affairs, and any discomfort is not sustained very long. Discussion too telling can be ignored anyway, particularly when it is conducted in much the same way that Swift characterized the academy of Laputa, where discussants held up objects to each other instead of using speech (Swift [1726] 1946, 182).

Others argue, however, that it is too easy to misunderstand the significance of TV. They say that we underestimate the perceptiveness of the viewer and overestimate television's power to sway an audience. Indeed, the whole literature about TV is far too ready, it is said, to identify it as the primary cause of effects produced elsewhere, effects produced by societies at large rather than by TV in particular (Lodziak 1986).

The point being made here is that people use TV. In practice they interact with it. They come and go from it. They contextualize it. And since the "eye" of the individual is situated in class, gender, and cultural terms, there are important differences in the social consciousness with which they contextualize and interpret what they "see." They are quite capable of making of the "news," for example, just one more story, just one more way of providing information, and one that fits their ideas, not those of the broadcasters. They are quite able, for example, particularly if they are aware of its many limitations, to treat "the news" with "irreverence" (Fiske 1987; Rushkoff 1997).

People manifest more awareness than they are given credit for, in other words. Life experience is more comprehensive than the experience of TV. It makes multiple meanings available from which we can and do make choices. It gives us the capacity to acknowledge the intentions of the channel-masters and to identify and allow for the kinds of language, both verbal and visual, with which they obscure those intentions. It gives us the capacity to decide what relevance TV may have, and the extent to which it is partial, patently false, simply irrelevant, or wrong. Perhaps we are not as isolated and as impotent as we appear. Perhaps there really is more to us than TV is able to make. Perhaps those who think the question is closed fail to appreciate how the social totality and the lived experience of those who use "news" may matter more than its mere televised representation. The argument goes on.

### Making a World Wide Web

The question gets raised again when we consider a medium like the Internet and the World Wide Web. Do people show more awareness than they are often given credit for when it comes to using linked computers on a global scale? It is early days yet, which means that it is not possible to do much more than speculate (Frederick 1993; Pettman 1997). Suffice to say, however, that the capacity of the Internet and the Web to disseminate the culture of the West, and thence to craft the culture of the world, may prove unparalleled.

The Internet was a Western invention. Indeed, it was an American and a Cold War one. The requisite technology is still being disseminated, however, and so its global potential has so far not been fully explored.

Will it result in intellectual entropy, overwhelming people's capacity to absorb information and create and store knowledge? Will it erode the sovereignty of the contemporary state? Will its main consequence be politico-economic, with money being moved in digital form around the world, revolutionizing in the process the nature of the global market and the value of national currencies? Will we become more individuated as a result, using the technology by ourselves, alone, rather than in solidarist groups? Will it foster rationalism, or nonrationalism, or irrationalism, or all three?

So many questions. As to the answers we can say, first, that there are the optimists, heartened by what the Internet and the Web make possible. Indeed, some see in recent events evidence of a new and higher level of human maturity (Rushkoff 1997). With the capacity for "citizen's diplomacy" growing, for example, state-makers find they are faced not only by their peers but by empowered publics as well. Hundreds of millions, even billions of linked computers, in private homes and transgressing all borders, offer intriguing possibilities for politico-strategic agenda-setting on a global scale.

Second, there are the rationalists, who note that the pattern of diffusion these computers make mirrors the uneven pattern of development that characterizes world affairs as a whole. They see computers and the capacity to connect and use them as mostly being a matter for the world's rich. These analysts are less likely to see mass emancipation resulting from Internet usage, at least not yet, since it is not the dispossessed and the unemancipated who get regular access to them.

Third, there are the pessimists who talk of new forms of social fragmentation and alienation, and wonder what they might eventually mean in terms of world affairs. They talk of decentered networks and of cyberspatial loss. They note the enormous amount of information already available on the Web, on both personal and institutional Web pages, for example. And they worry about people's capacity to absorb it all.

In particular they worry about people's capacity to absorb the information they find on the Web in an analytically meaningful way. During the so-called "Asian financial crisis," for example, that began in 1997, there were Web sites that cached large numbers of commentaries on the events involved. Those finding such a site might have assumed they had discovered an informational bonanza. As often as not, however, they had discovered a very limited version of events, cast in terms of the dominant analytical language of the day, and not offering any alternative interpretation to them. Such alternatives did exist on the Web, but they had to be looked for by those who knew what they were looking for. In other words, they had to be looked for by those able to seek out, access, and process the information they found in a knowing fashion. Such people would already have been familiar with the range of possible (as opposed to typical) interpretations, and able to tell, at any point on the Web, what they were not being told, as well as what they were.

It may be necessary, given not only the plethora of information the Web makes readily available, but also the ideologically loaded nature of all information, to rethink the role of the universities, for example, and particularly their role in regard to the social sciences. The role of memory, of the value of the human mind as an instrument for learning and storing information, may well be superseded now by machines that can perform this storage function more efficiently even than libraries can. Not more effectively, perhaps, since every mind carries around in it a working stock of information that makes thinking and creating possible. But the sheer amount of information that computers make available to those who have them, and the sheer ease with which this information can be accessed, is unparalleled, even by great stores of books (which, with the advent of a World Library, are online anyway).

The result, incidentally, may be much greater need for analyses like the one this book tries to provide—critical overviews that try to establish systematic connections between all possible information within a particular field and that construe the perimeters of that field as undefined. The value of the human mind remains undiminished. Indeed, it may be augmented as a result. Reasoning powers may become more important, not less, as they did, first, with the invention of the written word, and second, with the invention of printing. The key skills become: how to access not only some information, but also a broad range of information; how to acquire fundamental categories; and how to connect and apply them. This requires a priori understanding of a comprehensive kind, however, capable of making information out of noise and knowledge out of information. The more evidence the Web makes available, in other words, the more important our standards of evidence and our analytical maps must be. The more important it is that we be able to tell good information from the bad or indifferent sort. The more "frequently asked questions" we are provided with answers to, the more we need to ask, and be able to ask: who is asking these questions and why? Who is answering these questions and why? And in what particular way?

Prior comprehension is not only necessary because of the danger of information overload and of a consequent lack of discrimination. It is also necessary because "who knows what" is a power in itself and countering the fear of a vast rationalist conspiracy suspended in the electronic ether, and of digerati planning to take over the world using self-regulating intellectual systems that nobody notices until it is too late, is only possible by political understanding.

## World Affairs as Part of a Politico-Cultural Attempt to Make Modernity (Mind-Making)

These world affairs—the world affairs of our day and age—are characterized most fundamentally by the priority placed upon the use of reason in pursuit of truth, that is, as an end in itself. It is reason used in such a way as to see where the argument leads, and not to argue for some other end, like the good, the beautiful, the practical, the ethical, or God. By consciously valorizing the use of reason, we objectify the world and individuate the self. It is a mind trick, a sleight-of-mind. Nonetheless, it is a mental skill that makes possible new and reliable knowledge in marvelous amounts, especially with regard to nature and, more problematically, with regard to ourselves.

People in every society and in every era have valued human reason. Few societies have made it the definitive feature of their whole culture, however. Of these societies, the one that Europeans, and now also North Americans, have been building worldwide is the most committed and the most success- ful. In elevating so highly the power of human reason, these societies have been able to affect not only an ongoing scientific revolution but also an applied scientific revolution (the industrial/technological revolution). They have provided Old World Europeans, New World Americans, and their nu- merous global acolytes with enormous material power. This is a fact of some consequence for world affairs.

There are alternatives to using reason in this way, but they must contend now with world affairs made in these terms. There are premodernist beliefs in reason as a means to other ends, for example, and postmodernist beliefs in the limits to reason and the need to transcend them. These alternatives are viable and defensible but they are not hegemonic. At the moment, it is the deep belief in rationalism that globally prevails.

While some scholars have attempted to analyze world affairs in these terms (Lapid and Kratochwil 1996), doing so is still not considered by the disciplinary mainstream to be as legitimate as highlighting what it means for world affairs to be politico-culturally modernist.

The concept of a politico-cultural context, particularly of a global kind, is not yet common parlance in world affairs. The politico-cultural context is the most comprehensive one, however, being the context for all the matters of security, political economy, and society that currently constitute world affairs. The politico-cultural context cannot simply be added on to these other matters. It is not another dimension to modernist world affairs. It is what characterizes modernity per se, and therefore it characterizes every aspect of modernist world affairs—politico-strategic, politico-economic, and politico-social.

This is not to say that all the world has only one culture, but that at the moment there is only one world culture, and that this culture impinges on everyone on the planet, crafting the context to everyday experience, to a distinctive political purpose, that is, the prevalence of the West. It includes the global dissemination of one particular language (English), of singular

**Figure 1.** World Political Culture

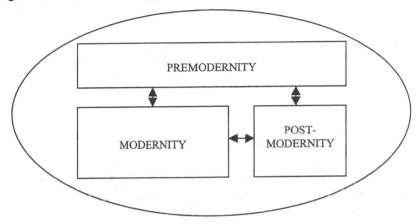

modes of dress (suits and dresses), of distinctive musical technologies (the symphony orchestra and the rock band), and of regional cuisines (French, U.S., and Italian). These are mere symptoms of a more radical cultural message, however, about the power and importance of emphasizing the use of reason as an end in itself.

The world *political* culture is this way of life as it pertains to politics. And since the most pervasive way of life on the planet at the moment is the Western one, it is the political value of that culture that currently has most consequence. Europe and the United States, and those prepared to imitate them, currently dominate world affairs. Their dominance has involved major attempts at planetary imperialism, the construction of world markets of production, investment, and exchange, and the global crafting of people not as individuals, which we are all born to be, but as individualists, which is a social status we have to learn.

The cultural mind-move that made all this possible took place more than three hundred years ago, though some would put it long before that. Since the seventeenth century Westerners have been building world affairs, as we know them (state-centric, market-made, and individualistic). They have been promoting not the fundamental value of ritual ("doing what has always been done"), nor of role-behavior ("doing what is expected of 'someone like me'"), nor of obligation ("doing what is 'my duty'"), but of reason ("doing what is rationalistic"). This is the context within which modernist world affairs take place, and any account of this context is the most radical account we can give of their contemporary making (see Figure 1).

The modernity that characterizes the politico-cultural context of world affairs arose first as a particular intellectual response to a particular set of constraints and opportunities experienced by sixteenth-century European thinkers. It came to receive global notice because of its instrumental power. In the process it has, for the moment at any rate, eclipsed all others (Calhoun 1997, 12–18; Anderson 1991, 163–185). Though pre- and postmodernity prevail regardless, people moving globally among all three along the arrowlines indicated, it is modernity that currently prevails.

### Making Margins—Within and Without

What would a map of the world's main politico-cultural practices look like? It would document first and foremost the global progress of modernist rationalism, that is, the location of the major sites of modernist and nonmodernist (premodernist and postmodernist) learning and research. It would document the practices modernists use worldwide to coopt, convert, and otherwise subjugate large parts of the global population—the appropriate gender socialization practices, for example, and the teaching of contemporary mathematics and science. It would also document the countervailing practices of feminists, indigenous peoples, environmentalists, the ethical, and the devout.

The heartlands of modernity, Western Europe and the United States, were nonmodernist once. Much of them are nonmodernist still, partly by choice and partly because of lack of opportunity. Making them modernist is not a process that will ever be complete either, since nonmodernist practices do not stop, even in those parts of the world that see themselves as the most modernist of all.

White West European and North American males were the first to privilege modernity in any great numbers, but the modernist project is not triumphant in either Western Europe or North America, even among white males. We do, it is true, have these world affairs rather than any nonmodernist alternative to them because of the global success of this project. It is an ongoing project, however, not one that was planned or executed all of a piece. It has margins as it is made, both internal to the project and external to it. As a consequence, it must contend with countermodernist critiques from within and with both postmodernist and premodernist critiques from without. All raise fundamental questions about modernist epistemology (the way modernists think about knowledge itself) and modernist ontology (who is doing this thinking, the nature of their existence, and what their reality means).

### *Modernity and Countermodernity*

The critiques made by postmodernist feminists, postcolonialists, and the representatives of indigenous peoples have been particularly cogent in this regard. A generation ago, the unspoken question in the study of world affairs was simply: "what are world affairs, that we may know them?" It was assumed that world affairs were simply "out there" and that we just had to study them to know what they were. Because of these countermodernist critiques, this assumption can no longer be sustained. Now we ask: "who are 'we' that we may know world affairs?" and "what is it 'to know'?"

In the study of world affairs, it was the so-called behavioralists, in the 1950s and 1960s, who first began to wonder about matters like these. It was the post-Vietnam countermodernists—on the margins of modernist world affairs—who took this question to its ultimate conclusion, however. They were the first to turn a debate about scientific method into a debate both about knowledge itself and about our being-in-the-world. It was a radical challenge that saw knowing about world affairs as having its own particular character—a character not neutral and not apart from what gets known.

Modernist knowledge, as noted already, is amazing. From astrophysics to zoology, we find extraordinary evidence of what the "light of the mind" can reveal when focused in a rationalistic way.

With regard to the study of world affairs, however, modernity has been notably less than amazing. No matter how highly we esteem reason, it does not generate large amounts of new and reliable knowledge about how the world works. To the contrary, it seems to obscure important aspects of just what it is that we most want to know.

This is not welcome talk in scientific terms. Indeed, to some it can sound downright dangerous, inviting unsystematic analysis—"arbitrary" analysis—that is wide open to abuse. If truths cannot be pursued by rational means, then deliberate fraud can no longer be exposed by analysis and any old purpose can be accepted as simply another way to know. This is to parody the argument, however. Though "truth" is only a Grail (or Grails) that we reach toward but never expect to grasp, reaching in such directions is still defensible. It is even arguably desirable, though it is arguably not enough.

The rationalist/modernist response is to say that there are no limits to what we now can know by rationalistic and objectifying means. At the very least, such an analyst would say, the question of limits is not a very interesting one, and at most it should be determined empirically, not decided in advance.

Countermodernists argue back, saying that we have all the evidence we now need to show that the light of the mind not only illuminates, but also blinds. And it blinds analysts of world affairs the same way it blinds analysts of anything else.

It is talk like this—of the limits to modernist rationalism—that has led to recognition of a role for hermeneutics ("interpretation"), phenomenology ("consciousness"), and participant understanding. It is the attempt to acknowledge those "many points in a cognitive structure beyond the reach of universal standards of logic and science . . . [where] there is no rule of logic and no law of nature dictating what is proper or necessary for us to believe" (Shweder 1984, 39) that makes nonmodernist talk so compelling. What are the implications of these complementary conversations for how we study world affairs?

## Making Modernist World Affairs in Three Dimensions: Politico-Strategic (State-Making), Politico-Economic (Market-Making), and Politico-Social (Self-Making)

If we lift the lid off the box marked "modernist world affairs," we find the modernist project going full swing. Picture this reality in all its complexity, and picture such concepts as state-making, market-making, and self-making as intellectual categories, imposed upon this reality in a bid to comprehend it (Watts 1989, 59). It will be immediately apparent from any attempt to do so that categories like these are conceptual conceits. The subject *is* complex, and what is more, it changes all the time. So how can we ever hope to explain and understand world affairs? Why bother to even try? Why bother to make sense of subject matter so obviously incapable of responding to it?

At this point I always think of the person who would have us perform major operations in sewers, because there is no such thing as completely aseptic surgery. Or who would have us commit blatant fraud because we cannot ever be completely honest.

In the face of the absolute limit set by human complexity, what can we do? We can only do the best we can, and so it is in the study of world affairs. We cannot know "the truth" about the subject. It is too complex and we are too much involved. We do not decide as a consequence to know nothing about world affairs, though. We do not despair and turn our backs on the whole enterprise and choose not to understand it at all instead.

We cope. Hence our concepts, our categories, our little intellectual boxes.

The question then becomes: what concepts to prefer? Here we find that many other people have done an enormous amount of work for us already. For many years—some would say, for millennia—analysts have attempted to explain and understand world affairs as they have seen them, and all that analysis is available for us to learn from and to use.

Here we also find that in acting in the world as if it were constructed of discrete dimensions, we do, in part at least, bring those dimensions about. It is not just a matter of trying to explain and understand the world, in other words, but also a matter of how explanations and understandings work, in self-fulfilling fashion, to construct the very world we then purport to find.

## World Affairs in Three Dimensions

Try another mental picture: put someone with her back to a wall and draw a line around her. Then turn her side-on and draw another line. Then tell her to bend forward so a line can be drawn around the shape she makes when viewed from above. One person; three different shapes. It all depends on your point of view.

World affairs are not a discrete entity like a single person. But world affairs can also be looked at from different points of view.

The most common ways of "drawing lines" around world affairs I've already mentioned, namely, in state-making (governance), market-making (sustenance), and self-making (coherence) terms. These are the process-labels for "polity," "economy," and "society," which are the conventional labels for the social sciences as liberals see them, and for the dimensions of world affairs referred to here as the politico-strategic, politico-economic, and politico-social ones.

Politicking is ubiquitous, which is why "politico-" is used in every case. "Politics" is usually defined as the work of governing a country. It is also defined, however, in terms of getting what we want. In this second sense, politicking takes place in any and every group. Depending on the culture, people strive, more or less overtly, to have their own way. Politics, there-fore, is everywhere.

Any attempt to talk about a separate "political" dimension to world affairs obscures the extent to which the process of politicking is ubiquitous. This is why I prefer to add "politico-" to the other labels I use, rather than designate it as a separate conceptual domain. Hence the use of the terms "politico-economic" and "politico-social." What about "politico-political" as a term, however? Does it not highlight the significance of the politicking process? Arguably, yes, though only by obscuring once more the ubiquity of all politicking practices. Instead of "politico-political," I prefer to talk of the "politico-strategic" dimension to world affairs. This label allows me to high-light state-making and all attendant diplomatico-military practices, in terms of global governance, without detracting from the political significance of the other dimensions of world affairs.

Why privilege governance, sustenance, and social coherence, however? What about the appreciation of art? What about religion? What about mo-rality? What about other dimensions of human practice that governance, sustenance, and social coherence do not account for?

My task here is to portray the modernist making of world affairs as clearly as possible. I cannot escape the fact that these three dimensions have been used since the nineteenth century to structure the way Western liberals in particular have sought to change the world. They have made these three dimensions dominant now, and, in self-fulfilling fashion, these three dimensions have taken on a life of their own. Enough people act as if they were the main dimensions of world affairs to make this the case in fact and to make the commonsense experience of world affairs comprehensible when described and explained this way.

## Mapping World Affairs in Three Dimensions

Just how pervasive this triune approach has become is immediately apparent if we pick up the map-making metaphor introduced earlier. Think of a world map of nation-states. Then think of a world map of global corporations. Then think of a map that shows the extent of the teaching of human rights. Imagine other maps as well, maps that depict differences in the division of labor by gender, for example, or that show the distribution of the world's ethnic groups or the world's religions.

Most world affairs analysts highlight states and their relations (IR), and maps reflect this fundamental fact. As a consequence, we associate contemporary world affairs most closely with the state-centric, geopolitical Mercator representation of them. It is a point of some significance that these maps—the ones with which we are most familiar—show states as containers, divided by clear lines, with no unassigned areas between them. The locations of the major cities are given, as are strategically significant geographic features like mountains and rivers, railways and roads. Not much else is depicted, however, since maps like these are largely meant to represent borders and the territories they enclose. More specifically, they tell us what happened when a seventeenth-century European politico-strategic practice (the post-Westphalian state) was turned by imperial means into the universal way of politically organizing humankind.

World affairs analysts also acknowledge the significance of the international political economy (IPE), which is the label most commonly used for the study of the world market and world capitalism, that is, the study of production, trade, and finance, and of the investment relations between states, firms, states and firms, and classes. These relations, and the practices they involve, can be represented by another kind of map that hangs, in a sense, behind the state-centric one. It tells us what happened when European entrepreneurs discovered the trade winds, began exploiting for profit new technologies in ship design and navigation, and began plundering the Americas. It also tells us how, with much of the transportable wealth of the New World colonies in their hands, Europeans went on to develop the industrial means to produce commodities and food (machino-facture), and a new mode of production, that is, capitalism.

It is not hard to imagine a map of the market-making practices that define the modern world economy and contemporary global capitalism. A map like this would not only compare states as producing and consuming entities. It would also show the major trade routes between states and within them, the location of major stock exchanges, banking and insurance centers, key production chains, the jurisdiction of the world's major firms, and global patterns of ownership, industrialization, and labor. It is instructive how rarely a map like this is displayed, despite the significance of its subject matter. It is an important fact in itself, therefore, that the state-centric map remains the main way in which world affairs are visually represented.

International political societies (IPS) are not widely recognized yet by the mainstream discipline, but behind the politico-strategic and the politico-economic maps lies another map again, a map of the major ways in which people socially cohere. A map of the main modes of coherence would document personal commitment to the "imagined community" of the nation (Anderson 1991), to the global practice of individualistic autonomy, and to the global practice of the (nonnational) collectivities that people create, largely as an antidote to individualism and its alienating effects.

A map of the world's international political societies would have to be drawn in terms of school syllabi and media content—indeed, of socialization practices of all kinds. It would be a hard map to draw in graphic terms, but it would show how these societies get made in people's minds. It would show how loyal they are to the state where they live, for example, and how far they have got in constructing doctrines of individual rights and collective duties. It certainly makes conceptual sense in terms of the significance of the liberalist trichotomy that currently structures the practice of world affairs. However, like the politico-economic map, the politico-social one is notable by its absence.

### All the World's a Stage . . .

If map-making seems somewhat mundane, consider world affairs as a stage play instead. We do, after all, talk of international "actors," "theaters" of war, and world leaders playing "roles." And though, like any metaphor, this one too has its limits, obscuring, for example, metaphors of work rather than play (Harre 1979), world affairs do get made in these three-dimensional terms, and these three-dimensional terms do lend themselves to the image of the stage. This is especially so since the making process is brought to many of us now on TV. The illuminated screen that sits in one corner of the room is like a little theater after all, enclosed in plastic and glass, within which we see enacted a small sample of the world's current events.

We sit, for example, as the world audience, watching as the diplomatic and military representatives of nation-states tread the global boards and play out the high dramas of international affairs. They give grand speeches. They build alliances and break them. They go to war, directing whole armies. They bring conflicts to a close, signing treaties, negotiating laws, and making interstate institutions. The whole vast spectacle unfolds before us, and unless we are unlucky enough to get pulled onto the stage (or into the studio), it never feels other than a distant show. It is "high" politics, done by people we will never meet, from parts of the world where we will never go, about problems of security and strategy we will never comprehend.

In the wings, all the while, lurk the theater company's accountants. We do not see them, but they see us, since this high drama is a "low" drama as well. It is a business. Performances are advertised. Nightly takings are counted. Players and crew are paid. The whole thing must make a profit or it folds. Behind and even as part of the spectacle on the stage we encounter the market that makes the performance possible and the behind-the-scenes deals done by statesmen and profiteers. In that market we find theater bosses who own and manage the means of theatrical production. Behind-the-scenes we find entrepreneurs who risk their capital to put on shows. We find firms determined to be seen on stage. We find workers, selling their skills for wages, constructing sets, for example, so that they and their families might survive. And we find audiences prepared to pay higher or lower prices for the better or worse seats. The high politics of the performance on stage is only possible, in fact, because of the low politics of all those who labor or manage, fashion or fund. Not for naught are plays called "productions," since many must produce what audiences sit and consume.

How does an audience get defined, however? Why do people assume the identity an audience requires? How do they get to know their part in the production, as people who spectate and pay? Here we find politics "lower" even than those of the market. The show would be nothing without the audience, since the social relationships that constitute a theater-crowd are an integral part of it. Without an audience, the little society that constitutes the theater would not exist at all. And yet nothing in the theater itself tells people what to do or how to behave.

The conventions the audience must observe in attending a performance on a stage are just as much learned as the performance itself. All these conventions are acquired. They are not innate. They have to be taught and as children we are indeed taught them. We are taught how to behave as members of a theatrical crowd, how to purchase tickets and find our individual seats (whether in the high-paying or the economy part). We learn how to watch, when to be silent, and when to clap and leave. Having the requisite identity is no small thing, in fact, since without a skilled audience the play

Table 1

**Modernist World Affairs in Three Dimensions (IR/IPE/IPS)**

| Colloquial label | Key process | Key concept | Core value | Type of power | Key power relationship |
|---|---|---|---|---|---|
| High politics (IR) | State-making (governance) | The state (polity) | Order | Diplomatico military | (Im)balances of power |
| Low politics (IPE) | Market-making (sustenance) | The market (economy) | Wealth or equity | Material | (Im)balances of production |
| Even lower politics (IPS) | Self-making (social coherence) | The individualist (society) | Conformity | Rational | (Im)balances of social identity |

would have no meaning. To paraphrase the greatest English playwright of them all, it would be a tale told by idiots. It would truly signify nothing.

The politico-strategic domain of "high politics" and the politico-economic domain of "low politics" are familiar to all students of world affairs today. They are the IR/IPE of the mainstream discipline and are taught accordingly.

Less familiar is the politico-social dimension, the "even lower" domain identified above. This domain includes not only the international society of state-makers that Bull and Watson talk about (1984) but also the international societies that ordinary people themselves create. There have been attempts, both current and of longer standing, to analyze world affairs in these terms (Walker 1989; Lapid and Kratochwil 1996), though it is still not deemed legitimate to spend as much time on matters of politico-social coherence as it is on matters of a more diplomatico-military or commercial kind.

As a consequence, the discipline is not referred to, as it ought to be, as IR/IPE/IPS. It is still referred to as IR/IPE.

The whole modernist project can be depicted schematically in Table 1, however. As noted already, the metaphor of world affairs as a stage play soon stops working if we carry it too far. It can be taken a step further, though. We can, for example, stand outside the whole theater and ask: what is this event? Where does "theater" come from? What does it signify? What norms, beliefs, and cultural values does it enshrine and transmit?

Not all peoples, it seems, have theaters and performances of this kind. It took a particular historical tradition to invent "theater" in the modern sense, to create a politico-cultural artifact of this kind, and to charge it with the significance it now has in the West. We might well, as a consequence, want to compare the form Western theater currently takes with forms it takes elsewhere. We might want to compare Western societies with ones where "theater" like this does not exist at all. We might then want to explore the limits that the conventions of the theater impose and how these limits might be transcended. We might want to ask who it is that theaters exclude so they can provide their performances, and what those excluded might want to do instead. Why are those on the stage of world affairs mostly men, for example, and what would happen if it were mostly women there instead? Would the play be the same?

Used like this, the metaphor locates these world affairs, modernist world affairs, "our" world affairs, that is, in their politico-cultural context. These world affairs are part of the modernist project and they promote and protect its primary norm, reason.

As pointed out earlier, this project was initiated in Europe in the seventeenth century when thinkers began to rely on reason rather than religious revelation. Eventually, reason and its use became an end in itself, and not just an instrument with which to enact God's ends.

The consequences of this "enlightenment" were radical indeed. They included the scientific revolution, the industrial revolution, and a revolution in the sense of self. They reduced space and time to quantities and everything else to matter, including any sense of a nonmaterial realm. They eroded the festive appreciation of life, the magic use of language as a means of casting spells, and much, much more. The modernist project was also male-made and ethnocentric, and all this acted like a stain, coloring all three dimensions of world affairs and the competing ways in which these dimensions were eventually described and explained.

### Competing Analytic Languages

If we take the practices that characterize modernist world affairs and talk of them in terms of three particular dimensions (politico-strategic, politico-economic, and politico-social), our next step is to ask: how are we to describe and explain each particular dimension? How are we to make sense of the issues each dimension involves?

The problem here is that there is no one analytic language that all analysts will agree to use. Most proponents of particular analytic languages would like to have everyone else share theirs. This does not happen, however, since there is no "true tongue," no analytic Esperanto, that allows us to talk about world affairs in the same analytic way. This is so for the simple reason that there is no agreement on the nature of human nature. This does not mean that Babel must result and that for every one person there must be a different analytic language. It does mean that we cannot expect agreement on how to talk about world affairs.

Table 2

**Modernist World Affairs: The Main Analytic Languages**

|  |  | Modernist World Affairs | | |
|---|---|---|---|---|
|  |  | Politico-strategic (state-making) | Politico-economic (market-making) | Politico-social (self-making) |
|  | Bad | Realism | Mercantilism | Nationalism |
| Human nature | Rational | Internationalism | Liberalism | Individualism |
|  | Good | Globalism | Marxism | Collectivism |

Modernist analytic languages do clump around the different assumptions modernist analysts make about human nature. Depending on whether they think human beings are bad, or rational, or good, modernist analysts identify more or less closely with particular points of view. The result is a three-by-three matrix that includes the dominant analytic narratives of our day (Table 2).

Those unfamiliar with these nine labels, or the analytic languages they refer to, or the analytic dialects each language entails, will find them briefly outlined in Chapters 3 and 4. They will have to be taken as read for the moment, as a comprehensive overview of the modernist study of world affairs and of modernist world affairs themselves. Those who are familiar with the analytic languages involved may want to take issue with this particular summary, in whole or in part. U.S. scholars, for example, might find the internationalist/globalist distinction untenable, dismissing it as a British invention that is worse than useless and even downright misleading as an analytic distinction. Once again, I would ask that disbelief be suspended until a more detailed account can be given of what the matrix involves.

The neatness of a matrix belies the radical entanglement we find in practice. The modernist ploy of discriminating between aspects of human nature, for example, quickly fails in reality, since all human beings incorporate all three aspects, and many more. And the analytical languages merge into each other. They are not as discrete as they look.

By the same token, it has not yet proven possible to collapse any one of these dimensions of world affairs into any other. Nor has it proven possible to dispense with any one of the main assumptions about human nature. None of the analytic languages this matrix highlights is dispensable either, since no analytic language has been able to prevail over the others in a definitive scholarly fashion.

Modernist world affairs are, first of all, modernist. As such, there is a rationalist/individualist cast to the whole project. Within this context, I see the main analytic narratives about state-making being realism, internationalism, and globalism. I see the main analytic narratives about market-making being mercantilism, liberalism, and Marxism. And I see the main analytic languages about self-making being nationalism, individualism, and collectivism.

Each language not only describes and explains world affairs but prescribes for them too. It offers policy alternatives. It makes value choices. Indeed, the whole modernist project is normative, from top to bottom. Since we cannot escape this consequence, we might as well admit as much and proceed accordingly, though it is a moot point how many do (Frost 1996, 33–39).

Modernist arguments about world affairs are ideological. They do not merely analyze. They advocate too. They recommend—implicitly or explicitly—particular kinds of change.

Ideologies are levers, made to move the mind, wielded by those who serve particular interests or causes (Berger and Luckmann 1966: 18). As a consequence, having an "ideology" suggests we have a very particular, and hence partial, point of view. Since it is not possible to have no point of view (though we might aspire to having no point of view by adopting the objectifying perspective of the rationalist—in itself a point of view!), we are all ideologists, whether we like it or not.

Imagine, for example, that you rule a poor country with a large debt that can no longer be serviced. Do you default, trade your way out of trouble, or try and fight the exploitation that put you in this plight in the first place? Each policy choice has a cogent rationale. Each involves a different approach (in this case, mercantilism, liberalism, or Marxism). Each employs a different analytic language with which to describe and explain that approach, since each is shot through with different assumptions. No choice at all is a choice for the status quo, and that is not a neutral place to be either. So what ideology do you endorse? And why?

As with language itself, what is said in one analytic language may not make much sense in another. Ideological nuance varies enormously. The same word can be used in different analytic languages to different ideological purposes, for example, taking on different meanings in the process. To a liberal market-maker, "capitalism" is a system where private individuals, not the state, own productive enterprise. To a Marxist class-maker, it is a historic mode of production, characterized not only by private enterprise but also by labor that is sold on a free market for a wage. The same word has different connotations, depending upon the analytic language using it and therefore upon the analytic context in which it is couched. This makes the translation of one analytic language into the other more than a matter of transliteration. It makes it a matter of interpretation, too, involving empathy, imagination, and tact.

At this point, it also becomes evident how wide a range of identities there is in world affairs. By *identity* I mean the sense we have, or the sense attributed to us, of who we are and how we differ from others. In terms of Table 1, for example, we find civil identities (defined in terms of states), market identities (defined in terms of caste or class), and social identities (defined in terms of a nation, a collective, or the self). In terms of Figure 1, we find modernist identities (defined in terms of reason), premodernist identities (defined in extrarationalist terms), and postmodernist identities (defined in postrationalist terms). We also find identities that pertain to those on the margins of the modernist project because of that project's sexism, ethnocentrism, secularism, and materialism—identities that are defined in gender, ethnic, religious, and ecological terms.

Modernist world affairs make most fundamentally for rationalism. Its proponents are more interested in value neutrality than any other value. In practice, however, all the analytic languages are prescriptive and therefore normative. They are in favor of particular values and against others. It is not possible, even at our most positivistic and scientific, to be amoral and value neutral. The distancing mind-move that is the dais upon which modernity is built is a bid to be objective, to not take sides. Rationalism is a side in itself, however. Thus, while morality may not be explicit in modernist world-affairs, except in terms of rationalistic doctrines like human rights, this does not mean norms are not there and that values do not play an important part in the making of these world affairs. This is immediately apparent, by the way, once we ask what construction ordinary people place upon the making of world affairs.

### Different Analytic Dialects

The main analytic languages that characterize modernist world affairs come in a wide range of analytic dialects too, more or less moderate and more or less extreme. Liberalism, for example, comes in different versions that are all clearly liberal but conceptually accented, each in its own way. "Extreme" liberalism, for example, promotes the freedom of the individual much more actively than "moderate" liberalism does, the latter being more willing to entertain state help in this regard. Realism comes in different versions too. There is "extreme" (or classical) realism, which grounds power politics in a view of human nature as competitive and aggressive. And there is "moderate" (or neo-) realism, which imports into power politics the rationalistic response any state-maker might be expected to make to the security dilemma the state system presents.

Within each dialect, whether moderate or extreme, there can be subdialects too. "Moderate" Marxism, for example, which is a dialect of the analytic language of Marxism, is discernible now in terms of subdialects like world systems theory, dependency theory, and neo-Gramscian theory. Each of these subdialects is notable for not anticipating proletariat revolution. That is what makes it "moderate" rather than "extreme." Despite being moderate, however, each of these subdialects differs from the others in notable ways.

### Each Dimension as a Continuum

The three dimensions of world affairs constitute continua. The politico-strategic dimension, for example, extends from an extreme preoccupation with state independence to cosmopolitan notions of transstate governance. The politico-economic dimension extends from an extreme preoccupation with economic nationalism and state-market protection to an equally extreme preoccupation with production and distribution by a range of other social collectives. The politico-social dimension extends from an extreme preoccupation with nationalism to the self-in-society conceived of in collectivistic terms.

### Each Dimension as Entangled in the Other Dimensions

Reading across the top of the matrix, we can see that politico-strategic realists are often the same people who are politico-economic mercantilists and politico-social nationalists. Running right through the middle of the matrix is the liberalist strand, which is pervasive at the moment. Liberalists are those most keen on constructing rationalist human practices. They are quintessentially modernist. As a consequence, they promote politico-social individualism, politico-economic liberalism, and politico-strategic internationalism (which is also known as "liberal institutionalism" or "neo-liberalism" and is used by liberals to carry liberalism over from the politico-economic domain into the politico-strategic one).

Running across the bottom of the matrix is the belief in the possibility of world government (the politico-strategic dimension), world communism (the politico-economic dimension), and world collectivist movements (the politico-social dimension).

Above the central, liberalist strand, therefore, we see analysts reaching back for or emerging from premodernist sentiments: the tribal sentiments of nationalism, the self-reliance of mercantilism, and the realpolitik of realism. Below the central, liberalist strand we see analysts reaching forward for sentiments that most modernist analysts see as still (if ever) to come: the cosmopolitan sentiments that a global government would require, the post-liberal sentiments that global communism would require, and the transindividual sentiments that collectivist social movements would require.

None of these analytical languages, with their component dialects and subdialects, was invented for this matrix. They all derive from historic debates about how best to explain and practice world affairs.

As the study of world affairs became more rationalistic, labels were given to different approaches, and the differences perceived between these approaches were read back upon authors from the past to create a scholarly canon that could be used to tell the historic story of each approach. Thomas Hobbes, for example, was read as a realist. Hugo Grotius was read as an internationalist. Immanuel Kant was read as a globalist. This meant highlighting only aspects of what these particular authors had to say, often at considerable cost to the integrity of their thinking and the context in which they thought. Any such canon is highly problematic as a consequence.

## Making What We Know by Subjectifying
## and Objectifying Means

As modernist rationalists, we are taught to objectify. We are taught to stand back and look *at* world affairs as they take place, in Bosnia, perhaps, or in Beijing. We watch the current events unfold on our TV screens. We read about them in newspapers and magazines. And we use the descriptions and explanations we find there in our own descriptions and explanations of world affairs.

As modernist rationalists, we learn to value a particular kind of experience. We are taught to sharpen our mental focus and to intensify our intellectual gaze so that our reason achieves maximum logical consistency and power.

It is also possible, however, to broaden out again the range of ways in which we engage world affairs. There are, for example, nonrationalist techniques, like listening in ways rationalism does not allow, and becoming engaged. Being consciously subjective like this brings to the task of knowing a feel for the texture of daily life. It also provides a better appreciation of how the world varies.

All knowing involves experience. The question is what kind of experience we choose to place a priority upon. Here I am discriminating between distal experience, which is objectifying and intellectualizing, and proximal experience, which is subjectifying and participative. I maintain that by objectifying, that is, by choosing not to take part, we set limits to what we learn. As I see it, the rationalist approach (whether conceived in strict scientific terms or, more broadly, in terms of systematic thought) distorts what we learn. Hence my determination to remedy this effect, to stand close to listen, and to take part as well.

### Standing Close to Listen

What does it mean to stand close and listen rather than stand back and look? When we stop objectifying and start attending to what ordinary (and not so ordinary) people actually say, we lose the clarity the "mind" makes possible. We win instead the chance to know with the clarity of "the heart." No amount of distanced reflection can provide this.

There are rationalistic research techniques that do allow us to listen, albeit in objectifying ways. We can do interviews, for example, or conduct public opinion surveys, though the more we make these techniques amenable to quantitative assessment, the more we lose the sense of what the research means to those we interview and poll.

Which is not to say that experiential proximity is unproblematic. Those we listen to may lie to us, for example. Advertently or inadvertently, we may lie to ourselves, because of personal prejudice, perhaps, or false consciousness of some other kind. Even when those we listen to do not lie, they may be inarticulate or otherwise less than capable of saying what is going on. Or they may fail to fully understand our questions. Or they may not be aware of what would constitute the kind of answer we want. Or we may fail to understand what they mean by what they say. For all these reasons and more, we do need to stand back to look objectively again at what we have heard by standing close to listen.

This said, what we learn by standing close to listen will complement what we learn from an objectifying distance. It will help correct the distortions that using reason alone entails. It will help transcend the limits that rationalism sets.

### Taking Part

We can go one step further again by taking part, in person if possible, and vicariously if not. There is no substitute for such an experience and the standpoint it provides. If we cannot have that experience, then we can still glean something of the meaning of standpoints other than our own by extrapolating from accounts of experiences that are available to us second-hand or by using our imagination.

Listening to what people say is one thing. Being involved is another. By immersing ourselves in the world affairs that we want to describe, explain, or otherwise understand, we get evidence available by no other means. Indeed, it is evidence that standing back to look may actively preclude.

Only engaged perception, in other words, gives us the feeling of what world affairs involves. Thus, while our rationalism may show us illuminating social constructs like "haves" and "have-nots" or "women" and "men," our participation (in social movements or the like) will show us how limiting such categorization can be. Taking part is one way of finding out how categories fail in their bid to capture the meaning of world affairs.

Engaged and participative research provides access to the life-worlds of those "other" than "us." In the modernist context, they make it possible for those on the periphery to know about the core, and for those in the core to know about the life-worlds of those that these world affairs marginalize and render mute.

The relevant techniques here are familiar to students of sociology and anthropology. They are known as "participant observation" or "ethnographic fieldwork." In disciplines such as these, the notion of experientially proximal as well as experientially distal research is long established, the pros and cons of fieldwork having been weighed up by anthropologists for many years.

The concept of fieldwork is largely alien to most scholars of world affairs, however. There are exceptions, especially among "development" theorists and conflict mediators and those who do case-study research. These are exceptions though. The norm is to be disengaged.

Rationalist/positivists say that the evidence resulting from experiential research, unless explicitly used to test a hypothesis, is merely anecdotal. They treat it as suggestive at best and are only likely to include it in their accounts of world affairs once they have objectified it. This is defensible. It also, however, provides a less comprehensive and arguably less accurate account than might otherwise obtain.

Participant research techniques do have drawbacks. These are many and varied and they can compromise severely the value of the evidence they provide. They do not invalidate participant research itself, however.

Rationalist/positivists query participant research because of its uncertainty, for example. We may feel we are taking part when, actually, we are not. What we want to know may also stop happening or may happen in some other way, because we are there. Our influence as a participant may inhibit the behavior we want to explain or understand, or it may change it into something else. In this way, the whole research experience can become a lie.

Another drawback is selective perception. The cause of this consequence is self-evident. Uncritical participation can swamp objectivity completely, in a number of ways. Those we are close to, for example, or those we most respect, may not be the best of informants, despite the fact that they are our preferred ones. What is plausible and comprehensible is likely to loom largest, too, obscuring in the process what is actually going on. As we become more familiar with the participant experience, we may also start overlooking the obvious or we may start thinking in the values implicit in the language of our experiential environment, likewise inhibiting our capacity to learn.

The most serious problem has to do with our own subjective status, however, since our participant "self" may be neither as constant nor as reliable as we think. Indeed, the whole research technique relies upon our having and maintaining an individuated awareness, which would only seem to exacerbate the limits that rationalism ultimately sets. It certainly does not mitigate them.

For reasons like these, we do need to stand back again. We do need to try in an objectifying way, which may be provisional at best (but which is no less worth doing because of that), to look at what it is that taking part reveals. We have to have a rationalist reprise, in other words. We have to reflect on the meaning of what we have experienced in taking part and ask whether the proximal experience actually does take us beyond the limits that objectifying reason sets or whether it only fixes those limits more firmly. This is where scientific enquiry can and does have a point.

Such a reprise is also necessary if we are to make available what we have learned by taking part in terms that positivists in particular and rationalists in general find appropriate. To begin with, we may feel it more apt to convey what we have learned by taking part in a poem or a play. If we present this to an academic audience as serious scholarly research, however, we cannot expect to get a sympathetic hearing. It would be futile, for example, trying to get the *International Studies Quarterly* to publish something so obviously extrarational and nonanalytic, regardless of how objective or informative it might be. There are conventional ways of presenting rationalistic knowledge about world affairs, and those who flout these conventions soon find themselves put beyond the disciplinary pale, into journals like *Alternatives* (Bleiker 1998).

### Explaining and Understanding

Going through this cycle—standing back to look, standing close to listen, taking part, and then standing back to look again—is not intended to dispense with objectifying reason. It is meant to complement it using other ways of knowing, thereby maximizing our chances of explaining and understanding world affairs. Explanation and understanding are said to be different ways of knowing. Explanation is knowing why things are the way they are "from without," as it were. Understanding makes what we are knowing meaningful "from within," as it were (Hollis and Smith 1990; Lakoff and Johnson 1980). Using this difference, we can see that it might be entirely possible to explain what we do not understand (science) or, conversely, that we might understand what we cannot explain (intuition). Combining the two is not as simple as it might seem, however. Explainers try to objectify. They tell stories of cause and effect. Understanders try to subjectify. Their story describes how reality seems and the "rules and meanings" this seeming involves (Hollis and Smith 1990, 6–7).

Within the intellectual frameworks of the West, these two different ways of knowing (or knowing about) world affairs cannot be added together (though Zen Buddhists have no problem resolving such seeming contradictions, albeit in a mystical way). If these two ways of knowing cannot be added together, however, they still can be placed in a complementary relationship, along the lines of the logic of the dialectic. This identifies first a thesis, then an antithesis, then a synthesis that becomes the new thesis, and so on. Dialectical logic does not blend opposing points of view. Rather, it allows the one to be played off against the other, each retaining its own way of knowing and each knowing in ways the other cannot. The two alternatives thereby complement each other, making it possible to come to a broader conclusion than either alone allows. This compensates in turn for the limits each sets.

Using explanation and understanding in an interactive way makes for a more comprehensive, less distorted way of knowing. This is why standing back to look a second time is not the same as standing back to look the first time. It is informed by all that gets heard and felt, by the listening and doing that goes on, between the first objectifying enquiry and the second. The second time we stand back to look, we get not only a different kind of analysis, in other words, but arguably a better one—more complete, better able to apprehend more and different kinds of evidence, and better able to account for both explanation and understanding.

As a process, this spiral of knowing leads out, providing a deeper and broader capacity to explain and understand world affairs. There is no reason why it should only be confined to one cycle, either. It can be repeated indefinitely.

The process may ultimately dissipate for lack of consequence since "[e]ach viewpoint is arguably incomplete—a mix of insight and blindness, reach and limitations, impartiality and bias." And even taken together, standing back to look, standing close to listen, and taking part can achieve "neither omniscience nor a unified master narrative." The best we can ever expect are complex assessments of what are "ever-changing, multifaceted social realities" (Rosaldo 1989, 128).

The process does work, though. Take, for example, the doctrine of politico-strategic realism (which I shall deal with in more detail in Chapter 4). The usual modernist approach would be to provide a rationalist analysis of this state-centric ideology. Why stop there, though? Why not then listen to IR realists themselves saying what IR realism means to them? And having done that, why not go further and participate in the practices IR realism recommends? Having stood close to listen and having taken part, we can then return to our objectifying mind-gaze for an analytic reprise. We can reflect once more upon what has been learned by these experientially more proximate means. We can get as a result a more nuanced appreciation of IR realism, an appreciation of a kind that a rationalist/positivist analysis alone cannot provide. We can get as a result a more accurate appreciation, too.

### The Eye/Ear/Nose Cycle: The Collapse of the Soviet Union

I call this cycle the *eye/ear/nose* cycle, since it involves, in a figurative sense, looking at world affairs with the eye of the mind, listening to people speak about world affairs with an open ear, and nosing out what world affairs involves by taking part. I find this cycle highly salutary. However, does it really make for more comprehensive and accurate accounts of world affairs?

Consider, for example, the failure to anticipate the collapse of the Soviet Union. Despite years of practice and immense material and mental resources, mainstream analysts of world affairs did not predict either the scale or the speed of the changes that happened in the Soviet Union in the 1980s. Specialists whose whole careers had been dedicated to the study of Soviet affairs, international relations theorists, journalists, politicians, entire intelligence establishments, were all found wanting. They were all found to have been working to reinforce the "deep, instinctive conviction that the world will always be as it is right now—except that it will become, gradually and harmoniously, even more as it is now" (Fairbanks 1993, 56).

There were a few, it must be said at once, who did predict the end of the Soviet superpower. This group included angry exiles, wishful Cold Warriors, and the occasional academic or journalist. Their predictions were always qualified, however. And they typically saw the weak point of the Soviet system, as did Soviet leaders themselves, as being the country's disparate ethnic groups and nationalities. In this respect, they were also wrong.

The kindest way to answer the question as to why so many failed so badly is to highlight the complex and contingent character of all world affairs and their intrinsic unpredictability. In these terms, the collapse was just one more instance of the whole subject's uncertainty. World affairs are like the weather. There may be patterns to it, but they are hard to predict.

for example, had a kidney complaint, and his successor only barely outlived him, as a result of which Gorbachev came to power, bringing with him a willingness to attempt major reforms. Who could have anticipated the collapse of a key protagonist's kidneys, let alone such radical consequences? Some specialists see this as quite enough to explain why so many of their number failed not only to provide the right answers but even to ask the right questions.

A less kind answer to this question might be the lack of imagination of the analysts concerned. This would not explain why the lack of imagination was so widespread, though.

Even less kind would be the charge of bias. There was, undoubtedly, a comprehensive bias induced by the Cold War itself, though it seems odd that such a bias should have so seized the analytic imagination as to preclude all but a mere inkling of what ultimately took place. One would have thought that, just as an academic exercise, there would have been schools of thinkers prepared to posit the possibility of the Soviet Union's demise and to elaborate variations on this theme. There were no such schools. There were old guard theorists who were profoundly antipathetic to the Soviet system. They seemed to believe we were stuck with a totalitarian party regime forever. There were younger Turks, the so-called "revisionists," who simply saw the Soviet system being sustained by the same mixture of "habit, consent, and coercion" that keeps most regimes going most of the time in most parts of the world (Rutland 1993, 117). And that, by and large, was it.

Common to the whole analytic culture was a bias even more insidious than the Cold War one, however, namely the reliance on rationalism and positivism. So significant was the shared predilection for doing research in this way that I believe we have a test case here for a whole way of knowing. The failure, in the main, to anticipate even the possibility of the collapse of the Soviet Union arguably exposed a weakness in the whole cultural apparatus that was being used to describe and explain the world. This weakness was the inability to recognize that there is more to knowing than intellectual abstraction and analytically generated data can ever allow.

World affairs theorists are not used to thinking in terms of such a shortcoming. For the last three or four hundred years, the protagonists of the modernist project have been making the world over into tightly governed, territorially bounded entities, embedded in a world market, where individualist identities prevail and where the objectifying use of reason is the politico-cultural rule. World affairs analysts are heirs to this Enlightenment tradition, and for those with global interests to promote and protect, the need for reliable knowledge can be acute. Hence the embrace of the scientific method and the attempt mentioned earlier to scientize the study of world affairs. Hence the failure to send astute poets to the Soviet Union, disguised as vodka sellers, to drink with people and to report what they learned when they got back.

Rather than stand close and listen, in other words, the relevant analysts chose to stand back and look. Even when the information was gathered up close (by spies and the like), it was treated as if it had come from afar. Highly symbolic here, for example, was the use made of space satellites to measure the growth of the wheat crop in the Ukraine. There were also doctoral students doing intensive work on a country they did not even visit. Thus, when an English academic surveyed the eighty-seven dissertations written in the United States on Soviet domestic politics between 1976 and 1987, he found that only seventeen of their writers had visited the Soviet Union, and of that seventeen "[o]nly a handful" had conducted "anything resembling fieldwork." (Rutland 1993, 115). Admittedly, the Soviet regime at this time was not facilitating fieldwork, particularly by students from the United States. But for seventy doctoral students of domestic Soviet politics not to have set foot there does lead one to wonder about the academic criteria for adequate knowing.

Perhaps some of the failure to anticipate the peaceful demise of the Soviet Union was due, in other words, to the pervasiveness of the faith in hypothetico-deductive analysis. One prominent U.S. historian certainly thought so, accusing IR scholars of favoring "method over subject." Even at the height of the Cold War, he said, it was easier to change the formal policy toward the Soviet Union than it was to change the mainstream preference for "behavioralist data-collection projects" (Gaddis 1992/1993, 25). The more that scholars relied on "observable, calculable evidence," the more they failed to account for the "critical variable of self-awareness." And the more they failed to account for self-awareness, the more "incomplete, misleading, and washed-out" their accounts of reality became. Little wonder, he concluded, that they failed to anticipate the end of the Cold War (Gaddis 1992/1993, 29). Not that the historians did any better!

In the light of this analytic debacle, Gaddis began to believe that the study of world affairs should be brought "up to date." Knowing means using every means possible to get at the unknown, and for Gaddis this has now come to mean using "not just theory, observation, and rigorous calculation, but also narrative, analogy, paradox, irony, intuition, imagination, and . . . style" (57–58). Presumably he is indicting himself here, too, since Gaddis is not known for using these means either.

### The World-in-the-Individual

In the case of world affairs, we are in a sense already up-to-date in that, as statist, capitalist, individualistic, and reasoning beings, many of us actually embody (or is it en-mind?) the dominant ideologies of our day. World affairs—

these world affairs, modernist world affairs—are constituted in us. We find the world-play, not on some distant stage, but taking place within. We are the players, the members of the audience, the inhabitants of the world.

Far from being passive observers of world affairs, in other words, we are active participants in them, too. This is not to say that we are necessarily to be found taking part in the world's wars, financial confusions, or crises of global identity, though the dynamic and interconnected nature of contemporary world affairs bring these closer all the time. It is rather to highlight how much we are implicated in the process of perpetuating these world affairs, rather than any of the alternatives to them.

Whether we know it or not, we actively collude in the making of these world affairs. They are made in us, and through us, all the time. We mostly take them for granted, like the air we breathe and the water we drink. These are after all "our" world affairs, not some other kind of world affairs, and as a consequence we mostly fail to notice how much they are there. They are there, though, primarily in the form of nation-states, capitalist markets, individuated societies, a rationalistic culture, and margins that highlight the patriarchal, postcolonialist, ethnocentric, environmentally unsustainable, secularizing nature of the whole project. And they are there in our own thoughts and feelings as citizens, workers, individualists, and rationalists, and as en-gendered, en-raced, en-classed beings.

Regardless of whether we appreciate the extent of our collusion, it does require certain kinds of human beings to bring these world affairs about. It requires human beings with particular attitudes, concrete skills, and specific concepts of themselves to perform the repeated patterns of practice that make all this possible. People learn these practices, and whatever is learned can be unlearned or relearned in different ways. It is thus that these world affairs are made and remade. It is thus, too, that despite all the constraints that the past bequeaths, new kinds of world affairs are brought about.

The constraints from the past are many and varied. They include the way the time scales involved extend far beyond our life-spans. The sheer size of the past is one important reason why we fail so notably to appreciate how much of modernist world affairs we get taught how to do. If we are born into a statist, capitalist, individualistic, and rationalist world, for example, and a sexist, ethnocentric, and ecologically unsustainable one to boot, then it could well seem that it was ever thus and that it will ever thus be.

Though these characteristics of world affairs are all bequests from the past, world affairs were not always like this. They will not always be like this, either. These are key features of world affairs at the moment, however. And though we tend to assume that it will continue to be like this for the foreseeable future, if the past is anything to go by, it will not.

Knowing the world-in-ourselves can allow us to transcend the constraints of the past. By becoming more mindful of the worlding-rules we already know and of the meanings imbued in us about what is and what is not globally appropriate—by being more introspective, in other words—we can learn much about these world affairs at first hand.

If we are to access our culture and our consciousness by introspection, however, what then is it to know? What becomes of knowing by objectifying?

We can introspect rationalistically. We can, by using our "unique ability consciously to separate ourselves from the socio-historical conditions of our own existence" (Ourossoff 1993, 281), try to determine what we think and feel. In doing so, however, we compromise our capacity for nonrationalist introspection. We are detached again, this time from ourselves. Our knowing is extraspective again, not introspective, and we cease to learn what listening or taking part can teach.

We need to introspect nonrationalistically as well, then. We need to listen to our own internal constructions and to take part in how we/they think and what we/they feel.

Who is to do the listening and taking part here, however? The rational mind will try to make another mental observer, to be this inner analyst and to do this from a distance, which is just what we are trying to preempt. The point is not the creation of an infinite regress of inner observers, but rather something else again, that is, proximal experience, or the intellectually unmediated awareness of what we think and feel.

To sum up and conclude, then: I have argued that the study of world affairs should be put in the most fundamental politico-cultural context that we currently can, that is, the belief in reason as an end in itself. This project—the project of modernity—has created politico-cultural peripheries both within and without its putative core.

The politico-cultural project of modernity has politico-social, politico-economic, and politico-strategic dimensions, each of which is deeply entangled with the others. Each of these dimensions is separate, too, at least conceptually so, since this is the way these world affairs have been made and continue to be made.

Each dimension has been described and explained in a number of competing analytic languages. These languages are all rationalistic. As such, they are part of the making of modernity. Individualism, liberalism, and internationalism are hyper-rational, however, carrying the politico-cultural logic of mental autonomy further than it has ever been carried before.

The limits that all the languages of modernist world-making set can be transcended by research of an experientially proximal kind. This is why in the remaining chapters I will first provide a discussion of each analytic language. I will then provide a short example of someone speaking in this language so that we can listen to it more closely. I will then provide a short sample of writing that shows, however vicariously, what it might feel like to take part in the world that such a language promotes and protects. And I will finally provide an analytic reprise. This four-part sequence will allow me to highlight the experientially proximal as well as the analytically distal aspects of the discipline, thereby giving proximity the analytic attention it arguably deserves.

Standing close to listen and taking part provide information not available any other way. Without such information, modernist/rationalist analysis is an account of a world of reason, which is not the world in which we live. World affairs involve the practice of reason, to be sure, and what could be better for describing and explaining this practice than rationality itself? The rational analysis of a feeling, however, like the will to go to war, the desire to make a profit, the desire to be oneself, or the belief in reasoning itself, does not exhaust our sense of what these feelings mean. Rational analysis allows us to talk about these feelings, but it does not document these feelings as we know them experientially. For that we need other research methods and other research reports, able to provide not only "facts" about world affairs but the "feeling" of these facts as well. For that we need research methods and research reports less indifferent, less likely to caricature what are fundamental concerns, and less false in this most fundamental respect.

# I

# The Neglected Aspects of the Discipline

# 2

# Making Modernity

The mapping exercise in the previous chapter puts modernist world affairs, with its three main dimensions, in their politico-cultural context. It depicts modernist world affairs as one aspect of modernity and of the modernist project, though by calling it a "project" again I do not mean to suggest that it was planned and executed as such. The whole process has been much more contingent than the project metaphor suggests. This is not to deny that there were many planners and policy-makers who had a modernist end in view. It is only to say that there was no grand plan, no conspiracy, no cultural plot to take over the world.

Most studies of the making of modernist world affairs do not begin by talking about them in politico-cultural terms, though that is arguably where they should begin. Being modernist is momentous. Highlighting only two dimensions of world affairs (the politico-strategic and the politico-economic), as the contemporary discipline does, is to obscure that fact. This has not only distorted the study of the subject. It has also helped craft these world affairs.

By rendering the making of modernity less visible, we help hide it. We help hide what is arguably the most important single fact about world affairs. This hiding ploy gets fed back into the practice of world affairs in the form of policies that do not adequately account either for the modernist predilections of state-makers, market-makers, and self-makers *or* for the nonmodernist propensities of those put on the margins of these world affairs.

When I say that these world affairs, the world affairs of our day and age, are modernist, I mean that their most characteristic features for the last three or four hundred years have been willed by the West in terms of the emphasis placed there on the use of reason as an end in itself. Most people in the West know little about this. It was a minority project in the first place, and some would say that it is a minority project still. What "the West" means has changed over four hundred years, too. This said, the priority placed upon the primary use of reason as a cultural norm, that is, as an end in itself, defines modernity as conceptualized above. And it is the extent of this particular emphasis, despite all the examples of the use of reason in other times and other climes, that is notably "Western," too.

Nonmodernist people are rational, I hasten to add, since I am not talking here about universal human capacities. Nor do I want to suggest that the West is the only culture to have ever placed a high value on the use of reason. Goody argues that it is "pointless to speculate about deep, continuing, cultural factors . . ." that assume the West is "marked by the presence or growth of rationality (or a special form of rationality) or by similar, unique features" (Goody 1996, 238), and while I do not agree with him, I certainly agree that there is abundant evidence of the use of reason by other cultures, both now and before. Needham's study of the sciences of ancient China (1954) is just one example, albeit an outstanding one, and contemporary accounts of universal rationality at work abound as well.

My point is different, and it is this: that nonmodernists, both non-Western *and* Western, but particularly non-Western now, are not taught to privilege rationalism. They do not as whole cultures actively promote rationalist thinking. They do not actively seek to follow the lines of argument that reasoning provides, wherever these lines may lead and regardless of the consequences.

They learn instead, whether knowingly or unknowingly, to put their reason to other purposes, which they get from their cultural context and which typically implicate the particular sense of cosmic authority their societies sanction.

In medieval Europe, before the advent of modernity, this purpose was mostly faith in the Christian concept of God. Reason was ultimately one way to know Him. This did not stop the ploughman from thinking about the most efficient way to plough a field, of course. Nor did it stop the carpenter from thinking through the best way to wield a plane or, indeed, how to improve upon the design of the plane itself. The *problem-solving* use of reason is endemic and universal. God remained, in the cultural vein, the cause and purpose of these people's best rationalist endeavors, however. The use of reason as a *critical* tool capable of assessing the truth value of God, and even of reasoning itself, was not taught as a matter of cultural course. It is now, though, and that is the difference.

The "modernist" label is one that Westerners have given themselves. They are the ones who talk about "modernity" and the "modernist project." The use of the word "modern" is part of the modernizing process itself, and all these terms are therefore incorrigibly contemporary and ethnocentric.

"Modernist" has a range of meanings that need to be held apart, however (Williams 1983, 208–209). The word is used, for example, to describe not only the world affairs of this day and age (how "contemporary" they are), not only the novelty of these world affairs (how "up-to-date" they are), not only the way in which world affairs are characterized by patterns of behavior that not all people yet accept (how "innovative" they are). It is also used to describe specific patterns of behavior deemed especially "progressive," that is, in terms of the "modern" state, the "modern" market and capitalist system, and the "modern" sense of the individual.

The "rationalist" label is one that Westerners have given themselves also. They are the ones who talk about rationalism and the use of reason as an end in itself. And they do a lot of talking indeed. Rationalism encompasses a very wide range of issues by now. As a doctrine, it is used to highlight what are deemed to be significant aspects of mind, matter, and the metaphysical, as well as of time, space, perception, emotion, morality, change, and truth (Hollis 1973; Rescher 1988; Harvey and Okruhlik 1992; Gellner 1992; Nozick 1993). Some of these issues will be discussed below, though only cursorily.

While well aware of the enormous number of concerns I do not address here, I try to focus on what is of primary interest to analysts of world affairs. This I take to be the notion that "modern" refers not just to the present, or to the newly fashioned quality of that present, or to the originality of what has been newly fashioned, or to particular features of that fashioning process, but to "modernity." And this I take to be the culture of Western rationalism (culture used here to refer not to the arts, nor to specific national cultures, but to whole civilizations and the ways of living and believing they hold most dear). This culture dominates world affairs at the moment, having made of the way we think a tool of extraordinary discrimination.

What caused Westerners to create such a civilization? This is a historical question that has not yet received a satisfactory answer. It probably never will. But create such a civilization they did.

One value stands out in the making process. It is the key to any understanding of the modernist project Westerners have been engaged upon for the last four hundred years. This is the value, noted more than once already, that gets placed upon the use of reason when it is used to "see" the world "objectively." It is the value placed upon the mental capacity to view the world from a distance, as a picture and to see in that picture what is not merely apparent but what is real.

Placing a priority upon this mental ploy is a fundamental aspect of world affairs today. Like the automatic rifle, the U.S. dollar, the business suit, and the English language, rationalism has become a universal tool. And as we shall see, it has been rendered progressively more formulaic in the process.

J.D. Mabbott once likened the use of this objectifying power to climbing the tower of a great cathedral. As the objectifier climbs, he says, "the common and particular details of life . . . shrink to invisibility and the big landmarks shake themselves clear. Little windows open . . . with widening views. . . ." Every turn of the narrow stair brings another casement, and though no one ever gets to the top, what draws people on is the dream of the tower's summit, where they think there's a "little room, with windows all round" where they can see everything—where there will be a view of the whole (Mabbott 1958, 1).

Accepting for a moment Mabbott's metaphor of the mental tower, what grounds, might we ask, is it built upon? What foundations underpin the project it represents? Who gets cast into its shade? Does anyone ever reach the top?

The idea of a cathedral obscures the sense of such a tower built, not upon stable land, but in the sea. It obscures the sense of such a tower being built as we climb it, rather than one that exists already, which we can then appreciate and explore.

Questions like these lead to different images—that of the garden, for example. Instead of knower-climbers, might we not speak of knower-gardeners instead? Instead of analysts, crouched by narrow windows, saying they can see the whole view, might we not talk of researchers tending the analytic soil, judiciously fertilizing and planting, weeding and nurturing, and with luck and good weather producing fine produce that all can enjoy (Carse 1986)?

Mabbott's modernist tower is built on the grounds of premodernity. The garden that Carse would have in its stead is the garden of postmodernity, though I do not wish to exaggerate the dichotomies between these metaphors. To do so is to essentialize their differences—a modernist ploy in itself. I do not, in other words, want to depict the study of world affairs in "either . . . or" terms. I do, however, want to highlight the way it is possible to go directly from one countermodernist position to another, to go from premodernity to postmodernity without having to go through modernity at all. Indeed, many people currently seem to be doing just this, taking selectively from what modernity has to offer, moving directly toward a world with postmodernist characteristics, while managing to maintain their premodernist integrity in the process.

This is not something many modernized Westerners readily understand. They see "modern times" as synonymous with what they themselves have achieved. Anyone who does not aspire to do and be the same as they is by definition nonmodern, a word they use to denote not only the noncontemporary, but also all that is backward, old-fashioned, and unprogressive. Modernity used like this is the ideology of modernism. It gets used to compare the "modern" with the "traditional," the latter term being a patronizing euphemism for "backward." Tradition is no longer deemed to be venerable, dependable, and constant. It gets deemed obsolete, retrograde, and unsuccessful instead.

In other words, what the West has been doing for the last three or four hundred years has been made, by Westerners themselves, the standard by which all other human endeavors get assessed. This is ethnocentric, as indicated already, and it is also arguably masculinist as well. Such is the power of the modernist project, however, that modernist Western acculturators are currently able to constitute themselves as the global ones. Key products and key preconceptions of modernist Western culture are now recognized worldwide, and where they are not acknowledged freely as such, they are directly imposed by neo-imperial means.

Which is not to say that all the earth's people share these products and preconceptions, since only a minority does. Relatively few find it definitive as a way of life, in fact. Thus, while the global impact of modernity is undeniable, and no one escapes its consequences, both good and bad, the project is contested. It is a matter of some debate, as well, how many people actually see modernity as the basis for the best of all possible worlds (Said 1993).

Subsistence villagers in the Solomon Islands, for example, do not speak the conceptual language articulated by European thinkers over the last four hundred years and made global by Euro-American imperialists. While self-evidently "in" this world, they are not "of" this particular version of the world. Nor do they necessarily want to be of this particular world, except in a highly selective way.

To take another example: most Japanese do not know this language either, though the most international of them, who have studied or worked abroad, have a capacity to "two-track" their minds. They speak in countermodernist/premodernist terms with their fellow cultural "insiders" while speaking in modernist ones when they deal with cultural "outsiders." When necessary, they mentally administer this distinction with great care, protecting aspects of their own way of life that they continue to prefer.

More North Americans than Solomon Islanders or Japanese tend to know this language, or know about it at least. Large numbers of them have never learned it well, though, or have never had the chance to. Canadian, U.S., and Mexican educators continue to fail, despite the best of intentions, to foster a vigorous spirit of rationalistic inquiry and the appropriate forms of mental speech in more than a few. Indeed, many of their students are quite pleased to fail in this respect, and rightly so, many might say.

### Premodernity: Reason as Means

If we are to put the modernist project at the center of our story, as its world-shaping significance suggests we do, then we can say that before the advent of that project there was only premodernity, in all its manifold forms. There were peoples, that is, as there are peoples still, who did not privilege rationalism; people for whom the rationalistic use of reason, and the way it can be made to work in critical as well as instrumental ways, is not the key cultural concern.

In giving modernity such prominence, I could be said to be colluding in the process whereby modernists legitimate what they make in this regard. I could be said to be endorsing modernist rationalism and the idea of an autonomous "self" that goes with it. In the process, I could be said to be helping exalt Western "selves" in relation to non-Western "others" (Said 1978).

This is very far from my intention, however. In using categories like premodernity, modernity, and postmodernity, I am, it is true, accepting the contemporary significance of the modernist project. I do not believe that this project is necessarily superior to particular countermodernist alternatives, however. As Foucault argues, it is not a question of distinguishing modernity from a "more or less naive or archaic" premodernity and an "enigmatic and troubling" postmodernity. Like him, I do not want to put premodernity/modernity/postmodernity in a simple sequence, like a train. Rather, it is a matter of trying to find out "how the attitude of modernity, ever since its formation, has found itself struggling with attitudes of 'countermodernity'" (Foucault 1984, 39) and with the premodernist and postmodernist aspects of other ways of being.

### The Anthropological Debate

Debates in disciplines other than world affairs help make this point clearer. Premodern cultures are the particular intellectual province of anthropologists, for example. Anthropology was originally created, as was world affairs, for an imperial purpose. It was developed as a rationalistic (objectifying, scientific) way of doing things, not to the West but to "the rest." At colonialism's end, the scientific validity of the work anthropologists had done heretofore began to be questioned. This led in turn to attempts to articulate the difference that social scientizing in general is supposed to make.

Rosaldo casts the story of early anthropology in mythic form. It is an engaging rhetorical ploy. "Once upon a time," he says, "the Lone Ethnographer rode off . . . in search of 'his native' . . . he encountered the object of his quest in a distant land. There, he underwent his rite of passage by enduring the ultimate ordeal of 'fieldwork.' After collecting 'the data,' the Lone Ethnographer returned home and wrote a 'true' account of 'the culture.'"

The mythic quest of this (typically male, Western, objectifying) individual was never an innocent one, however. "Whether he hated, tolerated, respected, befriended, or fell in love with 'his native,' the Lone Ethnographer was willy-nilly complicit with the imperialist domination of his epoch. The Lone Ethnographer's mask of innocence [or, as Rosaldo puts it, his 'detached impartiality'] barely concealed his ideological role in perpetuating the colonial control of 'distant' peoples and places."

The "eye" of the ethnographer, in other words, was an imperial, as well as a racist and sexist, "I." What was cast in neutral, disinterested terms, as serving a purely scientific purpose, proved not to be so in practice.

The point of the mythic quest, Rosaldo says, was self-validation, self-aggrandizement, and social control. Thus, in concluding his epic tale, Rosaldo notes how the Lone Ethnographer typically portrayed the colonized as members of a "harmonious, internally homogeneous, unchanging culture" who needed not only Western "progress," but also its economic and moral example. Seemingly timeless and traditional, the colonized thus served as "self-congratulatory reference point[s]" against which Western mind-makers measured their progress in the "long, arduous journey upward" that had led to themselves (Rosaldo 1989, 30–31).

Just as Vietnam, and the decolonization process of the 1950s and 1960s of which Vietnam was one awful symptom, marks the point at which the scientistic certainties of IR realpolitik began to unravel, the same war led to radical reassessment of the classic studies that the Lone Ethnographers had made. U.S. anthropologists, like U.S. IR analysts, began to question their most basic assumptions. As a consequence, what had been deemed analytic representation began to look more like analytic interpretation instead, and both disciplines began to take an interpretative turn.

The standard studies in anthropology, for example, which had been revered for years, were found to be inadequate, inaccurate, far from "true" accounts of how the object peoples actually felt. Being "intellectual," for example, the standard studies were seen to have avoided the confusing effects of emotional feelings such as indignation, frustration, anger, disapproval, or even sympathy. Feelings like these do cloud the capacity to be rationalistic. But so too does the self-conscious disinterest and intellectualizing of the kind these studies contained, which was shown to have distorted, skewed, and otherwise misled the makers of the accounts of the cultures concerned. More particularly, the classic ethnographies were found to impede our knowing and our understanding of how the social forms a culture exhibits are both made by cultural conventions and used in spontaneous and expressive ways.

The standard studies were shown, in a word, to be biased. The human capacity to live with doubt, to improvise, to create, if not actively suppressed, had been seriously inhibited by the objectifying mind-gaze. What to the ordinary person living in a particular culture might seem a meaningful compulsion, for example, had been invariably rendered, in the light of the ethnographical mind, into a mere ritual. The power and meaning of human behavior had been rendered more mechanical as a consequence—and more false. The classic ethnographies, that is, were seen to have reduced the vast diversity of the ways of human living down to a handful of preconceived theoretical frameworks, suitable for the doctrines of "structuralism" or "functionalism" current at the time. These anthropological doctrines were supposed to reveal the inner workings of any culture, anywhere, at any time. In practice, however, this was not the case (Gardner and Lewis 1996, 23).

The critical rethink of anthropology allowed modernist anthropologists to rediscover their subject matter. The peoples they study among are well aware, of course, of their cultural complexities. They do not need Western anthropologists to tell them that they are human beings, leading full and rich lives that have complex and meaningful patterns of behavior in them. For the anthropologists, though, it was something of a novelty to find out about other ways of living in terms of the "contested, temporal and emergent" forms in which other people actually experience them, rather than in terms of the intellectual frameworks that rationalism provides (Clifford and Marcus 1986, 19, 190).

The rethink of anthropology has been rethought in turn by now. In the process, the old rationalist agenda, in part at least, has been reaffirmed. The nonobjectifiers who do "postpositivist" (nonrationalist) anthropology are said by their more classically minded colleagues to have no good answers to critical questions about political economy or the loss of cultural variety as modernity becomes globally hegemonic (Marcus and Fischer 1986, 4). Turning away from objectivity is said to do little to answer questions like these. Classical modernism, the re-rethinkers maintain, does much better in this regard.

Some anthropologists never relinquished the old agenda in the first place. In one well-known "rethink" study, for example, specifically on the nature of anthropological understanding, Clifford Geertz discusses how "near" or how "far" the anthropological experience should be. Geertz is not interested in constructing a near/far cycle like the eye/ear/nose one, however. He wants to choose between two sides of a dichotomy instead. Should the social scientist opt, he asks, for total immersion in another culture (with the danger of becoming trapped within its mental horizons) or for abstract representation and interpretation (with the danger of becoming deaf to its special sounds)?

As it turns out, there is no choice, Geertz says, since he does not believe that one can ever get too close to another culture in the first place or, ultimately, perceive what other people perceive, a fact that immediately eliminates the dichotomy and replaces it with only one alternative, the objectifying one. The best we can do, Geertz says, is perceive what other people use for their perceptions.

Geertz is a rationalist. As far as he is concerned, describing the lives that other people lead can only document the fact that "we" would not want to lead them. He is happy to "go native" for a while, as a social psychological tourist, but only because he has Western rationalism to come home to (Geertz 1987). Thus, while on the face of it Geertz may find human diversity and human difference an "enduring, perhaps inevitable, perhaps even desirable feature of human existence" (Walker 1989, 4), in the brain behind that face we find the modernist penchant for putting the world at a distance. We find the choice, premade and utterly unalterable, to prefer experience from afar. We find no desire at all to entertain the notion that the experiences we have by coming close to "others" might modify and change, or even supplant entirely, our rationalistic ways.

In the wake of the rethink of the rethink of anthropology, new fields of study have emerged, such as cultural studies (Nugent and Shore 1997). The debate that all this rethinking involves is not unique to anthropology either. Historians, for example, also argue about the limits to rationalism, and the more they do so, the less premodernity seems a kind of absence and the less likely they are to depict premodernists as hanging about in the antechambers of global significance, waiting for the Age of Reason to reach them (Wolf 1982). Premodernists begin to appear, to historians like these at any rate, as having cultural presence and values of their own to promote and protect.

### *The Experience of Premodernity*

So much for standing back to look at premodernity in an analytical way. It is a basic thesis of this book that there are limits to what rationalism can reveal, however. The stories that rationalists tell are logical, hypothetically falsifiable, and empirically demonstrable. They are not all-powerful, however, which is why our next step is an experientially proximal one. I will now try to bring us closer to premodernity, at least as modernists construe it. I will listen to a premodernist speak about how reason should be used and what it should be used for.

I have chosen first of all an extract from Book 8 of St. Augustine's *City of God* ([1467] 1972, 306–311).

St. Augustine is a premodernist rationalist arguing that rationalism is limited. His rationalism is stuck at the tail, as it were. He cannot pull it free to allow the whole beast to range as widely as it likes. His mental means are modernist, that is, but his purpose is not.

St. Augustine of Hippo was born in North Africa in A.D. 354. He long predates, therefore, the advent of modernity, though from his writings it is very clear that he was a consummate reasoner. He never used his reason as an end in itself, however, to see where reasoning might lead. He used it in the service of his Christian faith, to demonstrate the power and importance of God, or, at least, of God as conceived by St. Augustine. What follows, then, is the voice of one historic premodern thinker speaking about reason as a means to an end compared with reason used for itself alone. In this passage he is praising Plato and the Platonists for their awareness of reason as a form of devotion, as a way to get to God.

> These philosophers [the Platonists] . . . recognized that no material object can be God; for that reason they raised their eyes above all material objects in their search for God. They realized that nothing changeable can be the supreme God; and therefore in their search for the supreme God, they raised their eyes above all mutable souls and spirits. They saw also that in every mutable being the form which determines its being, its mode of being and its nature, can only come from him who truly *is*, because he exists immutably. It follows that the whole material universe, its shapes, qualities, its ordered motions, its elements disposed throughout its whole extent, stretching from heaven to earth, together with all the bodies contained within them; and all life, whether that which merely nourishes and maintains existence, as in the trees, or that which has sensibility as well, as in the animals; or that which has all this, and intelligence besides, as in human beings; or that life which needs no support in the way of nourishment, but maintains existence, and has feeling and intelligence, as in the case of angels—all these alike could come into being only through him who simply *is* . . :
> . . . Plato defined the Sovereign Good as the life in accordance with virtue; and he declared that this was possible only for one who had the knowledge of God and who strove to imitate him; this was the sole condition of happiness. Therefore Plato has no hesitation in asserting that to be a philosopher is to love God, whose nature is immaterial. It immediately follows that the seeker after wisdom (which is the meaning of 'philo-soph-er') will only attain to happiness when he has begun to enjoy God . . .
> . . . There may be others to be found who perceived and taught this truth among those who were esteemed as sages or philosophers in other nations: Libyans of Atlas, Egyptians, Indians, Persians, Chaldeans, Scythians, Gauls, and Spaniards. Whoever they may have been, we rank such thinkers above all others and acknowledge them as representing the closest approximation to our Christian position.

Augustine clearly values the eye of the mind. He is a man who loves to think, and to think rationally too. That is not what he loves most, however, or what he values most highly. His ultimate purpose is to be with his God. Augustine has a personal and immediate sense of his continuity with the universe, a sense manifest in his belief in Christianity. Augustine thinks he thinks because of God, and for God. It is inconceivable to him that he might think beyond God. For him, there is no "beyond God," and so reason cannot be one of those goods that is an end in itself. For Augustine, there can be no end of any kind other than God. Rational thought can only ever be a means with which to think about God, and those who presume to think to some other purpose, Augustine says, are lesser thinkers. They are, as far as he is concerned, simply wrong.

This argument does not make Augustine right. Imagine trying to convince Augustine that he was not right, though, particularly in modernist terms. The argument would be a lively one, but if you wanted to regard reason as Augustine regards God, your argument would pass him by. You would be arguing to a radically different purpose. There would be no mental ground on which the two of you could meet, and you would both be left shaking your heads. This would be a fitting indication, perhaps, of how much the use of reason was involved in the argument, but there would be no conversion in either case. Augustine would likely consider you an inferior thinker, while you would likely find Augustine a Christian bigot. You would find him ultimately irrational. He, on the other hand, would consider you damned.

This argument does not make you, as the modernist, right either, though being "right" or "wrong" may not be the point. Perhaps the issue has more to do with the kind of knowledge that objectifying provides. What if the most "valid response" to the question "I don't understand" is not "objectify," as the modernist would say, but "develop your intuitions" or "change yourself" (Taylor 1987, 76–78)?

Modernists reject not only the premodernist argument that reason is a means to an end but also the postmodernist appeal to other points of view. They fear the irrationalism involved in a pre- or postmodernist point of view.

What can you say, the rationalist would ask, to the person who tells you that you have to change—to the person who says: "acquire my superior insights and understanding and wisdom—or else!" What can be said if there appears to be no rational grounds on which to say anything? Augustine does not insist that others believe in God. He merely considers them benighted if they do not. Other Christians, despite the compassion that Christ professed, have not always been so tolerant: hence the Catholic Inquisition. For this reason the modernist/rationalist would always reserve the right to question the authority on which any kind of true believer acts.

This is to bring the question once again within the limits of reason, although the extreme modernist/rationalist would acknowledge no such limits. A passion for dispassion allows of none. The faith that the modernist/rationalist professes in reason as an end in itself, like Augustine's faith in the Christian God, encompasses all.

If we do acknowledge limits, however, and if we do then attempt to move beyond them, what does this involve? What does it mean to have and to practice the basic values of another culture, for example? Is it even possible, or, as Geertz argues, are we only able to "see" from outside? If we are sunk in the well of modernist rationalism (or should that be perched atop a high cathedral tower instead!), can we imagine moving from such a place? It is no small thing to catch the feel of the way in which a premodernist way of life might actually be lived, and what such a life means for those living it. Taking part in premodernist living is the only way to understand what is involved, however. Personal experience is the next proximal step.

Taking part personally is not always possible. If it is not, then we have to find a more vicarious way of knowing firsthand. There are accounts by premodernists themselves, for example, of what they know and do, and I have chosen here the words of Confucius as one such account. Though highly problematic as a historical source (we do not know just who Confucius was or if he was even one single person), he provides a good example of premodernity in practice. He highlights ancient Chinese values that still feature in contemporary debates about Asian values. While these words come from a time and place very far from this one, they still get heard today.

Several concepts are central to the practical doctrine of ancient Confucius. One of the most important of these concepts is "li," meaning holy ritual, sacred ceremony, propitious rite. This is not a concept that makes much sense in a modernist context, though this does not mean that it makes no sense. The sense that it does make, however, can only be had by adopting the thought-world of the Confucians themselves.

What is this orientation? What is Confucius trying to say? I quote from Book 13, section 3, of the *Analects* (1989, 171–172):

> Tzu-lu said: If the prince of Wei were waiting for you to come and administer his country for him, what would be your first measure? The Master said: It would certainly be to correct language. Tzu-lu said: Can I have heard you aright? Surely what you say has nothing to do with the matter. Why should language be corrected? The Master said, Yu! How boorish you are! A gentleman, when things he does not understand are mentioned, should maintain an attitude of reserve. If language is incorrect, then what is said does not concord with what was meant; and if what is said does not concord with what was meant, what is to be done cannot be effected. If what is to be done cannot be effected, then rites and music will not flourish. If rites and music do not flourish, then mutilations and lesser punishments will go astray. And if mutilations and lesser punishments go astray, then the people have nowhere to put hand or foot.

It is time for an analytic reprise. Let's consider the significance of the short admonition above.

For a start, Confucius is not concerned with correct language in the way a rationalist objectifier would be. He is not concerned, that is, with using language as a way of accurately representing the world. He is concerned with appropriate speech, not "true" speech. He is concerned with what is right, not with what is true.

Second, Confucius is concerned with rites, which as he says, give you somewhere to stand, something to grasp. In a society that no longer practices sacred rituals and ceremonies to affirm a sense of the divine, its members float free, not knowing, in Confucian terms, where to put their hands or feet. To quote Fingarette (1972, 6–11, 71, 75–79):

> Characteristic of Confucius's teaching is the use of the language and imagery of *li* as a medium within which to talk about the entire body of the *mores*, or more precisely, of the authentic tradition and reasonable conventions of society. Confucius taught that the ability to act according to *li* and the will to *submit* to *li* are essential to that perfect and peculiarly human virtue or power which can be man's . . . Men become truly human as their raw impulse is shaped by *li*. And *li* is the fulfillment of human impulse, the civilized expression of it—not a formalistic dehumanization. *Li* is the specifically humanizing form of the dynamic relation of man-to-man . . .
>
> Let us suppose I wish to bring a book from my office to my classroom. If I have no magic powers, I must literally take steps—walk to my office, push the door open, lift the book with my own muscles, and physically carry it back. But there is also magic—the proper ritual expression of my wish, which will accomplish my wish with no such effort on my part. I turn politely, i.e., ceremonially, to one of my students in class and merely express in an appropriate and polite (ritual) formula my wish that he bring me the book. This proper ceremonial expression of my wish is all; I do not need to force him, threaten him, or trick him. I do not need to do anything more myself. In almost no time the book is in my hands, as I wished! This is a uniquely human way of getting things done . . .
>
> . . . Society, at least insofar as regulated by human convention and moral obligation, becomes in the Confucian vision one great ceremonial performance [therefore], a ceremony with all the holy beauty of an elaborate religious ritual carried out with that combination of solemnity and lightness of heart that graces the inspired ritual performance.

For Confucius the good life is relational, communal, ceremonial, dignified. It is about the subjective experience of civilized behavior. Moreover, the rites that constitute civilized behavior are self-justifying. They are ends in themselves. However rational we might be, there is no point to our rationality unless it is put to human purpose. This purpose Confucius sees as best expressed in emphatic, intensified, and sharply elaborated versions of our everyday intercourse, that is, in ritual.

This is very different from the objectified judgments that the use of reason alone recommends. To the modernist, a particular culture's rites are not self-justifying. There is nothing that prevents them from being scrutinized rationally. There is nothing that gives them generative power.

The rational scrutiny of a culture's rites also reveals no single civilized intercourse. There is rather a plurality of civilized intercourses. The dignity, the community, and the relationships that ceremonial rites involve are relative, rationalists would say. They would likely question as well the authenticity of the traditions and the reasonableness of the conventions that ceremonial rites represent. Are "reasonable conventions" actually reasonable, the rationalist asks, in terms other than their own? If ceremonial affirmation has the effect of further embedding a pernicious social hierarchy, for example, how reasonable is that? Whose interests do "reasonable conventions" like these serve? How warranted is the ritual affirmation of them? What of those "affirmations" that involve human beings being "punched, bullied, sent to jail, thrown into concentration camps, cajoled, bribed, made into heroes, encouraged to read newspapers, stood up against a wall and shot, and . . . even taught sociology" (Barrington-Moore 1967, 486)?

Critical questions about the reasonableness of rites miss the point that Confucius wants to make, however. For Confucius there is no premodernity, not only because he lived long before modernity was invented, but because its intellectual premises would have made no sense to him even if he lived today. He would, if he lived today, likely offer precepts, and precepts that did not valorize reason as an end in itself. He would not, as a consequence, have promoted the concept of modernity.

To the modernist, it is Confucius who misses the point. The light of reason is to be read in no other light. Rather, it casts any other human endeavor in the shade. The competition between the different orientations of the different life-worlds has been won. It is rationalism, modernists argue, that rightly reigns supreme.

What might this have to do with world affairs? How does trying to take part in the world that Confucius represents improve upon the modernist/rationalist approach to international relations?

Most people in the world want to enjoy the fruits of modernization. Many in it want to affect the scientific and industrial revolution that modernity has made possible (not least, those in China). Does this oblige them to let the root of the plant strike wherever its fruit might be enjoyed, however? Must everyone accept the primacy of the Cultural Revolution that took place in the West in the seventeenth century (and not just the scientific and industrial revolutions that were the result of that intellectual revolution), if they want to benefit from what modernist rationalism makes possible? Or might it be possible to have the scientific and technological revolutions without the intellectual and cultural one? Cultures like that of Japan would suggest so. The Japanese have shown a remarkable capacity for modernist industrialization while keeping the cultural and intellectual revolution that first made this possible under their cultural control. Their success has important implications for world affairs as a modernist project. It suggests that this project might be carried further in ways that modernists have not anticipated. It suggests, in other words, a more open-ended and unpredictable outcome.

## Modernity: Reason as an End in Itself

Modernity is characterized here in politico-cultural terms, that is, in terms of the use of reason as an end in itself. Used in this highly focused way, reasoning has produced not just science, but modernist technology, too. A vast human bounty has been produced by the knowledge, both theoretical and applied, that scientific reasoning has allowed. New kinds of power have been produced too.

The issue is the extent to which reason can be detached from other purposes and given cultural precedence. There is a point at which a culture gives reason such credence that it cannot be construed as a mere means any more. This is what is supposed to have happened, first, in ancient Greece and, later, in the Europe of the Enlightenment. Reason is used everywhere else at all other times. However, only in these two times and places, modernists say, does it receive so much attention that it becomes what can be called the superordinate cultural practice.

In a twentieth-century account of this process by one of its most eminent heirs, Bertrand Russell, the modern world "so far as mental outlook is concerned" is said to begin in the 1600s, in Western Europe. "No Italian of the Renaissance would have been unintelligible to Plato or Aristotle; Luther would have horrified Thomas Aquinas, but would not have been difficult for him to understand. With the seventeenth century it is different: Plato and Aristotle, Aquinas and Occam, could not have made head or tail of Newton" (Russell 1979, 512).

It is a moot point whether Aristotle or Democritus, once they had mastered Newton's language, would have been able to make out what he had to say. Aristotle would have wanted Newton's thought to express a sense of purpose very different from Newton's, or at least, the part of Newton (who was a religious man) that did not require a divine agent to do any more than set things up so they might mechanically interact. On the evidence of all that he wrote, however, Aristotle was a man of reason. He was not rationalist in the modernist sense, but he might have learned to be rationalistic if that was what was required to understand what Newton had to say.

The ancient Greeks were ostensibly the first to place primary emphasis upon reason, though they were mostly speculators, not experimenters. Russell says that "no one among the ancients, except perhaps Aristarchus" was both a speculator and an experimenter. Patient experimentation was found among the later astronomers of antiquity, but, Russell says, bold speculation was not. We find neither in the European Middle Ages (Russell 1979, 514).

Whatever we make of Aristotle and the other Greek philosophers, like Socrates, who loved a good debate, it is clear in retrospect that the rationalists of modernity are both speculators and experimenters. Those who established modernist science were different from the Greeks in that they had "two merits which are not necessarily found together: immense patience in observation, and great boldness in framing hypotheses" (Russell 1979, 514).

The rationalists of modernity are also better than the Greeks at holding the use of reason separate from revelation. They may be devout, and many both earlier and later rationalists are very devout indeed. But they are also able to use reason to know the universe with. Indeed, the universe they deem to be especially amenable to reason's ways.

Why modernity begins in seventeenth-century Europe is a question that becomes more complex, the closer one looks at the historical stories that are told about that time (Toulmin, 1992). Suffice to say here that the first steps were taken in the context of a protracted religious war between Catholics and Protestants, steps that moved the steppers away from the "self-incurred tutelage" of institutions like the Christian church. It was the church, and what the church represented, that had previously prevented people from using their reason publicly, freely, and "without direction" (Kant [1784] 1963, 3). And it was the priority accorded reason that was finally used to repudiate this prohibition.

### The Cartesian Offensive

Renés Descartes was the first to enunciate clearly the rationalist and, hence, modernist creed (Descartes [1637] 1912). He was a Catholic, he took part in the Thirty Years' War between Catholics and Protestants, and from personal experience he knew how divisive these religious differences could be.

Perhaps Descartes came to the decision to give so much credence to reason as a way of transcending such deeply felt differences. His creed of reason was a beginning only, however. There was much more to come. It is not as if Europeans went to sleep as premodernists one night and woke up as modernists the next morning. The creed had few adherents to start with, and it took hundreds of years before reason received the kind of cultural prominence that it has in Europe, in the rest of the West, and in the world today.

Reason as an end in itself holds nothing sacrosanct. It can be turned back upon itself and philosophers very quickly test just such a turn. David Hume, for example, became notorious for thinking through what our chances are of actually knowing anything in this particular way (Hume [1739/1740] 1874). Can we ever get "behind" perception, as it were, to know what is really there? Hume, thinking rationally, was not sure we could.

### The Greek Retreat

To rescue rationalism from skeptical self-defeat, it was necessary to beat what might be called the "Greek retreat." It was thought necessary to move away from knowing based primarily on perceiving and to recover a somewhat more intellectual approach. Thinking itself became once again a fundamental way to know. It was the German philosopher, Immanuel Kant, who led this strategic retreat ([1784] 1963), arguing that the basic assumptions that make science possible rest upon a priori categories that are not derived from what we might otherwise perceive.

The Greek retreat had its drawbacks. In the course of our biological descent, we have clearly acquired a capacity to model the key features of our environment in our minds, since without this faculty we would not have survived. Our reasoning skills provide no guarantee that the facsimile of reality we construct with them is what is real, however. While reasoning might have allowed us to survive in the three-dimensional, before-and-after world in which we live, thereby avoiding hungry tigers, there is no proof that it can account for reality in any sense more tangible than this.

Recent scientific conclusions, which modernist rationalism itself has led to, suggest that our capacity to know reality might, indeed, have limits. Quantum physicists, for example, have been suggesting for some time that reality is not only stranger than we imagine, but also stranger than we can imagine.

Does this mean that rationalism, in general terms, as one way of using the mind, or in specific terms, as the scientific method, is a waste of time? Certainly not. It has not stopped quantum physicists, for example. And world affairs are not quantum physics. They are human affairs, and as such they may be more amenable to rationalistic analysis than quantum affairs might be. We do, after all, use reason to do world affairs with, and though much of world affairs might be considered unreasonable, at least the reasoned parts of it should be amenable to rationalistic scrutiny.

### Modernity's Results

What has been the consequence of promoting the use of reason as an end in itself? What has modernity done?

## Objectification

One important result of privileging rationalist thought and experiment is "objectification." Heidegger calls this the "picturing" of the world. The research that characterizes science, he says, is done by "objectifying," which he describes as a "setting-before, a representing." Descartes' definition of truth in terms of the "certainty of representing" he sees as the initial move toward this basic practice, and Cartesian metaphysics he sees as being definitive of modernity as a whole (Heidegger 1977, 127).

To the ancient Greek philosopher "man is the one who is looked upon by that which is." To the modern rationalist, however, the world is "set in place before himself." To talk of a world picture is not to talk of a picture of the world, however, but of the world "conceived and grasped" as a picture. This is why Heidegger argues that the expressions "'world picture of the modern age' and 'modern world picture'" mean the same thing. A medieval world picture did not exist in this sense. The world picture does not change from a medieval one to a modern one. Rather, the world becomes a picture when it becomes modernist. Thus the world "as picture" is, for Heidegger at any rate, the definitive modernist fact. It is a logical consequence of giving reason the status it has now (Heidegger 1977, 131, 130, 134).

## The Creation of the "Self"

The second, equally powerful consequence of placing a priority upon reason (though some would say it was the cause of our placing such a priority, not the consequence) is the creation of the "self." It clearly goes together with the picturing process above. The significance of objectifying, that is, lies not in the change it signals in our position with regard to what "is." "What is decisive," as Heidegger argues, "is that man himself [sic] expressly takes up this position as one constituted by himself, that he intentionally maintains it as that taken up by himself, and that he makes it secure as the solid footing for a possible development of humanity . . . There begins that way of being human . . . for the purpose of gaining mastery over that which is as a whole" (Heidegger 1977, 132).

Imagine the society in which you live as a rubber mass. It is layered and lumpy since it is gendered and class-structured and racially split. It is hierarchic and hegemoniac and heteronomous and you are completely embedded in it. For the analytic purpose I am using it for here, however, it represents a singular human space.

Next, imagine that you have been taught since the day you were born to give priority to your reason as an end in itself. In being so taught, you have learned to pull up and away from the mass that is the society in which you are embedded. It is as if someone had taught you to push away at that mass at the point where you happen to be. You have as a consequence moved away from that mass using your own, socially acquired will to do so—a will that is specifically taught by the society in which you live.

At the peak of the pulled-up place—your place, your peak—is your rational persona, your "individuated" self. This persona looks down from a distance at the world and at the socially embedded being which is you in that world. It is still connected to the rest of the society, since the sheet is elastic after all. The society constitutes you in a wide range of ways, as a gendered being, as an ethnic being, and so on. The elasticity of the social sheet is not infinite, though. If you pull up or are pushed away too far it will snap, your connections to your society will break, and you will find yourself floating free in some asocial realm (a mental asylum, perhaps), looking down at the hole in the social fabric where you used to be. We are taught to stop short of this snapping point, for obvious reasons. Most never get anywhere near it. The potential is there, though, and extremely individuated individuals, living alone in huts in the woods, are one example of what can result.

Now, imagine that everyone in your society is taught to pull up or is pushed away in more or less the same fashion. Some, who are good at this sort of thing, or who get more practice at it, pull up and are pushed away more than others. Some, for whatever reason, pull up and are pushed away a short distance only. All, except for the ones who go too far, remain connected to the sheet. They are all part of society. But all have separate, individuated, rationalistic "selves" as well, standing out proudly from their social context as discrete beings.

From the top of their personal peaks, these selves talk to each other, constructing with their conversation a metasocial, intersubjective realm. This abstracted, second-order realm is socially constructed out of individuated individuals, rationalistic personas, and as such parallels the one where people are embedded instead. The emphasis placed upon the use of reason as an end in itself, and the will to think objectively, prevents this metarealm from falling back into the society below, though some individuals, not of this mind, do return to the social mass (or they may successfully resist leaving it).

Modernists are these rationalistic, objectifying, individuated individuals in this extrasocial domain. The whole ideological apparatus of modernity is designed to forge the will to make this realm and keep it going. The collective result is a metasociety of modernist mind-makers.

It is in this metasociety, this intersubjective realm of discrete, objectifying persons, that the doctrines of democracy, of the market, and of human rights get made. Doctrines like these are only possible if we have rationalistic individualists. Indeed, doctrines like these cannot be formulated without them.

Societies that do not privilege reason as an end in itself, that do not as a consequence have a rationalistic metarealm of this sort, do not practice these characteristically modernist doctrines, or they practice them in a much modified form. The Japanese, for example, actively educate for the opposite of the metaphor I have used above. A Japanese proverb—*deru kui wa utareru* ("the post that sticks up gets hammered down")—gives some indication of how Japanese get coached socially to conform. The cultural value placed upon conformity in Japan prompts the Japanese to police any personal attempt to pull up and away from the social space. This is much more than a matter of cutting down tall poppies. It is a matter of weaving dense social webs of social obligation that restrain the individual at every turn. It is a matter of binding the individual tightly within the social mass. Modernist mind-making of the sort just described does not obtain in Japan as a prime cultural value. Individualists (as opposed to individuals) are much harder to come by as a consequence.

*Reification*

Priviliging reason has a number of important consequences in addition to objectification and individuation. All of these are characteristic of the politico-cultural doctrine of modernity.

The most important of these consequences has to do with the way objectifying makes for "things" and "facts." Reason provides access to a version of reality that appears notably more reified and free of value judgments than that of the everyday world. This is the "fact-value" dichotomy that so excited the early modernists. In rationalism, they believed they had found a kind of knowing that was absolutely true. Here was a Grail that seemed really worth reaching for—one that made their former arguments seem limited and pointless. Beside this, all else appeared to be a matter of mere opinion.

We talk about "Japan" or the "Japanese," for example, using these words as if they refer to things. It is worth remembering, in the light of rationalism's subsequent success, however, that not only are these words not "things," but that the things themselves are not things either. They only appear to be things when we talk about them in this way. In reality, they are complex patterns of repeated human practice that get reified conceptually because it serves our purpose to do so. This purpose is control, mostly, and it is very important, because we would arguably not be here without it, but it does limit the kind of world we see. If we want a comprehensive understanding of the world, we need to appreciate what this kind of objectifying leaves out. In this particular case, it leaves out, most significantly, a sense of "Japan" as being contingent, contrived, and amenable to change. It makes it harder for us to see that the world is in change, that it is not fixed, and that emancipation from what prevails in the present is entirely possible, even emancipation from those patterns of behavior that constitute, in terms of their emergent outcomes, "the nation-state."

## Reperceiving Time and Space

Placing a priority upon reason profoundly alters our perceptions of time and space. The modernist perception of space is Euclidean: it can be mapped, given coordinates, commodified, and divorced from any sense of any particular place. The modernist perception of time is quantitative: it can be measured, gained, lost, wasted, commodified, and rendered uniform too.

Perceptions like these create abstract concepts of space and time, and then break the link between them. This makes it possible to lift social activities out of their local context, to create "genuinely world-historical" frameworks of "action and experience" (Giddens 1990, 16–17). These frameworks (like the Agricultural Revolution) can then be made part of a cosmic perspective and given "fixed, permanent constraints" (Bernstein 1983, 19).

A life led in the metarealm of reason is highly self-conscious. It can lack a sense of authenticity as a consequence. We have to decide for ourselves what to do, rather than accept what the past might have ordained for us. We must decide what to value and what to believe. It is a life where gods and festivals rapidly lose their traditional significance, where magic becomes mere trickery, and where the whole universe is a place of matter and force.

## Alienation and Discipline

As the modernist persona becomes second nature, so too do its affective aspects. Objectifying results in alienation, that is, because individuation results in isolation.

What kind of world affairs does this portend? Do disenchanted people make for disenchanted politics?

As world affairs are made more modernist, governance is said to become more instrumental. And as capitalist production and consumption spread, governance is also said to become less moral. People learn to worship shopping instead and through it . . . "the private authorities, the order and the corporate power their worship makes possible" (Shearing and Stenning 1985, 347–348).

## Westernization

The metasociety that rationalists create for themselves is highly abstract. It is social only in the sense that the rationalists, whose abstractions are those involved, make it so. This is not where most people live, since most people, in their ordinary lives, do not need or use abstractions like these to make sense of what they do or who they should do it with.

This is the modernist society Westerners aspire to, however. It provides great freedom within which to devise general intellectual rules and principles without previous cultural referents. It is possible to devise whole worlds there. These designs can then be imposed—rationally, of course—back upon the world from which those who did this designing originally distanced themselves. The modern state, the modern market and capitalist system, and the modern sense of the cosmopolitan, rights-bearing self are all made in this abstract, intersubjective realm.

The individuated beings who make these rational rules and principles use them not only to create new societies of their own, but also to create a world affairs that prioritizes reason as an end in itself. Modernizing Westerners have imposed these rules and principles on their own culture, the one that initiated the modernist project in the first place. They have imposed them upon other cultures as well. Thus, "Westernized elites," in other parts of the world, have "assimilated the ideas of Western Enlightenment philosophers." They have gone on to reproduce these ideas in their "eventual drive toward independent statehood." Cultural life across the globe has been reorganized in the process as people have learned to conceive of themselves as "solitary agents in large, industrialized, and abstract states" within a world culture of rationalism (Amaturo 1995, 5). The world has become, in two words, modernized and Westernized.

No one can ignore what has been happening in the West and what Westerners have been doing. Many nonmoderns have chosen not to embrace the rationalist revolution. Others have rejected it outright (as, to begin with, did many in the West). Most have tried to come to some kind of accommodation with it, however, if only to get access to its extraordinary power. Some of the accommodations have been highly selective, but all have had to deal with the success—martial, material, and mental—of rationalism in global political practice.

As just mentioned, some nonmoderns believe they can master the rationalist principles that allow for new scientific knowledge without having to compromise their core commitment to nonrationalist concerns. This is why Huntington argues that "[i]n fundamental ways, much of the world is becoming more modern and less Western" (1996, 38). It is entirely possible now to become more industrialized and perhaps even more scientifically minded, yet not be Westernized in the process. It is not possible to become more rationalistic and not get Westernized, though, since the West is characterized most definitively in rationalist terms. To be modernist is to participate with Westerners in their long-running politico-cultural project to privilege reason as an end in itself, now on a global scale.

## Emancipation

Those who see no reason why rationalistic Westerners should lose their global nerve in this regard applaud the emancipatory capacity that reason as an end in itself can confer. Much good, they say, can be done this way. Much bad can too, of course, and world affairs are replete with the appalling. Enough wars, holocausts, environmental disasters, and systematic patterns of exploitation and starvation can be attributed directly to the rationalist construction of world affairs to demonstrate that doing world affairs in this particular way can be highly detrimental. Nonetheless, there are those who believe that the modernist cause can be advanced to overall human benefit; that Enlightenment rationalism can be used "against itself" as it were, to "further the project of modernity" (Devetak 1995, 29–30); and that world affairs of this sort can be used to help more people than they harm or hinder.

Marxist theorists are prominent in this regard, since they have long attempted rationally to appraise human injustice and have long argued for rational rectification. Rooted in politico-economy, however, Marxists have never been given adequate credence by those with more politico-strategic or politico-social concerns. Thinkers like Jurgen Habermas have tried to compensate for this lack (1979), reworking the West's universalizing doctrine of "autonomous rational individuality" and "free public reason," trying to replace it with an "intersubjective" or "communicative" one (Osborne 1992, 79). In terms of the metaphor of the social mass that was used above, Habermas draws our attention to the significance, not of the rationalistic personas pulled up and pushed away to their separate points from the social space, but of the conversations that go on between these punctual personas—conversations that constitute the intersubjective metasociety. These conversations are essential, Habermas believes, as an emancipatory force, and a whole raft of so-called "critical theorists" have followed his lead in the study of world affairs (Linklater 1996).

Discussing modernity in this analytic fashion can only carry the discourse so far, however. The passion for dispassion that reason as an end in itself involves cannot be conveyed to others by the dispassionate means that reason used alone provides. Some more immediate account of this passion is required, if we are fully to appreciate it. Talking about reason rationally, we can ascertain its causes and consequences. We can assess its significance. We cannot know what it feels like by these means alone, though.

### The Experience of Modernity

To know more, to understand better what the passion for dispassion involves, we have to stand closer, where we can hear the voice of a convinced rationalist speaking.

One such speaker is Descartes himself, a man whose expression of the rationalist creed is still capable of making friends and influencing people. I quote from one of his main works, *A Discourse on Method*, written in 1637 (15–16, 26–27):

> I believed . . . the four following [conclusions] would prove perfectly sufficient for me . . .
>
> The first . . . never to accept anything for true which I did not clearly know to be such; that is to say, carefully to avoid precipitancy and prejudice, and to comprise nothing more in my judgment than what was presented to my mind so clearly and distinctly as to exclude all ground of doubt.
>
> The second, to divide each of the difficulties under examination into as many parts as possible, and as might be necessary for its adequate solution.
>
> The third, to conduct my thoughts in such order that, by commencing with objects the simplest and easiest to know, I might ascend by little and little, and, as it were, step by step, to the knowledge of the more complex; assigning in thought a certain order even to those objects which in their own nature do not stand in a relation of antecedence and sequence.
>
> And in the last, in every case to make enumerations so complete, and reviews so general, that I might be assured that nothing was omitted.
>
> The long chains of simple and easy reasoning by means of which geometers are accustomed to reach the conclusions of their most difficult demonstrations, had led me to imagine that all things, to the knowledge of which man is competent, are mutually connected in the same way, and that there is nothing so far removed from us as to be beyond our reach, or so hidden that we cannot discover it, provided only we abstain from accepting the false for the true, and always preserve in our thoughts the order necessary for the deduction of one truth from another . . .
>
> . . . as I then desired to give my attention solely to the search after truth, I thought . . . that I ought to reject as absolutely false all opinions in regard to which I could suppose the least ground for doubt, in order to ascertain whether after that there remained aught in my belief that was wholly indubitable. Accordingly, seeing that our senses sometimes deceive us, I was willing to suppose that there existed nothing really such as they presented to us; and because some men err in reasoning . . . even on the simplest matters of geometry, I, convinced that I was as open to error as any other, rejected as false all the reasoning I had hitherto taken for demonstrations; and finally, when I consid-

ered that the very same thoughts . . . which we experience when awake may also be experienced when we are asleep, while there is at that time not one of them true, I supposed that all the objects . . . that had ever entered into my mind when awake, had in them no more truth than the illusions of my dreams. But immediately upon this I observed that, whilst I thus wished to think that all was false, it was absolutely necessary that I, who thus thought, should be somewhat; and as I observed that this truth, I think, hence I am, was so certain and of such evidence, that no ground of doubt, however extravagant, could be alleged by the sceptics capable of shaking it, I concluded that I might, without scruple, accept it as the first principle of the philosophy of which I was in search.

In the next place, I attentively examined what I was, and as I observed that I could suppose that I had no body, and that there was no world nor any place in which I might be; but that I could not therefore suppose that I was not; and that, on the contrary, from the very circumstance that I thought to doubt of the truth of other things, it most clearly and certainly followed that I was; while, on the other hand, if I had only ceased to think, although all the other objects which I had ever imagined had been in reality existent, I would have had no reason to believe that I existed; I thence concluded that I was a substance whose whole essence or nature consists only in thinking . . .

Descartes is proclaiming here his faith in the individual's capacity to reflect upon the "matters of his experience" (11). And though his faith in what reasoning could achieve helped create a sense of the future to which both past and present could be "continually sacrificed" (Berman 1982) he himself remained committed to one basic part of his past, the Christian part. In this Descartes was a hinge-thinker. While casting forward to new ways to know, he remained part of that world where "all which we possess of real and true proceeds from a Perfect and Infinite Being" (31). Though he saw reason as an end in itself, that is, he still felt obliged to talk in terms of knowing God.

Rather than listen to an early modernist explain his passion for dispassion, we can go one step further, however. We can ask: what does modernity feel like when we do it? What is it like to take part in the modernist project?

We do not have to go far, in this regard. Introspection alone will do. We are all part of this project, so we can just ask ourselves.

If we want to share someone else's experience, however, we can turn to volume 58 of *American Anthropologist*. Here, next to articles on "Individuality in the Behavior of Chimpanzees" and "Matrilocality and Patrilineality in Mundurucu Society," we find Horace Miner's famous essay on "Body Ritual among the Nacirema." Miner is interested in the modernist as savage, and some of his participant observations of these contemporary primitives are provided below:

The anthropologist has become so familiar with the diversity of ways in which different peoples behave in similar situations that he is not apt to be surprised by even the most exotic customs. In fact, if all of the logically possible combinations of behavior have not been found somewhere in the world, he is apt to suspect that they must be present in some yet undescribed tribe . . . In this light, the magical beliefs and practices of the Nacirema present such unusual aspects that it seems desirable to describe them as an example of the extremes to which human behavior can go.

. . . [T]he culture of this people is still very poorly understood. They are a North American group living in the territory between the Canadian Cree, the Yaqui and Tarahumare of Mexico, and the Carib and Arawak of the Antilles . . .

Nacirema culture is characterized by a highly developed market economy which has evolved in a rich natural habitat. While much of the people's time is devoted to economic pursuits, a large part of the fruits of these labors and a considerable part of the day are spent in ritual activity. The focus of this activity is the human body, the appearance and health of which loom as a dominant concern in the ethos of the people . . .

The fundamental belief underlying the whole system appears to be that the human body is ugly and that its natural tendency is to debility and disease. While such is certainly not unusual, its ceremonial aspects and associated philosophy are unique.

. . . [Indeed, o]ur review of the ritual life of the Nacirema . . . [shows] them to be a magic-ridden people. It is hard to understand how they have managed to exist so long under the burdens which they have imposed upon themselves . . . [S]uch exotic customs . . . take on real meaning when they are viewed with the insight provided by Malinowski [however] when he wrote . . .:

"Looking from far and above, from our high places of safety in the developed civilization, it is easy to see all the crudity and irrelevance of magic. But without its power and guidance early man could not have mastered his practical difficulties as he has done, nor could man have advanced to the higher stages of civilization." (1956, 503–507)

Miner's ethnography of the culture of an American (Nacirema, spelt backward) shows clearly how much can get lost in translation when we objectify. Modernist rationalism, he suggests, when used to describe what goes on in the world, obscures and distorts. He satirizes concerns about personal appearance and health, but he could just as well have highlighted the cultural tolerance for particular kinds of violence, for extremes of social inequality, and much, much more.

The positivism that has stood over the study of world affairs for the last forty years is not a satire, but it too is an expression of modernist rationalism, and it too obscures and distorts. Positivists believe that casting accounts of the world in terms amenable to disproof, and testing them empirically, provides the most reliable knowledge possible. Their critics, however, argue that, carried to extremes like this, with regard to world affairs at any rate, rationalism trivializes and conserves. It trivializes because rigid protocols of verification make it hard to say anything of significance about world affairs. It conserves because behavioralists have to assume that world affairs change in consistent and uniform ways for their generalizations to hold. This makes them propagandists for the very assumptions on which the validity of their work depends.

Reason used as an end in itself has been carried to extremes in other ways, too. Placing a priority upon rationalism, together with realizing personal autonomy, is the impetus, for example, behind the liberal politics of individual freedom, unfettered marketeering, and interstate negotiation. Consider "rational choice" theory, which provides a systematic account of how people act in objectifying and individuated ways. It provides accounts of "prisoners' dilemmas," for example, where someone has to calculate the odds of opting for self-advantage or allying with others. These investigations, made by so-called games theorists, are then used to model decision-making in society, in the market, and in strategic affairs. The results are suggestive. They are rarely more than this, however, since they are too abstract.

Not only is much missed by carrying rationalism to extremes, in other words, but it is arguable how much can ever be achieved this way. The shortcomings of "rational choice" theory are only one case. The general failure to find scientific laws that are reliable enough to predict the future and improve policy is another. Both have been a major disappointment to state-makers, and particularly to those state-makers with extensive, diverse, and hegemonic interests to defend.

## Postmodernity: The Limits to Reason (and What Lies Beyond Them)

Postmodernists are those who contest the assumptions upon which modernist rationalism is built in modernist terms. They seek not only to render the claims rationalists make less legitimate, but to make in the process speaking spaces for those modernity has marginalized or rendered mute. They believe that the light of the mind not only illuminates but also blinds. And they believe that this light shines on some while casting others into the outer darkness.

What is this light? Who inhabits the margins it makes?

Modernists pull up (or are pushed away) from the world to look back down on it from afar. By "high-flying" like this, they seek to achieve the perspective that Mabbott's tower provides. They seek mental distance and the chance they believe this gives them to stress objectivity. They limit the use of the mind to conscious reasoning, in pursuit of enlightenment.

Those who prefer to "deep-dive" instead seek their knowledge in the realm of the irrational. Having learned to be rationalistic and individuated, those of a romantic disposition may prefer to plunge into the sanctity of their emotions to compensate. As self-conscious subjectivists, they pursue (as a rational choice) the depths of private emotion, rather than the heights of public thinking.

Postmodernists choose neither to high-fly nor to deep-dive. They prefer to watch the play of light on the water. They think it possible to understand the immediacy and complexity of this world only by exploring what modernist representation means and whom it marginalizes. They may use modernist reasoning but they turn that reasoning back on rationalists themselves to ask: how reliable is what they do? And who benefits? They seek to understand, in other words, the limits of the scientizing process and whom it puts beyond the pale. Refusing to be bound by those limits, they explore instead the way reason works in nonrational as well as rational ways. In the process, they give those excluded and silenced by the modernist project more of a chance to speak out.

### The Illusion of Objectivity

The key mental ploy here is the distancing one, as described in the section on modernity above. Postmodernists reject this ploy. Thus, while modernists believe that reality can be held apart from the self and is objectively knowable when we do, postmodernists believe that a mind-move like this one creates only illusion. As a consequence, postmodernists are much more likely to be Carsean gardeners, for whom reality is constructed "sociolinguistically." They see people as always having to make the meaning that the world has for them. They do not find reality "out there," and indeed, they believe it cannot be found "out there." For postmodernists, the world is not knowable in any absolute, abstract sense, because we are implicated in it, always.

How does the postmodernist argument square with the results of Western scientific thought? We do know that, by privileging reason, objectifying Nature, and individuating ourselves, we get new and reliable knowledge in large amounts. Classical physics is the example par excellence of what can be achieved by separating the observer from the observed, the subject from the object, and the mind from the world, and by assuming (and it is an assumption) that we can "step outside our systems of interpretation, our language, and somehow talk sensibly about the world as it really is" (Gregory 1990, 190). Even classical physics is constrained by some fundamental limits, however. These limits are set by the assumptions that all modernist rationalists make—that the world is tangible, tractable, and consistent, for example. These assumptions may be wrong, but modernists make them, because if they do not, they cannot know the world in an "all-seeing" way.

Assumptions like these are not neutral, however, as postmodernists are at pains to point out. They posit a certain kind of world even before it is described and explained.

Modernists assume that reality exists in material terms, for example. They assume that what they can sense, whether directly or indirectly, is something tangible and real. They assume that nature is some "thing" that is manifest enough to know about rationally. They assume a world knowable in the terms that rationalism requires if rationalism is to work as a way of knowing. This is one basic limit that rational objectification sets.

Modernists also assume that reality is tractable, that is, that it is simple enough for them to know. Perhaps there is no limit to the grasp of the human intellect. Perhaps we have transcended the limits that bound and bind other kinds of consciousness (those of the whale, perhaps, or the chimpanzee). Perhaps we really do have a mind capable of conceiving of the cosmos in all its complexity. We did evolve under very particular circumstances, and as a consequence we have specific mental skills. Perhaps one of these skills, as modernist rationalists assume, is the ability to comprehend all about everything. Then again, perhaps it is the other way around, and it is we who bring reality within our cognitive and perceptual grasp, reducing it to what we are able to know. Perhaps there are limits to what we do our knowing with, limits that prevent us knowing how complex the cosmos happens to be.

Modernist rationalists assume that nature is consistent, as well. Imagine a world where gravity worked here and not there, or only worked at random. Finding patterns where there are none is obviously impossible. We have to assume the world works in patterned ways; otherwise, it would be utterly unknowable. Modernists require a degree of consistency higher than pre- or postmodernists do, however, and this is another limit that rational objectification sets.

Happily, our experience of the world confirms its tangibility, its tractability, and its consistency, though we can never read our results as anything more than an approximation of nature's own language. Some believe that nature speaks in pure mathematics, but this is merely a belief. In practice nature's own language has to be guessed at. To portray the world as it really is, physicists invent versions of how nature speaks, and whole languages exist now that structure the best guesses physicists have made in this regard. No one knows which one of these languages is true, though, or even whether a universal language of natural truth is even possible.

Under such circumstances, "[t]he word real does not seem to be a descriptive term. It seems to be an honorific term that we bestow on our most cherished beliefs—our most treasured ways of speaking" (Gregory 1990, 184). We do not see nature by direct perception, and even direct perception is mediated by the mind. Nature does not speak in its own words. We hear it always on our terms and in our terms. We only ever see it interpreted, as it were, by what we have to know it with.

### How Objective Are World Affairs?

What about knowing world affairs? Can we know them objectively, like we can know the structure of the atom?

Here we are both better and worse off than the quantum physicist, because we are the reality we seek to understand. We are better off than the quantum physicist because world affairs are not a reality other than us. They are the affairs of other human beings and ourselves. Providing a general account of them, therefore, does seem possible. Unlike the atom, we are not forever consigned to knowing about them. However complex they may be, we can know them in ourselves. We are also worse off than the quantum physicist, since the problems quantum physicists face in knowing what is going on are compounded, in the case of knowing about world affairs, many times over. Unlike subatomic particles, the subject matter has volition, which makes the question of consistency, for example, considerably more urgent. State-makers really can act one way on Wednesday and another way by the time that Monday comes around. This problem may not be insurmountable, and modernist rationalists would argue that it is not, but it is certainly a dimension to reality that physicists do not have to deal with. The systems that constitute world affairs are profoundly chaotic. As such they require knowledge of the whole, if we are to explain or understand them in any particular part.

The problem is not intangibility. World affairs are real enough. Try declaring war on a state, or not honoring your contracts, or placing an advertisement in the *New York Times* inviting public recognition of your identity as a philosopher-king. You will soon find the protagonists of contemporary world affairs asserting their politico-strategic, politico-economic, and politico-social primacy.

The problem is with the constructed character of the reality of world affairs and with the way constructing world affairs of any kind requires power. Of course, if everyone should decide at the same moment to stop acknowledging the modernist meaning of the state and to organize their affairs in accordance with the dictates of one of the major religions, for example, then states, in the contemporary sense, would cease to exist. Or if the concept of personal property were repudiated worldwide, liberal capitalism would instantly become untenable. Or if everyone decided to give primary loyalty to some global clan, defined in terms of a totemic animal, perhaps, or a tree, then individualism would take on very different charac-teristics than those it has today. The point is that none of these things has ever happened or is ever likely to happen. The question then becomes: why not? What is the power that carries these world affairs from one day to the next? And how is this power mediated? How does it work?

The most important power sustaining modernist world affairs is the be-lief that this world is as it is and, therefore, is as it ought to be. We are taught to stand off from the world and to see it in particular ways. From our mental vantage points we emulate Archimedes, moving the world into those posi-tions that most closely conform to the modernist pictures we learn to see there. These pictures we learn along with modernist rationalism itself. We articulate them in terms of the analytic languages that dominate world af-fairs. Every medium of socialization is implicated in having these languages prevail.

To postmodernists, this is all very self-fulfilling. If you promote the use of reason as an end in itself, they argue, you make an Archimedean place to stand on. If, having done so, you then emphasize interstate competition ("re-alism"), you get an ungoverned world, obscuring in the process how much cooperation goes on at the same time. If you pursue private gain, you get a free market and you obscure how much exploitation exists. If you promote individualism, you get personalized societies and you obscure the emancipatory potential of social movements. You construct these world af-fairs, in other words, rather than any alternative to them.

Insist on certain knowledge in the study of world affairs, a postmodernist will say, and you end up not knowing world affairs at all. Theorize rational-istically about the need to protect national interest, for example, and you end up promoting war, not preventing it. Objectify intellectually about how to make us safe, and you put us in even greater jeopardy than before. Em-phasize rational market behavior and you get even greater inequality. Valo-rize individualism and you get the collective attempt to escape from it.

### Knowledge as Power

It is certainly tempting to seek certain knowledge of world affairs. Knowing the world in a reliable way allows for greater control of world affairs. The problem is that dependable knowledge of world affairs is not available, not in any "hard" scientific sense, not yet. It is not available, furthermore, be-cause of the extent to which we make what it is that we seek to know.

The assumption that certain knowledge can be had, which is the assump-tion that modernists make, can be dangerous, in fact, since it leads those who think like this to consider what they do know as being more true or more real that what anybody else knows. They may then project what they think they know onto the world as if it were absolutely real or true, thereby creating what they think to be real or true. This circular, self-fulfilling process serves the ideological interests their knowledge represents, but not the cause of reason they presume to serve.

How is it that sovereignty gets to enjoy such high status? What makes it the most significant attribute of the politico-strategic system? What (or more importantly, who) gets sidelined in the process? Likewise, how is it that international relations realism, politico-economic liberalism, and politico-social individualism come to enjoy such hegemonic standing in world affairs? And who has had to be put aside to get them there?

Once we think of world affairs in terms of authoritative interpretations, critical questions like these become obvious. To postmodernists it is immediately apparent, for example, that the present structure of world affairs is not the necessary, logical outcome of the past. Rather than review a concept like sovereignty by delving down through layers of historical meaning in a linear search for sovereignty's essential source, however, postmodernists chart the branching bush of historical opportunities that has sovereignty out there, at the end of one twig. In the postmodernist view, history is a story of who wins and who gets to tell who won. There are many histories and many such stories that form a web of narratives and power (Devetak 1995).

Once we stop thinking of world affairs in abstracted, rationalistic terms, that is, there is no essential state. There is only state-making, a never-ending ideological project that promotes the modernist concept of the state and the practices that constitute it, while actively precluding the many alternatives to the state that would prevail if this project ceased to be. There is no market either, only market-making. Nor are there selves, only self-making. World affairs cease as a consequence to be a place of fixed entities. It proceeds instead on a broad, interconnected front, moving moment by moment, becoming what we decide it will be. "We" are those who get to prevail in this regard, who get to define the character of the present. "We" are those whose concepts become the natural and normal ones, whose interpretations of world affairs predominate.

The question whether state-making (or capitalist market-making, or social self-making) provides the best possible answers to the world's current concerns remains open, therefore. Do these practices resolve issues of war and peace, production and distribution, coherence and self-awareness, in the best ways possible? Or are they merely the conventional solutions of the moment to issues that arguably require other forms of global practice if they are to be dealt with well? What other prospects emerge, in other words, once we look beyond the limits set by those strategies that are momentarily the most successful?

## Postmodernist Techniques

Postmodernists have developed a number of techniques that make modernity problematic. All of these techniques work by revealing the assumptions upon which modernist conceptions of world affairs are based, assumptions which may be extremely hard to see because of their taken-for-granted character.

In showing how modernists create historical canons that support their cause, for example, postmodernists show how modernists read the authors involved out of context and highly selectively. They go back to the writers that modernists cite, such as Machiavelli or Hobbes, Smith or Marx, Locke or Rousseau, and they demonstrate how these authors were read differently in their own times and what else they had to say (Walker 1993).

In showing how modernists use key concepts, like anarchy, to legitimate such ideologies as IR realism, postmodernists also critique these concepts. They "deconstruct" them, sieving them for meanings that modernist rationalism hides (Ashley 1988).

In showing how modernists craft world affairs that include some people and exclude others, postmodernists also reveal the partiality of the power relations that modernists endorse. Post-modernists are able to help those silenced by these power relations by showing how modernists inhibit their chances to speak.

In the process postmodernists proclaim modernist world affairs "a particular reading of (Western) philosophy and history become transhistorical/transcultural 'fact'" (George 1994, 216, 161). It is, they say, local interest writ large.

## Modernists Respond

Postmodernist critiques do not go unchallenged. Modernists find plenty of life yet in making the rationalist mind-move (Spegele 1992). After all, as Bernstein puts it, "[o]ne cannot consistently state the case for relativism without undermining it" (Bernstein 1983, 9). Vasquez makes a similar point when he highlights what he sees as postmodernism's "fundamental self-contradiction." Thus, "if everything is a social construction and nothing is permanently true," he asks, "how can postmodernism's view of the world and history as a set of constructions be anything but a social construction? And if it is a social construction, in what sense can it be true" (Vasquez 1995, 225)?

Modernists also point up the fact that postmodernists are much better at showing what is wrong with the study of world affairs than at putting matters right there. While postmodernists may be able to deconstruct the certainties of rationalist/modernist world affairs, that is, they seem to be notably less able to reconstruct them.

## Postmodernist Feminism

Tell that to postmodern feminists. If world affairs are deconstructed in terms of gender bias, they can then be reconstructed to bring women and gender relations back into view, and postmodern feminists do just that. They see it as their task to write "women, gender relations and feminist scholarship into 'the international'" (J.J. Pettman 1996, viii, x). The result has been a more accurate and comprehensive account of world affairs.

Deconstructing the male-made character of world affairs means making females visible in a field where their active exclusion has long been made to seem natural and normal. The "step to competence," as Kant describes the call to reason on the first page of his essay "What is Enlightenment?" is resisted, he says, by the "far greater portion of mankind (and by the entire fair sex)." Kant's offhand dismissal of the female half of humankind speaks volumes ([1784] 1963, 3). It is undoing just this kind of casual (and not so casual) damage that postmodern feminist deconstructionists see as their primary task.

Female invisibility is clearly evident in state legislatures, for example, where fifty percent of the world's population holds no more than ten percent of the world's parliamentary seats (Randall 1987). The same disparity holds for the bureaucracy, the judiciary, and the military. Women are there in large numbers, but only in support roles that make them hard to see and give them little public power.

This invisibility is also clearly evident in the global capitalist system, where people who are women are legitimately described as the world's "last colony" (Mies 1988). By the end of the UN Decade for the Advancement of Women (1975–1985), poor women worldwide had become poorer (particularly in relation to men) and more women were poor than at the beginning of it. A decade later, the situation was even worse (UNDP 1995). And this despite the massive ongoing contribution women make to global development.

Female invisibility is evident in the world's societies, too. People who are women have been "systematically excluded" from the creation, everywhere in the world, of "symbol systems, philosophies, science and law" (Lerner 1986, 5).

Evidence of politico-social exclusion of this kind also highlights the Euro-American Enlightenment as a project for men more than women. Indeed, this is a revolution that has only just begun in female terms. Little wonder that feminists call for a reframing of the whole history of Western thought in other terms than those that make the learning process such an objectifying, individuating, Western, masculinist one (Keller 1985, 47).

Is modernist rationalism really gendered, however? Is it really a male plot? Is it really patriarchical in practice? Or is this all a feminist fantasy, of the sort that rationalism is specifically meant to cure?

Lloyd argues that rationalism associates females with knowing that is dark, emotional, and mysterious, while it associates males with the opposite, namely, with the enlightened, the intellectual, and the understandable (Lloyd 1984). Merchant likewise contrasts rationalism (mechanistic) with its alternatives (holistic, harmonious) and finds the priority that rationalism now receives disadvantageous to females (Merchant 1980). Keller also posits masculine as opposed to feminine principles, the masculine associated with the head, autonomy, objectivity, purity, and domination; the female associated with the heart, sympathy, subjectivity, the erotic, and submission. She sees rationalism as characterized by the former, exalting masculinist principles, not feminist ones (Keller 1985).

Dichotomies like these beg many questions, but it is their abstract and essentialist character that is most problematic. They are all rationalistic themselves.

This would not matter if rationalism, in its strict, scientific sense, was gender neutral or gender free (or was able to move toward that goal), but rationalism is not, postmodernists say. It is sexist because it cannot be divorced from the standpoint taken by those doing the scientizing. So how are those above speaking? As female masculinist/rationalists, if the postmodernists are to be believed, and they are compromised accordingly.

Even the most rigorous attempts to free how we know from who we are, postmodernists say, must fail (Harding 1986). Scientizers may have objectifying pretensions, but these pretensions will be frustrated by the subjectifying fact of human difference. Postmodernists find absurd, therefore, any idea that scientizing how we know permits conclusions free of time, place, or cultural circumstance. Gender, race, class, and historical context, they argue, all skew scientific methods, not only in how these methods are used, but also in themselves and regardless of who uses them.

"Difference-tolerant" analysis is an imperative, in other words, not a choice. It puts us right on the "gender precipice," which, as Sylvester says, is to face the "biggest fight imaginable, something worse than usual battlefield combat." The "imagined prospect" is of "utter loss," that is, loss of "power, control, authority, dominance, prestige, [and] voice. Forever" (Sylvester 1994, 211). It is a radical prospect indeed.

There are limits to difference-tolerant analysis itself, however. Exalting human difference can also be used to obscure sexism, since relativism too thorough-going reduces the analytic landscape to rubble and, with it, conceptual purchase on the vast edifice of patriarchy. The belief in the absolute "heterogeneity of perspectives" is a fantasy "as improbable (and as potentially incapacitating) as locating an Archimedean point" (Harvey and Okruhlik 1992, 11). And it can be just as damaging to feminist points of view.

Hence, the timely reminder that the concept of the "female" is already crafted in intellectual terms that marginalize women. The modernist project relegates feminist critiques to every politico-cultural periphery, where feminists face a "double challenge." First, they must engage in "rational or philosophic discourse (a critique from within)." Second, they must attempt to "dethrone philosophy as the hegemonic 'master' discourse (a critique from without)" (Harvey and Okruhlik 1992, 11, 12).

To do this, they must not only document the history of this process to show how it has been constructed. They must also show that rationalism does not represent the real in any absolute, eternal, and universal way. They must show that it was crafted in context—in this case, a gendered context. Since it is constructed, it can be deconstructed and reconstructed, which makes it possible for feminists to subvert the hegemony of reason and provide alternatives, which is just what postmodernist feminists do.

### Other Social Movements

Feminists are only one of a number of social movements that take advantage of challenges like those the postmodernists provide. Many for whom modernist global culture is a home on the footpath—or a "reservation," or a place of existential angst, ecological hazard, or urban violence—seek alternatives to modernity. Some of them build social movements for peace, human rights, environmental sustainability, ethnic autonomy, or religious renewal. All bear witness, however, to the determination not to remain marginalized and to make world affairs more humane.

The key issue is voice. It is to get heard, to have a say. Postmodernists highlight the way people get locked out of the main analytic debates, and they seek to let them back in, in part by discussing what is "outside" these world affairs (Hoogvelt 1982, 214). This is no mere intellectual exercise, however. It is meant to give social movements a hearing, to give them a chance.

### The Experience of Postmodernity

Speaking of voice, it might be appropriate at this point to stop standing back to look at postmodernity (in good modernist fashion) and instead, to stand closer and listen to a postmodernist speak. Since a consistent postmodernist would not talk at all, especially in modernist terms, we could well turn here to a postmodern performance artist of some kind. Within the confines of a book this is rather hard to do. Listen instead to R.B.J. Walker, therefore, a leading late-modernist, as he talks in *One World/Many Worlds: Struggles for a Just World Peace* about the limits of rationalism and what might lie beyond them (1988, 51–52, 73, 98, 147–48, 150–51, 156):

> At the heart of the culture of modernity lies an insistent dualism. An autonomous knowing subject is presumed to be gazing at an objective world to be known. Knowing is then linked to the possibility of control of the known. Whether one thinks of the great philosophical systems of Plato, Descartes, or Kant; or of the heroic artist separated from but reproducing the world around him; or the political categories in which individuals are somehow assumed to be completely autonomous from the society in which they live; or even the division between the secular world of people living in time and the sacred space of eternity, the presumption of a radical split between human being and world is always in the background. In the foreground lies a cultural life permeated by debates about the relative claims of objectivity and subjectivity and the ever-present lure of utilitarian or instrumental calculation.
>
> This underlying dualism has been the unerring target of critique within the culture of modernity itself. At the popular level, "science" may remain a potent incantation supposedly offering protection from charlatans and subversives. But the actual conduct of much scientific research reveals a fundamental rejection of the dualistic categories constructed by Galileo and Newton—the categories that have become the prevailing "common sense" of modernity.
>
> Nor is it possible to avoid the darker side of modernity so readily visible in this century. From wars and extermination camps to impersonal bureaucracies, from the lonely isolation of the supposedly autonomous individual to the transformation of human life into a procession of commodities to be bought and sold, there has been no shortage of opportunities for scepticism about the progressive character of modernized life. And whether in terms of philosophy or science, of social thought or of aesthetics, there has also been no shortage of attempts to revitalize cultural traditions that have been dominant for so long and to take them in more creative and emancipatory directions.

In speaking as Walker does for the cause of critical social movements, he is also standing back to look at what he thinks they can do. His polemic is a modernist one in that respect. He does, however, articulate the cause of those rendered invisible by modernist mind-making and world-making. He serves the postmodernist cause in this respect, as he does when he talks about the limits set by modernist epistemology and ontology.

Standing back to look at Walker's advocacy of the postmodernist cause is to lay oneself open at the same time to the critique he makes of any attempt to objectify, however. It also highlights the self-denying character of this critique, since Walker's arguments about the limits to rationalist analysis are arguments against the rationalistic aspects of his own position too.

How do we break such a self-denying circle? In participative terms, we can either explore what it feels like to be ourselves in modernist world affairs, and not just of them, or we can explore the experience of others.

In 1984–1985, Carol Cohn studied with some of the leading defense intellectuals in the United States. These men (and they were, indeed, nearly all men) worked at the heart of the U.S. diplomatico-strategic machine, and of the modernist project. They worked as bureaucrats, consultants, academic advisers, and researchers, moving regularly between these different roles. Their task was to devise rational ways to live in a world that has nuclear weapons in it.

Cohn is a highly respected academic, rationalist and Westernized. Her identity as a female, however, gives her a perspective shared by many others on modernity's margins. She is able to see the modernist world in ways the males she works with apparently cannot. I quote from Cohn's report of her study year, an account she calls "Sex and Death in the Rational World of Defense Intellectuals" (1987, 687–690, 712–13, 717):

> Entering the world of defense intellectuals was a bizarre experience—bizarre because it is a world where men spend their days calmly and matter-of-factly discussing nuclear weapons, nuclear strategy, and nuclear war. The discussions are carefully and intricately reasoned, occurring seemingly without any sense of horror, urgency, or moral outrage—in fact, there seems to be no graphic reality behind the words, as they speak of "first strikes," "counterforce exchanges," and "limited nuclear war," and as they debate the comparative values of a "minimum deterrent posture" versus a "nuclear war-fighting capability" . . .
>
> As a newcomer to the world of defense analysts, I was continually startled by likeable and admirable men, by their gallows humor, by the bloodcurdling casualness with which they regularly blew up the world while standing and chatting over the coffee pot . . .
>
> Within a few weeks, what had once been remarkable became unnoticeable [however]. As I learned to speak, my perspective changed. I no longer stood outside the impermeable wall of technostrategic language and, once inside, I could no longer see it . . .
>
> One of the most intriguing options opened by learning the language is that it suggests a basis upon which to challenge the legitimacy of the defense intellectuals' dominance of the discourse on nuclear issues [though] . . .
>
> Much of their claim to legitimacy . . . is the claim to objectivity born of technical expertise and to the disciplined purging of the emotional valences that might threaten their objectivity. But if the surface of their discourse—its abstraction and technical jargon—appears at first to support these claims, a look just below the surface does not. There we find currents of homoerotic excitement, heterosexual domination, the drive toward competency and mastery, the pleasures of membership in an elite and privileged group, the ultimate importance and meaning of membership in the priesthood, and the thrilling power of becoming Death, shatterer of worlds. How is it possible to hold this up as a paragon of cool-headed objectivity?

Cohn's account of what at one point she calls "white men in ties discussing missile size" is vivid and detailed. The pervasiveness of the images of sexism, paternalism, male birth, male creation, domesticity, and nuclear divinity with which she was continually confronted provides her with many striking stories. Her commonsense appreciation of the experiential world of defense intellectuals is a graphic alternative to uncommonly abstract ones.

In standing back to look at Cohn's account itself, however, we may have questions that demonstrate how difficult it is to meet the "double challenge" alluded to above.

There is first the issue of rationalism itself. Cohn wants to mount a feminist critique of Western reason and rationalist objectifying. She wants to critique rationalism as an epistemological goal. She is obliged to use these very same tools in conveying her account of her year of participant observation, however, and in documenting how rationalistic strategists think. Second, there is the issue of sample bias. Perhaps these particular thinkers were unrepresentative, in which case Cohn's account is suggestive, not exhaustive, and we ought to look elsewhere as well.

Cohn's experience show unequivocally, though, how hard it is to be part of a particular thought-world and at the same time retain the critical capacity to understand the limits it sets and the critical will to move outside those limits. Her experience among the savages of strategic discourse, friendly and likeable as most of them were, is applicable to any thought-world, whether it be liberal capitalism, social individualism, or rationalist modernism itself.

Her participant observations also show how emotive and sexist the rationalist language of defense intellectuals can be. She does not show how much of their language is like this but she does show that they use this language, and that their claim to be rational and objective is compromised accordingly by a gender bias of which they are completely unaware. No account of strategic security can be given in the light of what she says that does not take this fact into account. The men Cohn met were clearly less rational than they liked to think they were. Since these men were also helping to legitimate a major means of species suicide, that is something worth knowing, and a very good reason why we should look beyond the limits that rationalist modernity sets.

# 3

# Making Sovereign Selves, Social Collectives, and Nations

These world affairs, that is, world affairs today, are modernist, which means that they are one outcome of a sustained attempt to privilege the rationalistic use of reason on a global scale. This attempt means that world affairs today are mostly made by those who—wittingly or unwittingly—want rationalism to prevail worldwide.

As the previous chapter pointed out, rationalism is the politico-cultural context in which today's world affairs are constructed. It is the most fundamental politico-cultural feature of the world affairs that result. If we want to know how world affairs work, therefore, the first and arguably the most important thing we should know about them is this, which is why I talked about mind-making first.

Making a modernist world, however, means not only making a modernist core. It also means making nonmodernist margins. It means the making at the same time of competing projects that are nonmodernist in character. Those who do not valorize rationalism, for example, are by definition premodernist. Those who do valorize rationalism, but who turn it back on itself to question its primacy, are by definition postmodernist.

Making a modernist world also assumes a particular kind of society, which is why some would put society first in conceptual terms. There are good grounds for doing so, too, though giving society priority obscures the world-shaping significance of the modernist politico-cultural context.

In practice, there is no culture without society. We cannot detach the two. Culture is always found in the social context that perpetuates it.

In principle, however, it is necessary not only to discriminate between the two, but also to highlight how pervasive culture can be and how it can set the context for other societies. This is particularly the case for world affairs where a particular culture, or important aspects of that culture at least, have spread beyond the social context in which they originated.

The definitive feature of these world affairs, I would argue, is the way Western rationalism has spread, well beyond the boundaries of Western societies. Because of the close association between culture and society, Western society has spread as Western culture has spread (hence the notion of Westernization worldwide, which is a social as much as a cultural process). If we do not separate the two conceptually, however, and if we cannot appreciate how cultures travel well beyond their formative social confines, then we will not understand these world affairs.

Western rationalism has been used to construct world affairs with distinctive characteristics. World affairs have been constructed in three-dimensional terms, each dimension built around three main analytic languages. If the state-making of soldiers and diplomats is seen as "high" politicking, and the market-making of marketeers and capitalists as "low" politicking, then the self-making the proponents of social coherence do is logically a matter of "even lower" politicking. Each of these dimensions is also now analyzed in ways that clump around particular preconceptions of human nature. The state-making dimension, for example, is described and explained in realist (people are bad), internationalist (people are rational), and globalist (people are good) terms.

Of the three dimensions of world affairs that Western/modernist/rationalists exalt, the politico-social is the least evident and the most neglected. Ordinary people experience world affairs in politico-social ways. Analysts of world affairs, however, until recently at any rate, have not accounted for much of this experience in studying world affairs. This lack has helped in turn to legitimate foreign policies that do not adequately account for politico-social affairs.

Redressing this neglect is part of any constructivist's agenda. Such is the power of "high" and "low" politicians to define what ought to be analyzed as world affairs, however, that there is still a long way to go before the politicians "even lower" than this get the hearing they arguably deserve. The hierarchical language is instructive in itself. Who says state-making is a "high" art, market-making a "low" one, and self-making beyond the pale? In part, the hierarchy is a product of the nature of the power that the respective politicians have at their disposal. State-makers wield diplomatico-military power. The disciplinary effects of their power can be and are used to highlight politico-strategic concerns. Market-makers wield material power. "Money talks," which is why marketeers are able to highlight politico-economic concerns with considerable success. Self-makers wield power over perceptions. This is a very great power indeed, but it is less tangible and harder to harness. There are not the same well-established formulas for operationalizing and applying it. It is also less predictable in its effects. It is readily apparent once we look for it. We tend not to do so, though, because of the more obvious impact of brute force factors and brute wealth ones.

In the chapter that follows, I discuss the politico-social dimension of modernist world affairs in more detail. I look at the three main analytic languages that characterize this dimension (individualism, collectivism, and nationalism) and I do so in nonrationalist as well as rationalistic ways. Because the literature (though not necessarily the world affairs literature) is extensive in every language, I shall be highly selective. I shall highlight key aspects and concepts only. I shall outline only the general shape of the main politico-social concerns as these pertain to world affairs, and I shall try not to obscure this shape by including too many of what I personally consider to be fascinating details.

Calling the politico-social dimension to modernist world affairs relatively neglected might seem rather odd when it includes such analytic languages as that of nationalism. Closer scrutiny reveals that "the nation and the national" are still "remarkably undertheorized," however (Deudney 1996, 130). It was only a decade ago that Mayall noted the "virtual absence" of any "authoritative account" of nationalism's "international impact" (1990, 5). Peterson also says that nationalism is "poorly understood and insufficiently studied" (1994, 77), and Guibernau decries the lack of a "systematic consideration of issues of nationalism," not only in world affairs but in "classical social theory" as well (1996). Recent studies have done much to redress this lack (J.J. Pettman 1996). It is still highly notable, however, when compared with what gets written and said about the politico-economic and politico-strategic dimensions of world affairs.

The politico-social dimension of world affairs is about more than nationalism. It is about individualism and collectivism as well. In the modernist study of world affairs (but not its practice), however, these two analytic languages suffer from even greater neglect.

When I refer to "individualism" I have a very particular ideology in mind. This needs to be clarified at the outset.

First, we are all individuals. We are all, with rare exceptions, genetically unique, and this is manifest whatever society and culture we are born to or grow up in. We all have peculiar and particular propensities. And while propensities are patterned, so that we learn eventually to recognize those who are optimistic, or sly, or artistic, or whatever, the particular combination of propensities we exhibit ourselves is biologically singular and without peer.

Second, there is the individuation that results from the objectifying use of reason. Modernist rationalism inevitably alienates us to some extent from the culture and the society in which we live.

Third, individualism is the outcome of the further development, once it is established, of this individuated and modernist sense of a "self." If a particular social value gets placed on the individuated individual, then individualism results.

We take the first step away from being socially embedded when we are taught by our society to stress reason. It is this process that creates the "self" per se and which is called above individuation. As we stand back mentally from the world to look at it objectively, we remain in that world, but we are encouraged at the same time to create a mental identity, a place in our minds, that is not of that world.

We take the second step away from being socially embedded when we are taught to place an especially high value upon this individuated self. If we accept these teachings (and we may get little choice), we develop a further sense of "Self" that is mentally more autonomous and emotionally more free. This is a social project, but the result is asocial—the ideology of individualism, which says that everyone ought to be, not only individuated, but also the sort of person who actively values the sense of separateness and self-fulfillment that individuation makes possible.

Having become individuated (by having learned to place a high priority upon the use of reason), we may, of course, be encouraged to become nationalists instead. We may get taught to identify with others who share our language, our history, and our way of life, submerging our individuated selves in that state-affirming project.

Alternatively, we may join the global environmental movement or the socialist international movement or the trans-Himalayan tap-dance and mime commune. We may, in other words, become collectivists instead.

If we do neither of these things, however, and learn to valorize our individuated status further (and this does have to be taught, I say again, since it is very rarely just ascertained), then we become individualists. We become hyperindividuated persons, twice removed, as it were, from the society to which we belong.

This is such an important process that it deserves to be explained again. When we mentally stand back from the world to look at it from a metaphoric distance, we mentally distance ourselves from our own society and from ourselves in that society. We become disembedded. We become what I call "enselved." (To a rationalist, this is the opposite of becoming enslaved, since it has emancipatory connotations. "En-" in English, when added to a verb, describes the process of putting someone into a particular state or condition.

To en-selve a person is to put them into the particular state or condition of being a "self.") What then gets made of that individuated being, what particular sense we subsequently acquire, depends on what we learn subsequently, however. Having been enselved, we might, for example, go on to learn to become individualistic, collectivistic, or nationalistic. The first step, though, is always individuation.

People learn first to be individuated. Then they learn to be individualistic, collectivistic, or nationalistic. Whatever the case, what they learn is a construct of modernist world affairs. And what they learn helps in turn to constitute world affairs in their modernist form.

People learn through all the avenues of socialization that surround them. They learn from their families, their schools, and their fellow worshipers. They learn from bureaucracies, the mass media, and the example authority figures provide. They learn the sort of sentiments that are appropriate to these world affairs rather than other ones. If they do not learn these world affairs, then they learn about some other kind of world affairs instead. They never learn about nothing. They are always taught something, and that something is world affairs as they come to know them. If they do not know world affairs as these world affairs, in other words, they know them as something else. This something else need not be "world affairs" either. It could be "our imperial affairs," perhaps, or "the affairs of our faithful."

The learning and teaching process is continuous. There is always a new generation to inculcate. There are always older generations to be reminded of who they ought to think they are and what they ought to feel.

In practice, the learning and teaching process also results in multiple senses of self. We never live in only one dimension of world affairs. We live in a world of states, and the sense of civic identity that state-makers demand has to be made and remade in all or at least in most of us if modernist state-making is to prevail. We live in a world of markets, capital, and work, and the sense of needing personal gain and private property, and of having to labor and be enterprising to achieve them, has to be made and remade also. We live as well as individuated selves who have to be convinced we feel nationalist fervor if state-makers are to foster the loyalty of the people who inhabit the territory they rule. And all of this happens because we learn to use reason as an end in itself. It all creates margins too, that is, other senses of the self that are gendered, for example, or ecologically aware, or indigenous, or post-colonial, or religious.

To summarize, then: individualism is used here to describe and explain the making of an individualistic Self. It builds on the individuated sense of human being that is common to all the cultures, including the globalizing modernist culture, that stresses the use of reason as an end in itself. It compounds the enselving process by creating a sense of Self even more highly conscious of its status than rationalism provides. A sense of this sort of Self is the basis of neoliberal concepts of the world market and of the politico-social doctrine of human rights.

Historically, this sense of Self can be and has been seen as more the cause of rationalism than its consequence. This leads in turn to complex discussions of what, in the West's intellectual story, was the source of and ground for what.

The analytic sequence described above, however, is able to explain how this sense of Self gets constructed today. It also explains how individualism gets disseminated around the world.

Individualism can be either more or less moderate or extreme. An extreme individualist is a narcissist and/or an anarchist who is likely to find living in any society an imposition. Since the preference for personal autonomy is likely to have been socially acquired in the first place, societies that actively foster highly individualistic preferences cannot last. They must ultimately reach the point where no society is left to do any more fostering. More moderate individualists, by contrast, are likely to dichotomize the Self and society in less drastic ways. They are likely to seek some kind of balance between their individualist sense of Self and their sense of belonging to a collective of some kind.

Collectivism is used here to describe and explain the making of a collectivist self. It denotes the attempt to make, of the individuated self, a more socialistic persona. Such a persona will act as a compensation mechanism for the emotional effects of individuation. Unless people are individualistic by nature, they tend to find individualism alienating. They try, as a consequence, to reconstruct more communal feelings. Rarely can they go back to premodernist communalism. They relinquished that capacity by becoming modernist and by learning to privilege reason. So they go forward to help develop a collectivist antidote instead.

Collectivism is seen here, therefore, as a form of redress. Any particular collective will consist of people already imbued with a sense, often very strong, of having separate selves. This makes collectivism difficult to devise and sustain. Thus, while many collectives have been attempted, ranging from small-scale communes like the kibbutzim in Israel, to feminist collectives, to environmentalist collectives, to neoindigenous groups, to religious cults, to international preparations for socialism on a global scale, all such projects are compromised by the nature of the material to hand. This material is the individuated human being, who may have gained a modernist persona by prioritizing reason, but who has most likely lost in the process the capacity for the nonreflexive feelings that make communal living possible. This is not to decry the considerable achievements that rationalism and individuation make possible. It is merely to highlight the considerable tension modernity creates between the self that results from modernist mind-making and any sort of human society.

Collectivism can be more moderate or more extreme too. More moderate collectivism merely decries individuation, while seeking to alleviate the worst effects of the alienation it can cause (crime, substance abuse, suicide). More extreme versions try to submerge the individuated individual in a solidarist alternative. This may well be nationalism and the nation-state.

Nationalism is used here to describe and explain the making of a nationalist self. Nations are a particular kind of society, much older than the modernist state and yet in their modernist state-made form the same age too. Not only are nations made of shared cultures, languages, and historical stories, but state-makers also use these attributes to build up, legitimize, and carry further the institutional fact of the state and to consolidate the singular civic status of those within its borders.

National fervor comes in more extreme and more moderate forms. The more extreme kinds of nationalism are associated with the tribal loyalisms manifest in times of war or by fascists. The more moderate kinds are the senses of shared self that are put to somewhat less competitive and more affirmative state-making purposes.

The modernist project has marginalized and rendered mute those who do not subscribe to the analytic languages cited above. Since no amount of self-abstraction removes individuals from their social context altogether, gender, for example, remains of relevance and the gendered nature of all these languages is apparent at a glance. All these languages play a part in rendering indigenous peoples less visible too, as well as environmentalists, and the proponents of religious faiths. A conscious attempt has therefore to be made to articulate the concerns of those rendered peripheral if the modernist project is not to prevail by default.

### Individualism: The Sovereign Self

To go back to the heart of the matter: individualism puts a high value upon having a Self. As Nietzsche once said: if you can't be a big exception, you can always be a little one. This could well serve as the motto for the individualist cause.

As a modernist doctrine, individualism is made, as indicated already, in two discrete steps. They usually take place together, but the first step is the most basic one. It involves placing a high priority on the use of reason and the creation in the process of a sense of a separate, individuated self. The second step, usually learned in parallel, takes this individuation process even further, valorizing the sense of self that stressing reason results in, to make a sense of Self, as it were. This second Self is what we normally understand "individualism" to be about. As an ideology, it promotes this sovereign Self as the globally preferred way to be.

Individualism is not possible without individuation, in other words, though it is possible to have individuation without going on to construct individualism (as alternatives like nationalism and collectivism attest). Individuated individuals can share their feelings of homeland and heritage instead. They may feel no need to cultivate their sense of self any further than this. Or they might place their highest priority upon collectivist sentiments of some kind.

I talked of modernist individuation in Chapter 2 and at the start of this chapter, so I shall not do so again except to emphasize the main features of this process and to highlight just how curious a process it happens to be in historical and anthropological terms. Geertz once argued that: "[t]he Western conception of the person as a bounded, unique, more or less integrated motivational and cognitive universe, a dynamic center of awareness, emotion, judgement and action organized into a distinctive whole and set contrastively both against other such wholes and against its social and natural background" is a rather "peculiar idea" within the context of the world's cultures (Geertz 1987, 136). And so it is. This point is debated, but it can also be made at considerably greater length than is warranted here (Shweder and Bourne 1984; Markus and Kitayama 1991; Spiro 1993; Morris 1994; Lindholm 1997).

A sense of self as a separate entity is part of every human's awareness of the work-a-day world, at least, every human who is not sick or sublime. This kind of self-awareness is perennial and universal and is not what I am talking about. Even the most nonmodern society is replete with individuals in this respect. Everyone knows who the moody one is, or the garrulous one, or the trickster, or the sage. Every group is made up of identifiably different individuals. Our unique personalities are facts of life, genetically demonstrable and universal.

Being individual is one thing. Being individuated is another thing entirely, however, while being rendered an individualist is different yet again.

Becoming individuated as an abstract and atomistic self who privileges reason is a particular cultural artifact. Becoming like this was not fully articulated until the nineteenth century, in fact, though it was prefigured in European thought in the sixteenth, seventeenth, and eighteenth centuries and much earlier by the ancient Greeks.

Modernist individuals are taught to objectify, to look at the world and at themselves in that world, from a mental distance (note the metaphor used in

Chapter 2 of pulling away—or being pushed away—from the rubbery mass of our politico-social context). Elias talks, for example, of the "we-less I" (1991, 199). Taylor talks of "atomism" and of the development of the notion of a human agent "able to remake himself [sic] by methodical and disciplined action" (1992; 1989, 160). Lukes talks (in conventional philosophic terms) of both "epistemological individualists," who see only individuals as being able to know, and "methodological individualists," who see all explanations in terms of "what individuals do" (Lukes 1973, 107–109, 110–21). All these analysts are circling the same practice and the same process, though not always self-consciously so.

As an end in itself, reason can be used to disengage the self from its social context and to treat all experience as, in effect, "someone else's." Reason can be reified and made "radically reflexive." It can be taught not to respond to custom, opinion, or any other authoritative voice. It can be taught to defer only to itself, to range free, to analyze, and to invent (Taylor 1989, 168).

Reason when it is used like this can be very useful. It has certainly been a very productive mental attribute in terms of our capacity to generate new and reliable knowledge about natural affairs. Reason used like this is also able to create the illusion of the self as "unprecedentedly radical." Thomas Hobbes was an early English exponent of this illusion, but its leading proponent was John Locke ([1690] 1894). A key part of Locke's intellectual arsenal was the idea of the "punctual self," or the individual brought to a point, an idea that corresponds nicely to the process outlined in Chapter 2 in which we come to view the world this way (Taylor 1989, 171). As part of this process, we find ourselves being pushed and pulled away from the society in which we are embedded. Taylor says that a "punctual" existence of this sort makes it hard for us to see ourselves "alongside whatever else there is." I would argue, contra Taylor, that we do see ourselves alongside others, though as discrete and separate selves and no longer as socially embedded ones (Taylor 1989, 175).

Once raised to self-conscious heights, we converse. From point to point, above the social fray, we talk with our fellow objectifiers—those who have been pushed or pulled into being detached too. By conversing we are able to make entire systems of thought and practice that those still socially embedded cannot. We construct metasocieties in which to reconfigure the contexts from which we have come, and, illusory though these reconfigurings might be, once brought back into the "real world" (as technology or democracy or the market or the state), we soon feel their world-shaping force.

The feeling of personal singularity is largely taken for granted in the West by now, though it has to be taught and retaught all the time to stop it mutating into something else and to stop people trying to revert to a more socially embedded way of living. Because it is taken for granted, we are largely unaware of it. Like the air we breathe and the water we drink, it exists, however, and we use it all the time. We think we "'have' selves as we have heads," as Taylor says (Taylor 1989, 176–177). We no longer notice that we are constructed like this. Nor do we notice how we collude in constructing others the same way. The failure to notice such a construction process does not mean it does not take place, though. Nor do we have to know it exists to visit ourselves as "selves" upon the rest of the world.

Lukes is reaching toward the same idea when he talks of the "abstract" individual, and when he decrees this abstract sense to be central to "many" versions of "most" of the forms that individualism takes (Lukes 1973, 73–78, 139). Lukes does not seem to appreciate the radical novelty or the radical significance of his own idea, however, and as a consequence he does not fully articulate the difference between the politico-cultural conception of the individual (the self) and its diverse politico-social manifestations (diverse doctrines of individualism). He runs the two together, as if the former were the same as the latter, much as they are run together in reality. They are not the same, however. Individuation is a much more basic attribute in mental terms.

Lukes' failure to appreciate the difference between the politico-cultural sense of an individuated self and doctrines of politico-social individualism is extremely prevalent. Once we do appreciate this difference, though, we can clearly see why individualism is so common in the wake of enseling, spreading as it spreads. We can see those so enseled beginning to explore the logical implications of their new mentality. We can see them using this mentality to politico-economic and politico-strategic, as well as politico-social, effect. And we can see one of its politico-social consequences as being individualism, or the heightened sense of the individualistic Self that an individuated self alone makes possible.

### The Self as Absolutely Good

The first thing that individualists do is to invest themselves with a sense of supreme normative worth. Social individualism, as an ideology, sees the individuated individualist as absolutely good. This raises cause-and-effect questions again, but the sequence is clear when cast this way.

Kant, for example, found in reason not only a way to think, but also a way to make autonomy mandatory. Individuals were, in his view, ends in themselves. They always deserved to be treated, he said, as having absolute and universal worth ([1785] 1991). It is not hard to see support here for the modernist doctrine of human rights.

The making of the politico-social language of individualism into an ethical principle is both cause and consequence of its ideological power. It is not only used to justify individuating people in the first place. It is also used to make people moral sites of irredeemable dignity.

### The Self as Purposeful

The second thing politico-social individualists do follows from the first, and that is to find the sense of an individuated self not only good, but also purposeful. The individual is deemed free, not in the negative sense of not conforming—though there is always something of that in throwing off the social shackles of authority and custom—but free in the sense of acting on grounds made for the self, by the self, using the full range of mental powers practically every human being is assumed to possess.

The sense of personal purpose and the freedom to pursue that purpose lead logically to ideas about self-maintenance and self-extension. The self is under the obligation to use itself to creative and affirmative effect. Having purpose and freedom is pointless, in other words, unless they are given full rein. The modernist life becomes a project in itself, an ongoing form of research into who the self might be and what the self can do.

### The Self as Private

The third thing individualists do is enclose the self and decree that enclosure essential in the pursuit of the kind of research indicated above. A line is drawn between public and private realms, with the latter said to be the domain of the individualist alone. Line-drawing like this requires specifying where such a line lies and when it is crossed, none of which is self-evident and all of which has to be constructed by individualists in formulating individualism as a politico-social creed.

The invention of the modernist Self made such a doctrine well-nigh inevitable. Once reason had been highlighted, it could be used for any purpose whatsoever. It no longer had to be dedicated to any other end. Its proponents were able to laud reason alone. Since rationalism individuates, reason was then able to laud individuation too. And it was used to do just this, in the ways discussed above, creating in the process the doctrine of individualism and the punctual realm in which it might be exercised.

### Individualism as Liberalism

In establishing the sense of Self as one of moral worth, personal purpose, and private significance, modernists also make possible politico-economic languages that promote individuated wealth-making and politico-strategic languages that exalt individuated internationalism. Individualism becomes the basis, that is, for a liberal, self-emancipatory language that can be and is used in both of the other dimensions of world affairs.

Individualism as a politico-economic project is called "liberalism" here, since, as we shall see in Chapter 4, that is mainly how the term is used in the study of world affairs. Liberals are free marketeers, and they see themselves and their analytic language as the ideology of emancipation, making freedom possible for all earth's people.

Politico-economic liberalism, in other words, exalts the sovereign entrepreneur. Under politico-economic liberalism, the rational and self-interested pursuit of material gain is supposed to be translated, via the mechanism of the free market, into public benefits for all. In liberalist terms, private competitiveness makes for public efficiency. It is a public moral good. Self-determination is the source of our productive drive. And private property is the basis of secure personal possession.

Exalting the sovereign entrepreneur also helps ensure that any attempt to hinder individualism does not succeed. Individualism is the antithesis, for example, of the kind of command socialism that characterized the Soviet Union. It is the antithesis as well, particularly in its extreme form, of the state planning many more democratic regimes do. Given that planning of this kind may be the only countervailing power able successfully to confront the large firms that now dominate the global market, setting so much of the global agenda for individual producers and consumers, opposing state power could well seem counterproductive. Such are the dilemmas modernist liberalists must face.

Individualism as a politico-strategic project is called here "internationalism." It exalts the sovereign civic individual, ultimately to anarchic ends. Politico-strategic internationalism, as we shall also see in Chapter 4, involves the attempt to reach beyond the state for laws that might make for a more cooperative and less competitive global milieu. It involves, for example, the international legislation and implementation of human rights, which is an individualist doctrine that privileges moral claims of universal standing. It also involves the attempt to implement democracy as the preferred system of state governance in the world, not only because this system maximizes individual freedom, valorizes individual consent, and respects individual privacy, but also because democracies are supposed (at least among themselves) to eschew the resort to war.

Individualism is the antithesis of the state-centric worldview that is traditionally known as "realism" (see Chapter 4). It proposes global cooperation and adherence to global norms, because these are thought to inhibit personal freedom less than states do.

Proposing global cooperation presents another paradox. State power may be the only power able in practice to implement human rights. Opposing such power would seem to run counter to the best chance we have, therefore, of seeing individualism succeed (at least in those countries where the state-makers are prepared to implement human rights, rather than practice policies that run counter to them).

Individualists can be state-centric "realists" if they are consummate rationalists. Rationalist realists, in the conventional disciplinary language, are "neorealists," which is a form of state-centric thinking that sees the system of states as being what rules (Waltz 1979).

To the "neorealist," the ungoverned nature of world affairs places exogenous constraints upon every state in the system, regardless of who rules it or what that rule is like. Neorealists hide their individualism behind highly abstract conceptions of structural determinism, or, rather, they treat states as individuated units which act as if they were human individualists. Microeconomists do the same when talking of firms. This is individualism taken to its dehumanizing extreme, since people per se do not appear to be important in either case.

This does not mean people are not there, however. In practice every structural determinant involves a personal choice. Somewhere, somehow, someone must make a decision. They may feel they have no choice in the matter, but they still have to decide what to do. "Neo-realists" assume that state-makers will always make rational decisions, and that the rational choice where global anarchy rules will always be a state-centric, self-help one. As a consequence, neorealists feel they don't have to discuss state-makers per se, since their behavior is entirely predictable. Nonetheless, the state-makers are still there, deciding like little machines to maximize their individuated preferences and making sure that anarchy is always the (largely unintended) result.

### Individualism as Personal Perspective

In more general terms, individualism creates a very personal perspective on world affairs. It stands world affairs on its head, as it were. Manning calls this the "pond-bottom purview." It highlights how ordinary people think and feel, rather than the clash and accommodation of reified entities called "states" or "firms" or "social movements" (Manning 1962, 77–87).

The systems, structures, and institutions that constitute world affairs are, after all, enacted by people. There are patterns to how people act when they organize, which may not be readily apparent in how any one person behaves. Nor may they be apparent as some sort of arithmetic sum of what all the people in an organization do. We must remain mindful, in other words, that patterns of repeated human practice (like states, firms, or social movements) have outcomes that no mere sum of their parts would predict and that these patterns of human practice cannot be discerned by focusing on repeated individual actions alone. This said, it is ordinary people who are the ones who think and feel the world's affairs day by day.

Individualism can be used to highlight how much world affairs are constituted by ordinary thoughts and feelings. It can be used to remind us of the enormous effort made every day to inculcate specific ideas about how the world works. In Chapter 1 I called this process the making of the world-in-the-individual. I find this hyphenated concept useful as a reminder. A model of world affairs has been built into all of us, and the idea of a world-in-the-individual flags that fact.

This is modernist thinking. Neither a premodernist nor a postmodernist would separate people conceptually from world affairs and then see them as enacting those affairs.

Premodernists either would not know about such a mind-set or would not want to know about it. In the life-world of premodernists, the community matters most and the self is embedded in the community in ways that require and get a great deal of conformity.

Postmodernists also highlight how the "rubber mass" of society remains intact, stretching up to include us regardless of how far we might be pushed or pulled away by our rationalistic pretensions. We live in relationship and in language, and we cannot detach ourselves from either without becoming divine or deranged.

The separate and abstract individual is a fiction, in postmodern terms. We are, first and last, socially constituted, socially determined beings. As such we are not only the subject of efforts to objectify the world, but we are also subject to the social relations in which we live. This is not voluntary. We cannot exist outside these definitive and constitutive relationships. We can never, for example, be undetermined in gender, race, and class terms. These are not "roles" we play, since there is no self outside such roles. We are not mere "subject positions" (Flax 1990).

Postmodernists see our constituted selves as multiple and interactive as well. Postmodernists welcome these interactions as potentially creative, though they remain mindful of the way these interactions can be used to mask attempts to determine social practices. White, university educated males, for example, typically depict themselves as rationalistic and objective. At the same time, they use their whiteness, university education, and maleness as measures and markers of rationality and objectivity. Particular values are made to seem universal when they are not, and universal values are given a particular meaning which they do not have.

Modernists see all this social constitution of the self as being largely beside the point. We are inescapably constituted by our society. Modernists do not deny this. What they do highlight, however, is how we can and do pull ourselves away from our social contexts, and how we can and do get constituted as rationalistic and detached beings. Given such detachment, they ask, how do world affairs seem? What does such a "subject position" tell us about world affairs? How does our "object-matter" appear from here?

### World Freedom

Worldwide, individualism liberates the self (or so individualists believe). By creating abstract conversations about the "rule of law," for example—by using reason to articulate neutral rules that hold for all—individualists realize an abstract realm that is governed by nobody, for nobody, and where there is no privilege, no disadvantage, and no domination. This realm is said, in individualist terms, to be where we are most free.

The problem is that individualism not only emancipates, it also alienates. It makes it harder to sustain the societies upon which human living depends. A world of utility-maximizing, rights-asserting, role-playing selves may be a globally compelling one. Their material choices may drive open markets, their civic choices may create open democracies, and their awareness of their sense of Self may nurture open societies, but people like these have not exhausted our potential for human being. The shopping, voting, self-affirming person that individualists prefer is a very particular way to live, but, despite its appeal and the extent of its acceptance, it is not the only way for human beings to live. It is not necessarily the best way, either.

Because individualism requires the making of mental distance, it can result in feelings of isolation. How widespread these feelings might be and what their significance is for world affairs if they become widespread remains unclear. If state-makers feel mentally detached, however, if they are advised by people who feel socially distanced, and if enough people feel existential despair, then these feelings are likely to have foreign policy implications. Those who feel intellectually disengaged and emotionally "absurd," for example, are quite likely to construct a commensurate kind of world (Goodman 1956; Berman 1980; Taylor 1991; Giddens 1991).

This said, individualism did help build the great European empires. The productivity, the military power, and the sheer impertinence of Europe were sustained in no small part by this particular analytic language. When these empires collapsed, however, individualism did not collapse with them. It went on to become a global ideology, competing with states and corporations for the chance to craft people's consciousness and with other ways of constituting the Self. Individualism, rather than being "swept aside or superseded" like other forms of imperial power, has proved to have "remarkable staying power, flexibility, and adaptability" (Wiarda 1981, 169–170).

## The Feminist Critique

Most feminists resent the extent to which individualism is a masculinist mentality. They see people as much more socially embedded than this mentality allows, and they are less likely as a consequence to seek to partition themselves off or to own their experience in ways that constitute discrete selves.

The autonomous, self-maximizing model of preferred human behavior is a masculinist one, feminists argue, and rather than being good and right, it is bad and wrong (Tickner 1996). Most men seek power over external things, which is not "obviously admirable" as a way to behave (Nozick 1989, 147). Most women do not behave like this, or as much like this, as men do.

In principle, individualism has no gender, no ethnic identity, and no class. As far as individualists are concerned, this is why it is uniquely suitable for universal use. Why then do feminists—with the exception of those feminists who are liberal—take exception to it? If it is for everybody, why does it not include women? If it is for everybody, it ought to appeal to all those who are taught to feel individuated and individualistic. If they are Buddhist (or green, or Amerindian) too, this ought not to impinge.

## The Experience of Individualism

Rather than stand back to look any longer, perhaps standing close to listen to a committed individualist speak will help answer important questions like these. The following comes from Robert Nozick, *The Examined Life: Philosophical Meditations* (1989, 128–129, 140, 144–150):

> It is reflexive self-consciousness that constitutes and organizes the self. Self-consciousness is reflexive when it knows itself as itself, not just when it thinks about what happens to be itself . . . Reflexive self-consciousness is the kind of consciousness someone has when he [sic] thinks of "I," "me" or "myself" . . .
> . . . Some Eastern theories condemn the self on three counts: First, the self interferes with our experiencing the deepest reality, and also with experiencing things in general as they are; second, it makes us unhappy or it interferes with our having the highest happiness; third, the self is not our full reality, yet we mistakenly believe it is.
> The terse recommendation of these Eastern doctrines, then, is to end the self. This is peculiarly difficult to achieve (short of ending the life also) and this difficulty gets attributed to the wiles of the self: We are attached to the

self—an attachment the self encourages—and we won't let it go. There are at least two other explanations of the self's tenacity, though, more respectful of the self. Although the self may not be optimal overall, it may be a somewhat good structure . . . Second, even if the self were suboptimal overall, it might be the very best and most efficient structure for certain delimited functions, functions we do not want to give up . . .

. . . [I]t acts [for example] as a central monitor . . . [I]t functions as an intelligence agency, as knower and noticer, and inquirer . . . The self also integrates its explicit verbal understanding with other modes of understanding and transmits the result internally to those semiautonomous portions that can make use of it . . .

. . . When the extreme heights of reality are to be scaled, perhaps, having more of a self will be a hindrance. The self then would [admittedly] be a local, not a global optimum, to be forgone carefully only for other more difficult ways of becoming more real still.

Until his Self goes global, Nozick is quite happy to have it and what it does for him. Nozick is not holding his breath, though, since as far as he is concerned, a "more real" self would mean suicide. This, he suggests, is hardly likely to mean a more acute sense of reality, at least, not for long. His nod to Buddhists and Eastern doctrines is only a nod. It is, in fact, his ethnocentric way of endorsing the pleasures of self-reflexivity. He likes his capacity for self-realization. He likes chatting to himself. He is, in a word, an individualist. Not for Nozick the silence of being sublime. Nor is he about to abide centrally planned economies either. Being real means being a marketeer too.

Having listened to an individualist discuss his ideology, I would like to ask what taking part in these terms is like. Those who have read this far, or opened the book at this point, are likely to be politico-social individualists, so I would first invite them to ask of themselves: what is it like to have such a sense of Self? What is it like to take part as a detached being in a wealth-making, state-making world, that valorizes the use of reason as an end in itself?

Since I cannot ask of readers what I am not prepared to ask of myself, I shall put the question this way: what does politico-social individualism feel like to me?

If I think about it, I can see that all my fundamental feelings are rationally mediated. Though I grew up in a world of nature and art, I was trained to prioritize reason, and I work now as a high priest in one of its larger churches (a university).

My faith in rationality is not all that it might be, since I accept the significance of unreason as well. I am not much of a heretic, though. All I do is try to complement Reason with other ways to know. I am not prepared to abandon rationality altogether.

Along the way I was taught to compete intellectually, to be self-reliant, and to value my status as an autonomous human being. I was taught as a consequence not to rely on intuition and to define the Good Life in terms of what I might ultimately get out of it myself. I was taught, in other words, not only how to individuate myself, but to valorize individualism too.

I have collectivist sympathies. These lie with working people, since my social origins were there, and I sell my own labor for wages. I am not much of a joiner, though. My sense of Self seems to make joining difficult for me to do. People of my ilk have been called "organic" intellectuals (Gramsci 1972) though I am not sure if that label fits. As a wage-worker I am supposed to be alienated too, though I get too much job satisfaction for that.

I have an Australian passport that says I am an Australian citizen. Unless I deliberately repudiate the identity this passport represents, I have a tether for life to the land where I was born and raised. The tether gets longer all the time, but it is never likely to be cut.

All and all, I would say I am a fairly predictable part of the modernist project. I am not on most of its margins, though I am on one or two. I am aware of how much my sense of Self is a modernist construct, and I wonder whether that sense could ever be transcended, and what transcendence would be like.

How does my experience compare with yours? Are the comparisons instructive? Does individualism feature in your feelings toward world affairs? Here is one answer from an author who considers abstract individualism a "manic defense," a form of denial, a way of stopping people from experiencing the social constitution of the subject, that is, themselves. It comes from Jane Flax and her work, *Thinking Fragments: Psychoanalysis, Feminism and Postmodernism in the Contemporary West* (1990, 42–43):

> Like many contemporary writers I have numerous questions concerning our and my expectations about adequate theorizing and desirable modes of social life. Although none of these questions is resolvable, giving reasons for why and in what sense one theory or concept of knowledge, self, gender, or power is better than another is still possible and necessary . . .
>
> I have . . . tried to confront a philosophical tradition and temptation—to speak as a disembodied, impersonal truth teller or critic. Adopting such a voice entails denying the limitations in vision necessarily imposed by any person's social location, including my own, which happens to be white, female, materially comfortable, someone who benefits in many ways from being a citizen of a rich and powerful First World country. I also feel pulled between the practices and knowledges arising out of the various kinds of work I do, as psycho-analytic therapist, teacher of political theory in a predominantly black university, writer, and mother.
>
> There may be no ways out of these dilemmas. Yet there may be at least better or worse ways of living with them. The better ways would seem to include a continuous struggle to be conscious of how philosophies and persons respond to differences and ambiguities: our fear of erasing them, our desire to do so.

### Collectivism: The Individual-in-the-World

The more we value our mental distance from the world, the more we are concerned not only with the maintenance of the cultural and social circumstances that make such distancing possible, but also with reinstating a sense of having a social self. The further we are pushed or pulled mentally away from the society in which we live, the further we move toward the point that the illusion of rationalist objectivity creates for us. And the more we do this, the more most of us feel the need to join this point to other such points in an analytic replica of the society to which we are still attached (Taylor 1992, 47).

Our need for a sense of social belonging seems to be due, in part, to deep predispositions on our part. With rare exceptions, we seem biologically to want to live in groups. This is evidenced by the fact that we cannot grow up outside society and expect to be able to come to maturity. This means that the need for society is radically exogenous and endogenous. We learn from others from the moment we are born. We learn from that moment on to prefer society itself. And we seem to have an inherited capacity to do so.

Whether by nature, nurture, or both, people want to be cupped by society, regardless of how highly they value their sense of being separate. They find individuation and the language of individualism that this makes possible very hard to bear. The "decision" to become individuated may be far less calculated than it sounds, and it is no accident that along with the spread of individualism has gone various attempts to repudiate individualism as well.

#### Societies of the Mind

We seek out in the metasocial realm, where reason and the objectifying use of it put us, other enselved individuals who are similarly unhappy with how enselving feels. We look for those who have the same mental "views" as ourselves, who see what we see. We establish with them an agreement of sorts that compensates for what is lost in becoming "we-less." We make societies of the mind that parallel the one we are still living in, but, intellectually at least, have left.

Because these societies are made in the mind, we can design them rationally to meet our desired specifications. Here are some examples of such societies and how they get made.

#### Scientists

Some prefer to keep using reason as an end in itself, for example, while seeking out others of their ilk. They may as a consequence found or join societies of scientists, where they can go on, among like-minded individuals, solving the puzzles that reasoning sets (Kuhn 1970; Latour and Woolgar 1979). Establishing "the truth" of the world is then done collectively, not individualistically. It is the society of scientists as a whole that determines what each of its members should agree upon, and what they should not, and what they should count as evidence in the process (Addelson 1994, 166).

## Social Movements

Some use reason as an end in itself, while also pursuing a cause of some other kind. They found or join movements that promote "scientific" socialism, for example, or environmentalism, or a faith.

Such societies are mixed. Their members are modernist, striving to retain their rationalist credentials. They are also likely to find a sense of collective purpose in utopian causes, however, like workers' revolution, women's liberation, environmental sustainability, or indigenous peoples' rights. Some serve more dystopian causes too, like the Mafia. Whether utopian like Greenpeace or dystopian like the Cosa Nostra, the causes are both individualist and collectivist.

## Romantics

Some use reason instrumentally only, drawing their sense of society almost entirely from non-rational sources. This is the "romantic" response, that is, the eschewal of mental "high flying" for the embrace (though still rationalist and individualist) of emotional "deep diving." It is the reversion to what are imagined to be premodernist thought-forms, but by those already modernist. It ranges from shared notions of biological destiny to the shared appreciation of verse.

Romantic soul-searching can take a nationalist turn and, in its most extreme manifestations, even a fascist one. Romanticism does not have to result in brownshirts and torch-lit rallies, however. It can result just as readily in white shirts and candle-lit poetry readings. The point is that both are romantic reactions to modernist individualism, and both have featured in the nineteenth and twentieth centuries as individualism has spread.

While fascists may feel the need to foster the fervor of ethnic essentialism, as symbolized by a charismatic leader, perhaps, they are still modernists first, seeking solace in a sense of solidarity second. There has to be a rationalist initiative before there can be an irrationalist response. There has to be an appeal to reason before this faculty can be put to unreasonable ends. This helps to explain the paradox of 1930s and 1940s Germany. Here we find large numbers of erstwhile rationalistic individualists consciously or unconsciously responding to Hitler's emotional appeal, while at the same time continuing to use their considerable thinking skills. How could such a modernistic culture have taken such a countermodernistic turn? Having done so, how could it continue to use modernistic means? Only an understanding of how modernist collectivism works can answer these questions. (A similar paradox lies at the heart of Cohn's account of nuke-speakers, quoted in Chapter 2).

All the uses of reason above foster a sense of society in the face of individualist fragmentation. They are collectivist antidotes to social atomism, whether high-flown, mixed, or deeply delved. Objectively conceived, they compensate for the alienating effects of objectifying rationalism in general and objectifying individualism in particular.

### Collectivism Versus Individualism

Defining collectivism this way puts me somewhat at odds with more common parlance. The more usual way of defining collectivism is in terms of the ownership and control of industry, either by the state or by the people.

Using collectivism in a more comprehensive sense, however, allows me to characterize socialism and communism as versions of collectivism. Otherwise I would have to use them as synonyms for it.

While collectivism, used in this more comprehensive sense, does not dichotomize individuals and societies (since individualists are social beings, and societies are made up of individualists), it does dichotomize collectivism and individualism. These are different analytic languages and ideologies. They are used as analytic languages to describe and explain different patterns of human behavior, and as ideologies they quite deliberately make for their preferred ends, that is, for how they would have the world to be. Individualists valorize the individuated person's normative worth (self-good), purposive worth (self-determination), and enclosure (self-reference). Collectivists see *society* in these terms instead (Triandis 1995, 43–44).

### Collectivism and Rationalism

Can collectivism transcend individualism? When individualists try to reconnect, to re-create a sense of society for themselves, the reconnection is still rationalistic, since individualism is an outcome of rationalism, as explained above. Collectivism is a response to the feeling of being made an individualist in this rationalistic sense. Does it transcend individualism in the process, however?

I would say that it cannot, since both are outcomes of the same rationalist, modernist project, and neither can escape its consequences, even the one (collectivism) designed to do so (Taylor 1989, 197). Collectivists and individualists alike are both going to feel cognitively superior to someone who believes you can offend a forest, for example, as a premodernist might. Both the individualist and the collectivist sense of self are stained, in other words, by the sense of detachment that objectifying mandates. Only complete reversion to premodernist embeddedness, or complete acceptance of the mind at play, could allow anything else.

This only repeats the point made above about collectivism being seen in the context of individualism. Though the two are ideologically counterpoised, the nature of that counterpoise has to be understood as the attempt of collectivism to rescue the sense (that individualism erodes) that society matters. As we become more individuated and as this sense gets valorized more and more to make us individualistic, we feel the sense of society receding. Any rescue attempt, however, has to be mounted in the face of ongoing individuation and, maybe, individualism too. It has to contend with the modernist project, in other words, which does not stop and which has hegemonic global force.

### Comparing Societies

The discussion so far has made little of the fact that whole societies differ in individualist and collectivist terms. Comparing societies in terms of individualism and collectivism, for example, is a ploy often used to contrast the social behavior of the citizens of Japan and the United States (Triandis 1995, 12–13).

Contrasts like these must be made with great care, however. In discussing the Japan/United States case it is easy to miss the difference between the premodernist character of Japanese communality and the modernist character of Japanese collectivism, between premodernist Japanese individuals and modernist Japanese individualists. Since similar distinctions can also be made for the United States, comparing the two means comparing all these different characteristics. The contrast we draw between the two countries is much more nuanced than a simple distinction between personal autonomy and social solidarity allows.

### Gemeinschaft and Gesellschaft

The distinction between a community and a collective is long-standing. The most notable exponent of it in modernist times is the nineteenth-century German sociologist Ferdinand Toennies ([1887] 1955), whose concepts of

*Gemeinschaft* (community) and *Gesellschaft* (society) have passed by now into the common stock of sociological categories.

With the global spread of individualism, it becomes necessary to distinguish with greater care than Toennies does between its politico-social and politico-cultural aspects. It becomes necessary to distinguish, for example, between different kinds of *Gemeinschaft* and different kinds of *Gesellschaft*.

This is why I prefer to talk only of premodernist societies as "communitarian." I prefer to reserve "collectivism" to describe modernist attempts to compensate for individualism. It seems clearer that way.

Westen's attempt to think not in terms of a dichotomy here, but of a historical process, is useful too. In premodernist times, he says, the individual is either completely embedded or (with luminous exception) very partially enselved. At first, we find preagricultural, hunter-gatherer societies. In cultures like these, the group-needs are paramount, the group is believed to have magical potency, and nature, culture, and the person are only minimally differentiated. There is no conception of a "separate and unified self." Later, as the means of production evolve, we get agriculture or a "massive ecological windfall that permits the growth of private property and some rigidification of class structure." In cultures like these, the primacy of group-needs is harder to maintain, the group itself becomes more internally specialized, and nature, culture, and the person become more differentiated. A sense of the "individual" begins to spread, though it is not yet considered the most legitimate social sense. Indeed, there is usually a concerted "cultural attack on individual desire (especially when opposed to group needs)," and notable efforts are made to maintain the moral primacy and authority of the group in the face of the rising challenge that individualistic desires represent (Westen 1985, 245, 252, 256, 263, 328).

In modernist times, industry and individuation proceed apace. The "locus of value and power" moves from the group to the individualist. We begin to get a third type of society that Westen calls "individuated collectivist" (266). Kinship relations become more role-like. Morality is increasingly self-made. Group cohesion is increasingly a function of self-interest. Religious faith is manifest more in personal devotion rather than public display. Individualists begin to see themselves in the mirror of the group, rather than as a mirror of the group. They begin to explain themselves not in cosmic or communal terms but in terms of themselves.

Finally we get "social contract" liberals and unabashed existentialists. The end of this particular philosophic line is reached when individualists are no longer seen as existing "for society," but when society is seen as existing entirely for the individualist.

At the end of this line, the individualist either feels indifferent to society, or triumphant in the face of society, or "nauseated" at the lack of it. The indifferent are content to play with their brains or, like Cratylus, the ancient Greek philosopher, to do no more than wag a mental finger. The triumphant celebrate their personal freedom as a victory without historic parallel (Rand 1961). The "nauseated" look for a collectivist leg to walk with to stop them going around in circles on the individualist one (Sartre 1965). "[P]athological narcissism" becomes the norm, as the culture completes the transition from "philosophy to insanity" (Westen 1985, 273–279).

### Collectivism plus Individualism

Late modernists proclaim the possibility of a synthetic form of collectivism wherein the individualist comes to full flower as a social being too. Rushkoff calls this the "next necessary phase of human evolution." He talks of a "community of individual creatures who form a networked whole in order to promote their collective survival," envisaging a liberalist utopia wherein the good of the collective is furthered along with that of the individualist (Rushkoff 1997, 157).

The Cold War precluded a global synthesis of this kind for fifty critical years. Perhaps, with the collapse of the Soviet Union, we may see the world move in this direction, particularly with the growth of a global market.

Liberal capitalism is too individualistic to qualify as a form of synthetic collectivism. It pays too little heed to the good of the collective. This is also why its contemporary triumphs are likely to be short-lived.

Social capitalism might achieve such a symbiosis, though only Japan has so far managed anything like this en masse. The politico-cultural context of Japan is still a premodernist one, however, which helps to explain this particular achievement.

"Humanity," Westen wrote in 1985, "will be lucky enough to survive the current century," let alone manage a culture that simultaneously affirms "individual liberty and collective sentiment" (281). He is wrong on both counts. Not only has humanity made it to the millennium, but, as individualism spreads, attempts are repeatedly made to strike precisely the balance he recommends. The whole socialist movement might be seen in these terms, and other notable social movements strive to realize this balance too. In the Japanese case, noted above, the intellectual revolution that in the West preceded the industrial one is yet to take place. As the Japanese move from premodernist communalism to modernist individualism and collectivism, however, they may be able to strike a viable balance between individualism and collectivism, inspiring others to follow suit. Their circumstances may be too particular, though, to be of global relevance.

In modernist terms, the reconciliation between individualism and collectivism must be made in the suprasocial realm, where "punctual" selves try to re-create a sense of community that can compensate for the alienation caused by objectification. Intimations of this kind were common in the nineteenth century as individualism began to be used to exacerbate individuation on a large scale and as the alienation that individuation caused became more widespread and more acute. Ever since then, many have sought solace, either in the most rationalistic utopia of them all, namely science, or in romantic reversions to what they can recall of premodernity (or can reinvent in its name), or in any number of rationalist utopias and dystopias (socialism, communism, apatriarchialism, and conservationism).

### The Experience of Collectivism

The movements above are rich with resources when we want to listen to a collectivist speak. Of the modernist social movers, though, the most famous is surely Karl Marx.

Marx sees states being taken over by proletarians, who then use the powers of the modernist state to dismantle states themselves. As we will see in the next chapter, this will pave the way for an advanced form of communism, the ultimate social formation, transcending all that has come before. It will allow the rational realization of an integrated and harmonious world. It will allow our industrial revolution to be put to civilized and humane effect. It will allow a new kind of utopia, one analogous to the life of hunter-gatherers, but hunter-gathers able to use much more complex productive means.

In *The German Ideology* ([1846] 1977, 54), Marx and Engels paint their most luminous picture of what this postcapitalist, rationalist utopia will be like:

> . . . nobody has one exclusive sphere of activity but each can become accomplished in any branch he wishes, society regulates the general production and thus makes it possible for me to do one thing today and another tomorrow, to hunt in the morning, fish in the afternoon, rear cattle in the evening, criticize after dinner, just as I have a mind, without ever becoming hunter, fisherman, shepherd or critic.

How society is supposed to regulate production is not clear. What is clear, however, from Marx's other writings, is that dismantling states is a whole-system procedure. If it does not take place "across the board," then socialism reinforces the state, as Lenin and Stalin demonstrated. It fails as a way of getting to communism. It gets stuck, and, in Marx's terms at any rate, it is not communism at all.

This is why Marx says, quite explicitly, that "communism is only possible . . . 'all at once' and simultaneously" and that it presupposes the "universal development of productive forces . . . [and] the world market" (Marx and Engels [1846] 1977, 56). A dictatorship of the proletariat that is not the end result of such an "all at once" global process, that does not wait for the maturation of the global production process, is not a dictatorship of the proletariat, in Marx's terms. It is a dictatorship of those who say they represent the proletariat. It is a dictatorship, period. Under these conditions the rational realization of a sense of society for all becomes the irrational realization of a sense of society for only some. The rest are left alienated, in a modernist limbo, waiting for revolutionary change.

Having heard a collectivist speak, we might ask what taking part in collectivism might be like, too. Since no collectivist utopia has yet succeeded, we can only imagine such an experience, which is what Eric Frank Russell does in *The Great Explosion* (1963, 178–180). The book is a satirical account of a planet where a group of followers of Gandhi have built a society based, paradoxically, upon both radical equality and absolute personal freedom. The single premise of their society, in line with Gandhi's notion of civil disobedience, is the ability to say no. Hardly the basis for social cohesion, one would have thought, but as those who were subsequently sent from Earth to survey the planet's culture were quick to discover,

> "This world runs on some strange system of swapping obligations. How would any person cancel an ob unless he recognized it as his duty to do so?"
> "Duty nothing," declared Seth. "Duty hasn't anything to do with it. And if it did happen to be a matter of duty every man would be left to recognize it for himself. It would be outrageous impertinence for anyone to remind him, unthinkable that anyone should order him."
> "Some guys must make an easy living," interjected Gleed. "There's nothing to stop them that I can see." He studied Seth briefly before he asked, "How can you cope with a citizen who has no conscience?" . . .
> Elissa suggested, "Tell them the story of Idle Jack."
> "It's a kids' yarn," explained Seth. "All children here know it by heart. It's a classic fable like . . . "
> "Red Riding Hood," offered Harrison.
> "Yes . . . something like that . . . Idle Jack came from Terra as a baby, grew up in our new world, gained an understanding of our economic system and thought he'd . . .become a scratcher."
> "What's a scratcher?" asked Gleed.
> "One who lives by accepting obs but does nothing about wiping them out or planting any of his own. One who takes everything that's going and gives nothing in return . . . Up to age sixteen Jack got away with it . . . All kids tend to scratch . . . We expect it and allow for it. But after sixteen he was soon in the soup . . . He loafed around town gathering obs by the armful. Meals, clothes

and all sorts for the mere asking. It wasn't a big town. There are no big ones on this planet. They are just small enough for everybody to know everybody . . . Within a few months the entire town knew that Jack was a determined and incorrigible scratcher."

"Go on," said Harrison impatiently.

"Everything dried up," responded Seth. "Wherever Jack went people gave him the 'I won't' . . . He never reached town number twenty-eight . . . He took to the open country, tried to live like an animal feeding on roots and wild berries . . . until one day walkers found him swinging from a tree. Loneliness, self-neglect and his own stupidity had combined to kill him. That was Idle Jack, the scratcher. He wasn't twenty years old . . . But don't let it worry you. Nobody has been driven to such drastic measures in my lifetime . . . People honour their obs as a matter of economic necessity and not from any sense of duty. Nobody gives orders, nobody pushes anyone around, but there's a kind of compulsion built into the circumstances of the planet's way of life. People play square—or they suffer. Nobody enjoys suffering . . ."

Russell's imaginary Gands have a simple code, that is, socially negotiable self-assertion. What makes their society possible is a rationally conceived form of reciprocity. This allows the individuals in it to dress how they like, have no leaders, and still sustain a viable society. Freeloaders, like Idle Jack, are simply ostracized. They are put outside the society and all that the society provides.

The hidden dimension is not economic necessity, however. It is trust. Money is not used, for example, not only because the society does not require a "printed record of every ob" (Russell 1963, 165), but because it is a face-to-face society, with a simple technology and no collective aspirations other than those required to maintain the society itself.

### Nationalism: Civic Ethnicity

Besides turning to collectives of one kind and another, those individuated and alienated by the modernist project have another important ideology they can turn to, namely, nationalism. State-makers use nationalism to legitimize the idea of the state itself, and where it does not exist, they invent it. What ingredients go into such an invention? What does nation-making entail?

People are typically born to a place. In that place they learn what nationalists conceive of as national traits. It is where they grow up, in other words, that people usually learn the tongue they speak, their customs and beliefs, how these customs and beliefs came to be, how to organize and make a living, and what the cosmos means. Thus people become peoples, ethnic groups, imbued with a common sense of location and with a common language, culture, history, polity, material base, and religious faith. None of these attributes, in their specific form, are genetically endowed. All are socially acquired.

Upon the feelings of "here-ness" and "we-ness," in other words, the idea of the nation gets built. Outside of the family, this is home.

### National Attributes

Attempts to itemize the main attributes of a sense of nation highlight "homeland . . . common myths . . . public culture . . . legal rights and duties . . . [and] a common economy" (Smith 1991, 14; Calhoun 1997, 4–5). Not all nations manifest all such attributes, which is why we recognize any particular nation by the syndrome of factors it manifests rather than any essential one (Calhoun 1997, 5). Nor can we specify this syndrome in its entirety. However comprehensive the list of attributes might be, we are never likely to exhaust the subtleties and complexities of what nationalism involves.

While attributes like those mentioned above are culturally acquired, there is a definition of the nation that is couched in biological terms. Those who subscribe to this definition try to establish a person's heritage in terms of shared "blood" or common genetic origin, which is supposed to determine the shared sense of national identity. Since there is no scientific evidence for national attributes of this kind, however, we have here not a biological fact but a culturally acquired belief masquerading as a biological fact. I prefer therefore to categorize this notion of the nation as a subset of the culturalist one, rather than give it separate status.

The first attribute listed above, that of a homeland, is the most important, which is why some see it as definitive. Homelanders define the nation as the "totality" of all those who think in these terms, regardless of who they might otherwise be (Oommen 1997). National identity, in terms of a sense of place, has the highest priority.

There is a problem with this point of view, however, since it excludes those who have a sense of nation that does not rely on land. There are many people who are far from typical in this regard. Those raised in more than one place, for example, will usually have a more complex sense of where they belong and who they are. Whole peoples may be atypical too, like the Gypsies, whose "we-ness" is strong but whose "here-ness" takes a less fixed territorial form.

The idea of a homeland also begs the question of how we should know one when we see one. What is such a place? To answer this question we cannot just say "home" again. "Here-ness" alone does not suffice to explain what nationality means. We need to define it in other ways.

### Essentialist Nationalism

Most of us recognize sentiments like the sense of place that specifies nationality because, in varying degrees, we find them within ourselves. The atypical are by definition exceptional, and in their own way they serve only to affirm what has been called the *essentialist* concept of the nation, a concept that evokes attributes like ethnicity, language, custom, and shared human experience (Guibernau 1996, 1–2).

With the advent of the modernist concept of the sovereign state, the essentialist concept of the nation acquired extra force and took on new meaning. Those making states began trying to create these sentiments where they did not already exist. The "state" concept gradually acquired a hyphen-cognate, becoming the nation-state instead. The nation as an ethnic narrative was wedded to the state's territorial story to make of citizenship more than the mere fact of being born within a country's borders or residing long-term there. Nation-statehood made citizenship into membership in a "community of common descent," and though citizenship could still be acquired for considerably less, the sense spread that those truly deserving of civic status were those defined by civic ethnicity and not just civic location (Smith 1991, 11).

### Institutionalist Nationalism

With *institutionalist* nationalism arose another great river of meaning as a rival to and also as a channel for essentialist nationalism. This river stemmed from the notion that a state, if it did not have a nation, should be a nation nonetheless. The corollary to this, of course, is that a nation that is not a state should be one too.

It is easy to imagine the problems that have arisen. Nationalism used in an institutionalist way is highly problematic. Drawing that simple hyphen between the nation and the state has proven a very complex task and a source of considerable conflict over time.

Essentialist nationalists who decide they want their own institutional sovereignty, for example, and their own state, can and do secede from the state in which they find themselves. Civil war typically follows as the state-makers seek to deny their claims. Even when conflict does not ensue, state-makers who want to make one nation out of one territory, although their land contains a range of nations, have to strike bargains between the major cultures involved (as in Switzerland or Canada). Or they have to impose one sense of nationhood upon the rest, dressing the imposition up as a new kind of culture, even though in practice this is cultural imperialism (as in Indonesia). Enough state-makers have actually succeeded in making new nations like this to suggest that the attributes that constitute old, preexisting nations can be consciously manipulated.

What does the institutional use of nationalism mean for essentialized notions of nation? If nations can be made, how can they be found? Are they actually irrelevant? Hardly, because state-makers always impose something. They do not fabricate new national attributes with no historical referents at all. They get the attributes they seek to impose from the cultures around them. The line between essentialist and institutionalist forms of nationalist feeling can be hard to see as a consequence.

## Nationalists Versus Statists

Another problem follows from that above, though it is more specifically to do with the modernist nature of state-making and the premodernist components of nation-making. The languages, customs, and beliefs that characterize a people have considerable emotional appeal. This affective component is at odds with the rationalist character of modernist state-making. As a result, the nation and the national are seen as a "somewhat embarrassing and mysterious anachronism, a disease of the transition to universal society, a residue of the prerational that is expected to decline and eventually disappear" as Western Enlightenment spreads (Deudney 1996, 130). At the same time, we find state-makers trying to fabricate national sentiments (in rationalist fashion), calculating consciously what is required to have such sentiments widely shared and crafting educational curricula, civic rituals, and official histories to create the requisite traditions (Anderson 1991).

Once state-makers start reaching for premodernist sentiments, however, who is to say where the process ought to stop? There are probably ten thousand nations in the world, defined in essentialist terms. If nation and state are to be linked institutionally, what is to stop any one of these thousands of nations from claiming its putative sovereign birthright? If a state can be a nation in principle, regardless of whether it is one or not, why cannot nationalists decide to be a state too? This kind of thinking can quickly set nationalists and statists on a collision course, especially when state-makers think that the nation should be only what they want it to be, and when self-determining nationalists use force to resist them.

## Why Risk Proliferation?

Raising up enemies like this is no way to run a state. We might well wonder, therefore, why state-makers risk evoking such terrible resolve. Why appeal to ethnocentric sentiments when they are potentially capable of destroying the state in the process? Why make nation-making part of the state-making agenda when to do so—to call up nationalism's emotive power—can jeopardize states themselves?

Some modernists hazard an answer to questions like these in technological terms. They highlight industrial capitalism and the way this momentous set of events created integrated transport and communications systems. They note that industrial manufacturers need literate and numerate work-forces. And they note the capacity state-makers acquire, with the advent of large-scale printing technology, to provide mass education to meet this need. These developments make in turn for a more widespread sense of social loyalty. In a word, they make for nationalism (Deutsch 1953; Gellner 1983).

Other modernists see nationalism having been fostered historically by European state-makers afraid of other states, or wanting to expand, or both. A united nation is much harder to defeat and much stronger as an expansionary platform. European state-makers as a consequence ran the risks involved, thinking that a sense of nationhood would make statehood itself seem more tangible and justified. National sentiments would consolidate and legitimize the concept of the state itself, which, in turn, would allow them to do more abroad (Guibernau 1996, 140).

Yet other modernists see nationalism having little to do with state-making at all, being a deliberate move, not from the top down but from the bottom up, to capture state institutions on behalf of the people as a whole. They highlight Rousseau's feeling, for example, that the nation is constituted of its people rather than its rulers or its ruling class (Rousseau [1758] 1960, 135). They note the practical effects of such an assertion, particularly the effects of the eighteenth-century revolutions in America and France. And they note the democratic claims these revolutions articulated and the nationalistic form these claims subsequently took (Carr 1945, 7–8).

### The Success of "The State"

Nationalism did not, in the event, destroy the state. State-makers, more often than not, were able to turn nationalist feelings to their own account, particularly where the two were more or less congruent anyway. It was the modernist state, in other words, that became the "mould and measure" of the nation, not the other way around (Carr 1945, vi).

As Mayall puts it, "The nationalists moved into the building which had previously been occupied by dynastic rulers and religious authorities, creating in the process much new real estate. However, the new sub-divisions, like so many condominiums and flying freeholds, left the building itself more or less intact." Essentialist nationalists mostly ended up working within the context of institutional nationalism, that is (Mayall 1990, 25–26).

How did this happen? How did the modernist state come to prevail in this regard?

Carr tells the story in three parts. In the first part, we find early modernist state-makers disentangling themselves from trans-European Christendom. Indeed, much of the history of this period, in statist terms at any rate, has to do with the making of state-based churches. The state at this time was also highly personified. As a consequence, so was the concept of the nation. It was synonymous with the person of the prince or the king, and the international relations of the time were thus the relations between these princes or kings. In the second period, the idea of the nation became more democratic. Power was in the process of passing from sovereigns to propertied middle classes, under whose aegis state-makers turned outwards in a massive wave of imperial expansion. Aristocratic mercantilism gave way to bourgeois liberalism, with Britain in the lead. The third period saw the completion of the democratic project and the "socialization" of the nation. This process brought the material conditions of whole populations into view, replacing a "single world economy" with a "multiplicity of national economics, each concerned with the well-being of its own members" (Carr 1945, 2, 3, 19, 22).

Carr's account is contested. Gellner, for example, accuses Carr of focusing too much on the formation of the modern state, and of not giving institutional nationalism its full due. In his view, for example, the first period had little to do with nation-making. The princes and kings shared a "French High Culture" at this stage. They were too busy making modernist states too, and to talk of nationalism is to undermine the importance of what happened next (Gellner 1994, 24). While Carr characterizes the second period in terms of bourgeois British internationalism, Gellner sees it instead as the source of the idea of institutional nationalism that was to triumph after the First World War. Carr, Gellner says, does not acknowledge the full significance of the nation-making revolution that was going on at this time. Gellner also adds a fourth and a tentative fifth stage to the process. The fourth, he says, involves nation-building by "mass murder and forcible transplantation of populations." Once in the hands of state-makers like Hitler, Stalin, and any number of other ethnocidal leaders, nationalism takes a destructive turn and gets used for "ethnic cleansing" and other appalling purposes. The fifth stage is one where institutional nationalism wanes, however, having been overwhelmed by the way the modernist project makes all states and nations more alike (Gellner 1994, 27, 29–31).

### Democratic Nationalism

Despite the differences in the accounts these two analysts provide, they are not radically at odds. Both note the transition from international relations to world affairs, and both see nationalism going from a matter of aristocratic whim to one of mass consequence. Both mark the emergence, that is, of a democratic concept of the nation. And both see this concept as "new . . . popular . . . [and here] to stay" (Carr 1945, 8). Whether it is here to stay depends on late modernist changes of a kind Carr does not explore. At the time he wrote, the homogenizing effects of world capitalism were not so chronic. The democratization of nationalism was clearly apparent, however, and by dichotomizing Frederick the Great (who treated his subjects as objects) and Napoleon (who posed instead as the "champion . . . of the emancipated French nation . . . [and] the chief missionary of modern nationalism"), Carr was able to document a key historic transition. He was able to get the whole historic plot into one apt nut (Carr 1945, 8). On this point, Gellner concurs.

### Nationalism in Decline?

Which still leaves unresolved the issue of Gellner's fifth stage. What will happen to institutionalist and essentialist nationalism as communications and transport systems spread? Will they survive the advent of global awareness? Will homogenization prevail, and will nations—whether made by social or statist means—then disappear?

The first point to note here is that global awareness is not neutral. Global awareness is awareness made global by the dominant politico-cultural project of modernity. As such it has the characteristics of that project. It globalizes not only the use of reason as an end in itself, but a preferred language (English), preferred customs (the handshake, the business suit, golf), preferred stories of the past (World War II), a preferred form of governance (liberal democracy), a preferred mode of production (liberal capitalism and mercantilism), and preferred dreams for the future (more of the same). Other languages, customs, and socio-cultural stories get marginalized accordingly.

Those marginalized by the globalizing of particular politico-cultural preferences may accept the loss of their local sense of themselves or they may not. They may accept the loss of their own distinctiveness or they may resist it, or they may try to blend the two practices somehow.

Essentialist nationalism can be used to foster resistance to globalizing sentiments. It can then be stood alongside the "peace, ecological or feminist movements" as a way of championing the "different, [and] the powerless" (Guibernau 1996, 133), though it can be used (as in the "ethnic cleansing" alluded to earlier) to devastate the different and powerless, too. Using essentialist nationalism to resist marginalization can have mixed results, in other words. It can be used to a legitimate and reasonable purpose to oppose universalism and hegemony. It can also be used to impose its own kind of conformity and exclusivity, its own kind of particularism, its own kinds of ethnic intolerance, racial prejudice, or ethnocide.

None of the above will be unfamiliar to students of world affairs. Despite being under-theorized, much thought has been given to nationalism of late. For one thing, the end of the Cold War has lifted the lid off a number of ethnic confrontations which have often had nation-state implications. Since most students of world affairs are modernists, they tend to see such implications in institutionalist terms. They tend to find the essentialist components of nationalism somewhat paradoxical. This in turn has prompted a new round of analysis as to what nationalism involves.

While modernist objectifiers categorize and reify the nation, reducing it to a concept with attributes, it remains "subjective, fluid and elusive" too (Duara 1996, 151). It *is* the cause of terrible resolve and violent conflicts. State-makers tell themselves that nationalism should be subservient to statism. Like the man who awakens the sleeping giant, they expect the nationalists to do their bidding and not the other way around. Once roused, however, nationalists can be keen to construct "self-conscious political communities" of their own (Duara 1996, 153). One part of the modernist project (state-making) can then find itself at odds with another part (nation-making), with unhappy consequences for both.

## Nationalism and "First Nations"

The modernist state and nation are only one of the way in which tribal loyalties can be organized. And though the modernist state has been globalized now, and with it the sense that this is the only legitimate way to order world affairs, institutional nationalism is nonetheless a highly reductionist politico-social practice.

The institutional nationalism that characterizes nation-statehood is only one possible manifestation of solidarist sentiment, in other words, and for many indigenous peoples, nation-states are only possible because they actively suppress alternative notions of what social solidarity entails. And while the indigenous "first nations" are relatively small in number and are likely to find state status denied them in perpetuity, this does not stop them asking why state-makers think they deserve a monopoly over what makes a nation-state.

On what basis, other than that of might alone (which never of itself made for right, though it does make for considerable amounts of compliance!), do state-makers claim sovereign privilege? Or to quote Duara again, "on what grounds can the present nation-state make a special claim to legitimacy as the first embodiment of the people-nation" (Duara 1996, 160)?

All claims to sovereign legitimacy are invented. There is no reason why those of "first nations" should be any more valid than those of state-makers. Prior possession is felt to support prior claim, however, and on this basis "first nations" contest the predominance of nation-states. What is more, they do so now on a global scale, pooling their physical and intellectual resources and coordinating fight-back strategies on the same world-spanning basis as the state and state system itself.

In containing such strategies, state-makers must not only suppress all nations other than their own, but also suppress all other ways of being socially solidarist. In seeking to get their existence acknowledged, "first nations" invent and revive alternatives to state-nationalism that draw upon premodernist thought-forms. State-makers tend to give these no more than token recognition.

The reduction of this kind of global diversity to whatever suits the modernist state has been called "ethnification" (Oommen 1997, 13). Globalizing the state system has turned many of earth's inhabitants into minority peoples in their own lands. This has been a harrowing process, if only because of the degree of dispossession involved. Pushed to the margins of the nation-state system, or outside of it altogether, indigenous peoples are some of the best placed to understand that system's ideological power. It may be scant recompense for the members of "first nations" themselves, but analysts wanting to describe and explain institutional nationalism are well advised in the first instance to ask indigenous peoples what it means.

### Nationalism and Gender

Institutional and essentialist nationalism is also gendered, which is why those wanting to understand it are also advised to ask what it means in feminist terms as well (Yuval-Davis 1997). For example, some feminists argue that, because men cannot bear children, they appropriate an "abstract concept of the blood-tie" which they then use to promote bonding among males and a "group identity based on male-defined needs" (Peterson 1994, 78). Do men create nations to allow them to club together, thereby compensating for the fact that they cannot have babies? Put like this, the feminist account of nationalism can sound a bit far-fetched. Put like this, however, and we (women and men) are forcefully reminded that nationalism not only fosters essentialized feelings of loyalty and solidarity, but that its practices are made by men, who make it as men. In this context, being not-woman matters. Men make institutional nationalism, for example, to foster the feeling that "the people" are one. Their doing so is highly misleading, however, and notably masculinist in practice. "The people" are only ever one in principle. In reality they are men and women and, in terms of access to "rights and resources," it is the men who prevail.

Here, as everywhere else in world affairs, gender makes a difference. A woman may be born to a place, just the way a man is, but her chances of enjoying the benefits of that place are much slimmer than his. She may become symbolic of the nation, but her body then becomes a target for abuse by enemy men, with rape in war the most obvious result. She can have children and she can teach them what to think and feel, but she cannot do any of this without masculinist/nationalist supervision. She can have citizenship in a nation-state, but she can not use that citizenship the same way a man can. The nature of her citizenship is different in a wide range of publicly administered ways.

## Nationalism and Rationalism

Nationalism is a modernist doctrine. It is part of the modernist project. The rationalism at the heart of this project not only individuates the sense of self, however, but can heighten the sense of a nation as being made up of individuated individuals too. For example, rationalism heightens the sense of the human body as being indivisible. It can make it easier to think of the nation also as an indivisible body. Rationalism heightens the sense of having a singular history and a life trajectory. It can make it easier in turn to think of the nation having a similar history (Calhoun 1997, 44). Rationalism objectifies such personal attributes as ambition, idiosyncrasy, volition, self-determination, drive, and will. It can make it easier to endow the nation with these same attributes.

The modernist concepts of nationalism and the "punctual self" (Taylor 1989, 159) can be and are used to reinforce each other. The separate sense of self that objectifying reasoning results in reinforces the sense of the nation as separate as well. This in turn helps to endorse the existence of sovereign states. A state-made world of clearly demarcated territories seems to be easier to build, in other words, if it has clearly demarcated peoples in it too.

As it happens, the world does not have clearly demarcated peoples in it. Ordinary people manifest complex social realities. Clean nationalistic distinctions can be hard to make. Divisions like these are easier to draw in the abstract, metasocial realm that individuated individuals inhabit when they talk to each other rationalistically. Hence the use of modernist rationality to create the nationalist distinctions convenient to the state-making cause. And hence the propensity to "download" such distinctions into the commonsense world of ordinary human experience.

## The Experience of Nationalism

Demarcating the peoples of Europe along nationalist lines intensified in the nineteenth century. Not coincidentally, this was a time of intensifying rationalism too. Standing back to look at these practices highlights the issues discussed above. What do we find if we stand close and listen, however?

Giuseppe Mazzini was the leading nineteenth-century advocate of Italian unification. In February 1861, he wrote to one of his German counterparts (1979, 168–169, 173–175):

> On the one hand, you have us . . . convinced that no continuous and pacific evolution of the faculties and forces of Humanity, on the road of common progress, can take place if . . . the arbitrary distribution of the Nations, caused by conquest or by the pretended right of royal families, does not undergo a fresh partition founded on geographical conditions, on language, and on traditions. I need not repeat . . . that by Nationality we only mean the organisation of the work of Humanity, of which the nations are the individuals.

In the following month of the same year, likewise to his German compatriots, he wrote:

> Be Alemmani, you say . . . What sense do you give to this expression? Of what Alemagna do you speak? Of the Alemagna which oppresses in the name of violence, or of that which blesses in the name of the power of the intellect? . . .
> . . . She needs Unity . . . she needs to concentrate her own forces and make the best possible use of them on the soil where her speech is spoken, where the mothers repeat her popular legends over the cradles of their infants . . .
> . . . I am an Italian, but also a man and a European. I adore my Country, because I adore a Country in the abstract; I adore our Liberty, because I believe in abstract Liberty; our rights, because I believe in abstract Right.
> Nationality is sacred to me, because I see in it an instrument for the good and progress of all; geographical conditions, historical traditions, language, and special tendencies, are for me only indications of it . . . The Nation ought to be for Humanity what the family is, or ought to be, for the Country. If it does evil, if it resorts to oppression, if it becomes a missionary of injustice for a temporary interest, it loses its right of existence . . . These are my inmost feelings about Nationality.

Mazzini was a modernist. He required the conscious rejection of premodernist aristocracies. He believed in the power of reason, in liberal progress, and he saw nations as analogous to individuated individuals. He rejected any kind of nationalism put to anything other than an emancipatory purpose (and he saw the nation as a figurative female, with women at home beside the cradle!).

Most of us inherit the kind of world he wanted and were consequently taught some form of civic ethnicity. We do not, therefore, have to reach far to find examples of what this means and how the nation gets made.

Not all of us have had to suffer nation-making at its most extreme, however. The following passage by Urvashi Butalia gives a vicarious sense of how this feels (1997, 14–15, 22):

The political partition of India caused one of the great human convulsions of history. Never before or since have so many people exchanged their homes and countries so quickly. In the space of a few months, about twelve million people moved between the new, truncated India, and the two wings, East and West, of the newly created Pakistan . . . Slaughter sometimes prompted and sometimes accompanied their movement; many others died from malnutrition and contagious disease . . . As always, there was sexual savagery . . . Thousands of families were divided, homes were destroyed, crops left to rot, villages abandoned. Astonishingly, the new governments of India and Pakistan were unprepared for this convulsion. They had not anticipated that the fear and uncertainty created by the drawing of borders based on headcounts of religious identity—so many Hindus and Sikhs versus so many Muslims—would force people to flee to what they considered "safer" places, where they would be surrounded by their own kind. People traveled in buses, cars and trains, but mostly on foot in great columns, called *kafilas*, which could stretch for dozens of miles. The longest of them, said to comprise 800,000 refugees, travelling east to India from western Punjab, took eight days to pass any given spot on its route.

This is the generality of Partition; it exists publicly in books. The particular is harder to discover; it exists privately in the stories told and retold inside so many households in India and Pakistan. I grew up with them . . . My mother [for example] tells of the dangerous journeys that she twice made . . . to bring her younger brothers and sister to India. My father remembers fleeing to the sound of guns and crackling fires . . .

The partition of India made two national-states out of one, at a cost far higher than anyone anticipated. Though Mazzini specifically rejected state and nation-making that exacted such a price, nationalists have not always heeded him. The events documented above have been all too common in the annals of current affairs. And though the experience of nationalism can be beneficial too, since constructing national sentiments does have an emancipatory side, the dreadful exceptions abound.

# II

## The Dominant Aspects of the Discipline

# 4

# Making States and Making Markets

State-making and market-making are the two remaining dimensions of modernist world affairs. They are also the discipline's current core concerns. State-making is International Relations (IR), and market-making is International Political Economy (IPE).

International Relations has been integral to the discipline's concerns much longer than IPE. Politico-strategic affairs were the main concern of disciplinary practitioners when IR was first founded. IPE became a disciplinary staple only recently. Its origins lie in the seventeenth century, when the concept of political economy was first coined. It was not accepted as a mainstream component of world affairs until the 1970s, though.

How do IR/IPE look in the light of the preceding discussion? What should we make of them with respect to what has been said about the other dimension of world affairs, that is, IPS (the making of international political society), and the macrocultural context of all three dimensions, WPC (the making of a world political culture)?

If we return to the discussion of the media in Chapter 1, we find state-making and market-making of major concern there. The media bias in this regard is one of the most important ways, in fact, in which our daily awareness of world affairs gets skewed.

The media do not report regularly and explicitly, for example, on the progress of the modernist project. They do not detail the politico-cultural dynamics that underpin the world state-system and global capitalism. There are very few updates, for example, on the number of schools in the world that give students the chance to practice critical scientific thinking and experimentation skills or that teach the first principles of neo-Darwinian evolution.

The media do not report regularly and explicitly on the third dimension of world affairs, either, which is the third map I mentioned at the beginning—the one that hangs behind the politico-strategic map (of global states) and the politico-economic map (of global markets). This only gets seen in the pages of the world's press or on the world's television screens when it impinges on these two other maps. As a consequence, there are very few updates on the spread of the ideology of self-realization, or on social movements, or on ethnic movements, except where these implicate the state- or market-making realms.

The neglect of self-making and mind-making does not mean that these processes do not matter. The failure to highlight the third politico-social dimension of modernist world affairs, or to highlight politico-cultural modernity per se, does not mean these do not feature in the making of world affairs. They do matter and they do feature. They are just not remarked upon in the discipline or, at least, not much, not yet.

The objectifying, neutralizing worldview that modernity fosters may make culture and society seem less relevant, but the experience of ordinary people confirms their significance. This is why commonsense constructivists consider global acculturating and socializing practices so profoundly important, practices that no comprehensive account of world affairs can and will neglect. Valorizing reason, the main acculturating practice, has extraordinarily significant consequences, as the lives of ordinary people amply attest. The intellectual revolution this practice involves radically changes every aspect of being and, as a result, the whole of world affairs. Valorizing the individual, the main socializing practice, has equally far-reaching outcomes. So does valorizing nationalist sentiments or collectivist ones, the dominant politico-social practices besides individualism.

The failure of the discipline so far to fully accommodate self-making and mind-making points up its partiality. State-making and market-making are only two ways of making modernist world affairs. Chapters 2 and 3 show that. So why are they promoted as if they were the only ways? Is the discipline so ill conceived that most of its proponents cannot see what is in front of their figurative faces? Is modernist knowledge so fragmented, perhaps, that it prevents the knowledge-makers from appreciating the shape of the disciplinary whole?

This is a question for the historians of the study of world affairs. It is an important question, but, whatever the answer, we must still look beyond core disciplinary concerns if we want a more comprehensive account of world affairs. We still have to augment the version of reality that modernists provide with nonmodernist insights. We have to add to the analysis of IR/ IPE, that is, the analysis of IPS and WPC as well.

How likely is it that adherents to the discipline will respond as suggested? Not very—not for the moment at any rate—in part because of the way partiality serves particular interests. It allows world affairs practitioners, for example, to disguise the extent to which they are implicated in promoting the modernist project. It also allows statists and marketeers to inculcate a version of world affairs that benefits relatively few. If people can be persuaded of the primacy of modernity, or of state-making and market-making, then they are less likely to question the self-serving logic of those who promote rationalism, or the global state system, or the global capitalist system. They are less likely to notice that a global state system requires wars, or that a global capitalist system requires accumulation and exploitation and large disparities in wealth, or that rationalism requires materialistic, individualistic, and secularizing selves. People are less likely, in turn, to require anything different. They will go on thereby helping those concerned to distort world affairs, in principle and in practice.

How important, after all, are politico-cultural and politico-social affairs? Here ordinary experience is paramount. Despite the long-standing determination by most analysts of global politicking not to talk about these kinds of affairs and to help craft the world accordingly, ordinary people's lives do involve politico-social and politico-cultural practices. The significance of the IPS and WPC is evident as soon as we look at what ordinary people do. Self-making and the privileging of reason are global issues now. Modernity makes margins too, where core components of world affairs get put on notional peripheries. All of this is obvious from the experience of ordinary people. It is not, however, if one reads the main scholarly works on world affairs.

The experience of ordinary people also confirms the ongoing significance of state-making and wealth-making. Regardless of the above, a comprehensive account of world affairs will include these affairs too.

Those familiar with the particular practices that characterize IR/IPE will find what follows to be summaries of them. It is organized in terms of the main analytic languages that dominate each dimension (realism, internationalism, and globalism in the case of IR; and mercantilism, liberalism, and Marxism in the case of IPE), but it does not pretend to provide more than the briefest of sketches of each one.

The ensuing summary, uncluttered by debates about particulars and details, lets us see more clearly what accounting for state-making and wealth-making does *not* cover, however. It lets us appreciate what the relevant analytic languages do *not* say. It lets us tell, particularly in the light of the preceding chapters, what IR/IPE obscures.

The ensuing summary will continue to feature experientially proximal readings as well, short examples of writings by proponents of each analytic language, and of writings that provide some sense of what it means to take part in the world affairs they describe.

Most analysts of politico-strategic and politico-economic affairs construe them in rationalistic terms. Few of them yet employ more proximal and less rationalistic means.

As noted already, this is not a history of the study of world affairs. Before discussing state-making and market-making, however, it is worth recalling briefly the historical context in which these practices developed. The how or the why of the way they achieved their manifest success, not just in shaping the discipline, but in shaping world affairs, remains unresolved. We cannot appreciate the character of the present without some awareness of where it came from, however.

The key point here is the way the scientific and industrial revolutions in Europe made possible new and overwhelming kinds of military power and a new kind of capitalism. In turn, these revolutions made possible (some would say inevitable) land-grabs on a scale rarely matched in antiquity. And they made possible (again, some would say inevitable) international accumulation on a scale equally unprecedented.

In making their huge imperial push, the nineteenth-century European state-makers destroyed most of the non-European empires and replaced them with their own. To Europe's east, and America's west, the Japanese state-makers followed suit.

The European imperialists took with them their Christian faith. They also took with them their ideas about state-making, market-making, and self-making, and about the efficacy of using reason as an end in itself too. Scientific progress was believed to token civilizational excellence, and those who prevailed believed it was their destiny to do so.

As the above account might suggest, European rationalism had a long-term effect on global assumptions about what is morally good. After World War II, this effect was given concrete form in a "universal declaration" of human rights. The European sense that moral norms exist that are known to all human beings (provided they can be shown to be human beings—an issue with important implications for nonwhites and women) was put into a globally compelling form and promoted accordingly.

In practice, the Europeans had fashioned the content of this rational morality and of the "natural" laws that decreed it from their own moral traditions. Hence the sense that the natural law doctrine, and the subsequent human rights doctrine, were mere ploys used by European imperialists, and their heirs in the United States as well, to legitimize their global reach.

Euro-U.S. claims for the universality of their notions of natural law became harder to sustain as non-European rulers began to achieve more equal status and to compare the substance of European claims with their own conceptions of morality and natural law. Once the European empires collapsed, the contest became more vigorous again. Indigenous peoples, trapped within states, were the most disadvantaged in this regard. They were the ones who found it hardest to get heard. No new state in the postimperial world had an easy time of it, however.

It was two disastrous wars in the European heartland that brought the European empires down. One obvious result was the globalization of the European-style state and state system. The Europeans bequeathed to the rest of the world their concept of state sovereignty. This bequest—the concept of legal state equality—became the organizing principle on which the interstate society of the second half of the twentieth century was built. All the new, state-making elites joined this interstate society. None tried to stand outside it. Nearly all chose to take their place in its central organization, the United Nations, and most subscribed, despite their many specific reservations, to its basic international laws (Bull 1984, 126; Pettman 1979, 229).

All of this is relatively recent. At the end of World War Two there were only fifty states in world affairs, though several of these were empire-states, not nation-states. The last of the great European empires, the Soviet Union, collapsed at the end of the 1980s, bringing the sum of states to nearly two hundred. In fifty years, from 1948 to 1998, the number of states quadrupled. It took until the year 2000, that is, more than three and a half centuries after the modernist concept of the state was first invented, for the world affairs implicit in what is known as the "Westphalian formula" to be finally realized. There was nothing necessary about the realization of this formula. By courtesy of human contingency, it was realized, however, and to world-shaping effect as well.

There were gendered logics at work, since state-making is done mostly by men: women do not command the process to anywhere near the same degree as men do. The process was driven by profit-seeking capitalists, too, whose productive powers required expanding markets in which to acquire resources and to sell their industrially produced goods and commercialized services. The historical story is a chapter of accidents, however. No one planned this particular kind of world.

The "high politics" of diplomacy and war have long been disciplinary reference points. This is the state-making dimension of world affairs, referred to in the disciplinary parlance of the day as International Relations (IR).

As indicated above, the three main analytic languages that characterize the disciplinary debates about politico-strategic affairs are realism, internationalism, and globalism. The so-called English School calls realism a Hobbesian language, after the English political theorist Thomas Hobbes (though it has also been called a Machiavellian one, after the Italian political theorist Niccolò Machiavelli). The English School calls internationalism a Grotian language, after the Dutch jurist and putative father of international law Hugo Grotius. And it calls globalism a Kantian language, after the German philosopher, Immanuel Kant (Wight 1978; Bull 1977). Those not happy with the names of historic authors use other nomenclature, like realism, rationalism, and revolutionism. "Rationalism" is also known as "(neo)liberal institutionalism" or "pluralism," particularly by American analysts. "Revolutionism" is more likely to be known as "globalism" in the United States, and that is the label used for it here.

*Realism* highlights power politics and interstate competition. According to realists (of the IR kind), we live in a world of sovereigns, self-determinators, territorialists, boundary maintainers, arms racers, power balancers, treaty makers, alliance forgers, United Nationalists, disuniting nationalists, and warmongers, plus the odd mongers for peace. This is the world affairs represented to us by the major media and the world affairs Louis XIV had in mind when he stamped his cannon *Ultima Ratio Regnum* ("the last argument of kings"). It is the aspect of world affairs that most of the discipline's proponents still consider paramount, the one they strive most diligently to articulate and defend.

In its extreme versions, power politics is deemed inevitable given the kind of creatures we are (bad) or the kind of constraints an anarchic state system places upon state-makers (rational). In its moderate versions, we are merely told to be prudent, to pursue the national interest by diplomatic rather than military means.

*Internationalism* highlights the amount of cooperation as well as competition that takes place in the interstate system. Contemporary Grotian/rationalist/liberal institutionalist thinkers point up the amount of international law that actually works, the extraordinary range of international organizations in the world, and the extent to which state-makers do considerably more than prepare for war. On the whole (and with the exception of the structural neorealists) they see people as more reasonable than realists do, declaring the dense network of interstate obligations as important to world affairs as the sovereign capacity to go to war.

Extreme internationalists see international organizations and laws as viable alternatives to power politics. Moderate internationalists, like moderate realists, are content to foster interstate diplomacy and alliances.

*Globalism* highlights the human capacity for cosmopolitan behavior. Contemporary Kantian/revolutionist/globalist thinkers are all notably more universalistic than the previous groups. They highlight the human capacity to do more than compete or cooperate. They see people as capable of doing better than having to resort to war or make cooperative gestures that only enshrine self-interest. They see them devising transnational ways of ordering the state system, up to and including world government. Because they see people as not only rational, but potentially good as well, they consider the state-centric system ultimately amenable to globalist reform.

The extreme globalists envisage a world government with world citizens and no more states. The moderate ones see world affairs building up to such a government, with blocs of states (like the European Union) coming together in a grand, state-based global confederation.

The "high politics" of state-making are now seen to have their counterpart in the "low politics" of marketeering. As a consequence, we find the discipline documenting the daily endeavor by states, corporations, classes, individuals, peoples, and genders to produce and exchange services and goods. This is the market-making dimension to world affairs, referred to in the disciplinary parlance of the day as International Political Economy (IPE).

In the Euro-U.S. study of the international political economy, there are three main analytic languages, namely, mercantilism, liberalism, and Marxism. Mercantilism includes a broad range of analytic languages, known variously today as "neomercantilism," "protectionism," and "economic nationalism." Liberalism also comes under various labels, such as "neoliberalism" and "economics." And Marxism is sometimes called "structuralism," particularly in the United States.

Each of these analytic languages describes and explains the international political economy in its own characteristic way. Together they generate very different policy prescriptions. They also generate their own in-house debates about the relative probity of the different dialects in which each language is spoken.

*Mercantilists*, like their realist counterparts in the politico-strategic realm, are the most state-centric. They talk of a world where state-makers seek to maximize their autonomy, mainly by securing economic sovereignty and the wealth of the state. The extreme mercantilists are autarchic or imperialistic. The moderate ones are prepared to compromise economic sovereignty if such a compromise furthers such sovereignty in the long run.

*Liberals*, like their internationalist counterparts in the politico-strategic realm, move away from such statist language to talk of interstate cooperation and the emergence of global markets. They feature the promise of trade and of international investment. They highlight the human propensities that make marketeering possible. The extreme liberals talk of a minimal state presence and the maximum individual freedom to create wealth. The moderate liberals bring the state back in, locally and globally, to act as an arbiter or umpire and to conserve market efficiency.

*Marxists*, like their globalist counterparts in the politico-strategic realm, are the least interested in the state as the unit of analysis. They see the global political economy in very different terms, that is, in terms of the capitalist mode of production. They highlight competing classes, not competing countries, and the capacity for radical change and a more egalitarian global society. The extreme Marxists anticipate working-class revolution and world capitalism's demise. The moderate Marxists are more convinced of capitalism's capacity to effect self-repair. They talk as a consequence of ongoing capitalist exploitation and how it might be minimized.

Realism and mercantilism, liberalism and internationalism, globalism and Marxism do not exhaust the subject of IR/IPE. As the grand narratives there they are contested, for example, by those, both within the modernist project and without it, who do not find themselves well represented in the stories they tell. These antagonists include feminist groups, environmentalists, postcolonialists, indigenous and religious communities, and groups of those kept or rendered poor.

There are realist and mercantilist feminists, for example, internationalist and liberalist feminists, and globalist and Marxist feminists. All question the gender implications of each analytic language from within the modernist project. There are also post- and premodernist feminists who question the gender implications of modernity as a whole. Since IR/IPE are part of the modernist project, they question the gender implications of IR/IPE too.

The hegemonic status that all these analytic languages currently enjoy was and continues to be made and not found. In the making, many people were, and still are, marginalized and rendered mute. The process of marginalization was, and still can be, violent and prolonged. The contemporary lack of prominence of many of those marginalized has to be understood in this light.

Remaining mindful of the alternative voices that speak from marginalized perspectives is a counterhegemonic practice, therefore. It is to heed the voices of the "nonelite, the nonwhite, the non-Western, the non-Christian, and those who . . . in their dissent against gendered and class givens . . . have illustrated their desire to think and speak for themselves, to face their worlds as creative, imaginative human beings capable of both understanding the processes that 'objectively' define them and changing these processes" (George 1994, 229–230).

Not all the voices that speak from the margins of modernist world affairs are worthy ones, of course. Hitler was able to "think and speak" for himself. He was creative and imaginative and he understood, in his own warped way, the processes that he saw as "objectively" defining him. He sought to change these processes, too, and many people were pleased to help him try. Not all those voices made mute, in other words, are ones that should be heard. Rejecting hegemonic, modernist concepts in favor of those found in the thinking spaces that lie beyond them does not guarantee better world affairs. Some of these concepts should arguably stay marginalized, because they are malignant and seek to enslave.

How are we to know which is which? How can the good (whatever this is) prevail? First, there are many moral principles that discriminate between the two. Second, there is the use of superior power to discriminate in this regard. In a state-made world both moral principle and brute force are mediated by state-makers, which brings us to the two languages most statist in construction, namely, realism and mercantilism.

## Realism and Mercantilism

Realism is the most state-centric of the analytic languages that characterize modernist world affairs. Realists talk of a world where state-makers are obliged to take matters of security into their own hands. In a state-made world, state-makers are obliged to help themselves. War is always imminent, therefore, though the point of any war is not the restoration of peace, but the preservation of the system of states itself. Only states, it is argued, can provide local order, albeit at the perennial price of interstate disorder (Bull 1977, 107).

### *Classical Realism*

*Classical* realists believe that people are fundamentally fearful of the aggressive aspects of their nature and that world affairs are characterized by an endless series of conflicts as a consequence. Classical realists are to be distinguished from the so-called *neorealists*, who believe that the effect of having states with different capacities, in a system of states with no government, is self-help in foreign policy terms, regardless of who the foreign politicians might be.

Defining what is "real" in terms of power politics has been problematic since antiquity. Classically minded realists like to cite the Melian Dialogue, circa 400 BC, discussed in Thucydides' *History of the Peloponnesian War* ([416 BC] 1945) as an early example of might confronting right and prevailing in intergroup relations, though doubts occasionally get expressed about the efficacy of such a citation (Onuf 1998). Scenarios like these are to be found in the ancient Chinese and Indian worlds too.

Two thousand years later, classical realists find Niccolò Machiavelli arguing likewise. In the hard world of conquest and colonization, Machiavelli argues, only might can deal with right. To extend one's rule is to imperialize, and a successful imperialist has to be ruthless to stay in control. Any generosity of spirit will be its own undoing, particularly where the colonial casualties are libertarians (Machiavelli [1513] 1961, 48).

Thomas Hobbes is the next touchstone in the classical realist canon. Hobbes wrote in England at a time of intense civil strife, concluding that "without a common Power to keep them all in awe" people will go to war and "such a warre, as is of every man, against every man." Hobbes thought of people as fundamentally greedy and insecure. They fight, he says, for each other's possessions, for their self-esteem, and for their good name, and without a government these natural desires get the better of them. Life as a consequence becomes not only violent, but also "solitary, poore, nasty, brutish, and short" ([1651] 1957, 65).

The same applies, Hobbes believes, to "Persons of Soveraigne authority"—kings and the like—all of whom are obliged, because of the ungoverned nature of the world in which they rule, to confront each other "in the . . . posture of Gladiators; having their weapons pointing, and their eyes fixed on one another; that is, their Forts, Garrisons, and Guns, upon the Frontiers of their Kingdomes; and continuall Spyes upon their neighbours." Hobbes doesn't believe that this state of affairs is irredeemable. Kings and the like do provide security. They do fear death, love the good life, and use reason (Hobbes was an early modernist). Attributes like these are capable, he says, of prompting agreement on "Articles of Peace." People do not want such agreements for their own sake, however (Hobbes [1651]1957, 65–66).

Classical realists believe Hobbes to be saying something highly salutary here, namely, that to survive or prevail one must pay close regard to the importance of physical strength. One of the leading realists of this century argues, however, that "[t]he impossibility of being a consistent and thorough-going realist is one of the most certain and most curious lessons of political science." Realism, Carr says, "excludes four things which appear to be essential ingredients of all effective political thinking: a finite goal, an emotional appeal, a right of moral judgement and a ground for action" (Carr [1939] 1991, 89).

Is Carr correct? Realism would seem to have at least one finite goal with emotional appeal to it, namely self-preservation. The desire to survive provides grounds for action, too, though whether it confers a right of moral judgment or not is more problematic. Many have made the moral claim that they are entitled to survive, and many have seen the moral judgments involved as entirely defensible, which suggests that there is more to world affairs than force. This said, classical realists see the need to defend oneself enough of a reason to assume that a cooperative outcome to world affairs will always fail. The prudent, they say, will always plan accordingly.

Thus, while rational reformers may like to imagine international peace resulting from the democratic resolution of international conflicts, for classical realists this end will never be attained, and appeasement will only ever be a ploy. Physical force is the ultimate measure of state-making resolve. Analysts like Carr, writing in the lead-up to World War II, saw only those with superior might as likely to survive, and as then, so today, classical realists think that hopes for international cooperation will always be dashed by the trials of strength that state-making has historically involved.

The most influential twentieth-century purveyor of this influential language was the German-American analyst Hans Morgenthau. International politics, Morgenthau said, was a struggle for power in the pursuit of national interests. Like Carr, Morgenthau was well aware that power had material and mental as well as military aspects. When he talked of power he mostly meant "brute force," however, that is, the physical capacity to prevail (Morgenthau [1948] 1972).

Morgenthau was not only a realist. He believed that realism was objectively true and that it fitted the empirical facts. We are a selfish species, he said, for whom contention and conflict are inherent. We may in the process appropriate the power of belief, creating moralities convenient to our cause, but given what we are and how we behave, moral principles are no sound ground on which to act. In Morgenthau's world, moral outcomes are only possible where the balance of power favors them, which is why diplomatico-military prudence should always be the basis on which we conduct world affairs.

### Neorealism

Morgenthau became the text-book authority for Cold War U.S. administrators, though as a refugee from a major European conflict he was more inclined to highlight irrationality rather than rationality. His regard for power had first to be "purged" and "domesticated" to make it compatible with liberal capitalism (Kahler 1998, 920–991).

Until Vietnam, that is. Many politico-strategic realists believed the United States had no business getting involved in such a conflict, since it did not serve the national interest and was a waste of money and blood. Having got involved, however, in realist terms the United States should have won. It had the physical might to do so, which is what supposedly matters most. When it lost, U.S. realists were forced to ask how realism could have been so unrealistic? Why had superior martial might not prevailed? Did the measure of might have to be reconfigured to include other indices, like measures of morale? And if that was the case, then perhaps Thucydides was wrong or, at least, was right only some of the time. Perhaps a freedom-loving people could prevail, as Machiavelli certainly believed they could, in which case ideals could be as real as brute force and realism itself had to be reconfigured to take account of that fact.

In reconfiguring realism, analysts were not allowed to get any closer to their subject, however. Rather, they were put at an even greater distance than before. This "neorealism" (sometimes called structural realism) was supposed to be even more objective than Morgenthau's. Thus we find Kenneth Waltz, taking his cue from the most successful of human studies in this respect, namely, microeconomics, rewriting realism as an abstract, logical, whole-system affair. To Waltz, the structure of the state system (anarchy) creates its own politico-strategic outcomes. At one end of the spectrum sit states determined to conquer the world. At the other end sit states merely hoping to survive. And though each state is formally the equal of all others, the system is decentralized, asymmetric, and ungoverned, making its operating principle the balance of power (Waltz 1979, 117).

By recasting realism in a more abstract fashion, Waltz hoped to renew its status as the predominant doctrine of interstate behavior. Most analytic onlookers could see at a glance, though, that this was the same militaristic, mechanistic idea as Morgenthau's, only more so.

The whole neorealist turn was a singular bid to find an analytic language that "worked," that is, one able to generate reliable knowledge about world affairs. It was modernist rationalism applied to the classical, now compromised version of realism, ostensibly to restorative effect.

This attempt served only to impoverish the doctrine further, however. It did not make it more nuanced or persuasive. Consider, for example, the key issue of rationalism. Neorealists say that state-makers need not be rational. Those who do not help themselves, where self-help is the name of the game, will suffer. Their fear in this regard leads to balances of power, which occur with "no assumptions of rationality" (Waltz 1979, 118). Who says fear is not a rational emotion, however? Why deem fear "irrational," as Waltz clearly does, when it might well be the most reasonable response possible? To answer these questions we have to understand how far Waltz is prepared to go to put the world at a mental distance. He wants to describe and explain world affairs objectively. He wants to arrive at a theory that remedies the "defects of present theories" in order to approximate truth (Waltz 1979, 1). He does not think truth can include subjective emotions as well as rational responses, however, and he is prepared to sacrifice the subtlety (and cogency) of his own theory to keep it free of sentiment.

### Antirealism

One consequence of neorealism was the opportunity it gave so-called "neoliberals" to counter realist pessimism with an equally rationalistic account of international cooperation. It was through this door that U.S. analysts were also able to bring IPE .

The conflict in Vietnam stimulated a much more radical rethink of modernist/rationalist analysis than the neoliberal one, however. It prompted a rethink of the whole concept of truth, allowing the claims of those like Waltz to be characterized as rhetorical, rather than analytic. Ashley, for example, called it an "orrery of errors" and a "self-enclosed, self-affirming joining of statist, utilitarian, positivist, and structuralist commitments . . . that anticipates, legitimizes, and orients a totalitarian project of global proportions: the rationalization of global politics" (Ashley 1984, 228). He was not alone.

Neorealists, it was said, fail to live up to their scientific aspirations. They fail as predictors and controllers, because they do not recognize how much they are responsible for creating the world affairs they claim to find. Particular aspects of human nature may well account for the use of force throughout human history. This does not mean that these aspects need predominate today, and even if they do, as Ashley says, it may well be because we choose to exacerbate them; because we choose to make these world affairs, with a realist bias, rather than any other kind of world affairs. To the postrealists, realism of any kind is only "one story among many." It is "neither the only plausible explanation nor the only possible world" (Beer and Hariman 1996, 7), and its rationalist pretensions give it no precedence at all.

As far as the realists and neorealists are concerned, their analyses are representations of the one knowable truth. It is the modernist (rationalist, objectifying) way of knowing that ensures the accuracy of this representation. It is modernist knowing that ensures that what they say is actually so. To read their writings is to know, therefore, how world affairs really work. To prevail in academic debate, therefore, is not to win an argument but to win the chance to present the most objective account of world affairs possible—the one true record, based on the one true set of assumptions about how we know and who we are. There is no alternative.

To postmodernists like Ashley, realism is not about how world affairs work. It is about how realists say they work. It is not about the way international relations get made. It is about making up people's minds for them, and, more particularly, it is about the modernist project itself. It is about furthering the belief in reason, including all the assumptions that make such a belief possible.

To Ashley, therefore, the "balance-of-power" schema is not a "logical relation deduced from a prior structure of states in anarchy." It is rather the "constitutive principle of a pluralistic states system" (269). World affairs is not the pregiven entity that neorealists assume it to be. Statesmen succeed, Ashley says, "to the extent that they . . . strike balances among all aspects of power—e.g., industrial capacity, population demands, military capability, nationalist labor, internationalist bankers, and the consent and recognition of other statesmen." It is this equilibrium, Ashley argues, that defines the state and state interests. It is *this* balance that the art of state-making entails and that produces the (IR realists') balance of power (269).

To R.B.J. Walker, another cogent critic of neorealist language, the way it counterposes a pluralistic state-made system on the one hand and utopian notions of world government on the other makes for a world affairs where fragmentation is to be feared. Such a dichotomy makes power politics, in turn, a prerequisite of order. It makes the simultaneous realization of greater local difference and greater global solidarity seem less possible, less likely, and less desirable too—and for no good reason at all, as far as he can see (Walker 1987, 83).

Realists do argue back, though not to the same avail of late (Gilpin 1984; Spegele 1996). They find it much harder than Morgenthau did, for example, to have their analytic narratives preferred. Realism is not as self-evident, or as natural, or as comprehensive an analytic language as it was once believed to be.

### Realism as Self-Evident?

How "self-evident" can IR realism be, for example, when the history of the state-system involves so much more than the mere "accumulation of successive power-struggles" (Rosenberg 1990, 301)? How can realism be necessary *and* sufficient as an explanation of world affairs when the powers of those ostensibly powerless (in realist terms at any rate) are so numerous and so extensive (Carroll 1972)?

### Realism as Naturalistic?

How "natural" can IR realism be when feminist analysts have demonstrated a gender bias to the whole state-making project? To realists, this is not a relevant issue. To gender analysts, however, sexism is all-pervasive and those who fail to acknowledge it manifest not the global insignificance of gender but the global power of patriarchy (Peterson and True 1998). The state-system has been made for the moment into a "natural" fact of world affairs. But the modern state-system is not any old state-system. It is a male-dominated one. Thus Tickner argues that, "[w]hile realists claim that their theories are 'objective' and of universal validity, the assumptions they use when analyzing states and explaining their behavior in the international system are heavily dependent on characteristics that we, in the West, have come to associate with masculinity." On the basis of the experience of particular men, in other words, realists have built a progressively more global but nonetheless still parochial world, peopled "almost entirely without women" (Tickner 1992, 30–31, 36–37). This fact alone is enough to render realism highly unrealistic.

## Realism as Comprehensive?

How "comprehensive" can IR realism be when it fails to account for world markets and for global capitalism? How can it claim to describe and explain world affairs when it fails to describe and explain major aspects thereof?

This failure is apparent at once when we consider the Marxist critique of realism, for example. In the middle of the last century, Karl Marx developed an analytic language that described world affairs in terms of modes of production. Concentrating on state-making, he said, only served to obscure the significance of the contemporary mode of production, namely capitalism. In his view, state-making was nothing more than a cover, a smoke screen, a bourgeois front for the more serious global process of expropriating the worth of the world's work. Behind the map of states on the wall was another map, he argued, of owners and workers, that determined particular world affairs at every point.

This was a reading of global events very different from the realist one. It was arguably a more comprehensive one as well (Marx and Engels [1848] 1975). Despite the collapse of the Soviet Union—a state that arguably had little to do with Marx's ideas anyway—it is still a relevant reading, highlighting tangible aspects of world affairs that realism does not.

It is not a reading that realists condone, however. Lenin's use of Marx's ideas to mount a revolution in Russia in 1917, and his justification of this revolution as only the first in a world-shattering series of them (Lenin [1916] 1985), deeply troubled the founders of the international relations discipline. They coped with the threat of Marxist theory largely by ignoring it, but after World War Two, with Stalin in Moscow and Mao Tse-tung in Peking, there began a countercrusade of Cold War. Part of this war involved the systematic relegation of Marxist analysis to the far periphery of the international relations discipline. It was, after all, the ideology of the enemy. It poked through in places, in studies of "development," for example, and later in discussions of the international political economy, but only peripherally.

In an age of triumphalist liberalism, Marxism continues to be treated as marginal. It is generally seen as irrelevant and outmoded, rather than any kind of intellectual threat. It is tolerated, but it is still largely ignored.

Marxism is a critique of realism nonetheless, since it implies the "total rejection of the state-centrist model." It constitutes a "direct challenge to much of the base of existing Western studies on International Relations," since Marx completely rejected the idea of a state system separate from the global system of production and exchange (Kubalkova and Cruickshank 1985, 13).

By behaving as if the state system is separate from the capitalist one, realist state-makers have brought about the very dichotomy (between the system of states and the system of production) that Marx explicitly rejected. This is why, despite the importance of what Marx says, state-making remains a primary aspect of modernist world affairs and, with it, realist readings of world affairs.

### The Experience of Realism

So far we have looked at realism by standing back from it. What do we learn by standing closer to listen to what contemporary realists themselves have to say? Since we are talking here about a major analytic language, which over the years has been used not only by many eminent analysts but also by world affairs practitioners, there is a wide range of writings that articulate realist concerns.

As one example of a realist speaking, I offer Frederick Schuman's pithy summary of the history of war, from his text on *International Politics: The Western State System and the World Community.* I follow it with a brief statement he also makes on the implications of war-making for a state-made world (1948, 382, 384):

> The prime objective, as in the days of Lagash and Ur, is still to put the enemy to flight or render him *hors de combat* by dissecting nerves, muscles, viscera, and bones through the subcutaneous introduction of pieces of metal into his body. All technological progress in warfare has consisted in devising more efficient means of producing and delivering to the ultimate consumer more metal, more swiftly, more cheaply, over greater distances, and at less risk to the producer and the middleman. Not until the invention of the atomic bomb was a truly novel means hit upon to end enemy resistance by ending enemy existence . . .
>
> . . . Analysts of world politics, along with the rest of the human race, ignore such developments at their peril. But they are necessarily more concerned with the links between strategy and diplomacy in the formulation of policy and with the liaison, in specific governments and particular situations, between professional specialists in force and professional specialists in fraud and favors.

In realist parlance, state-making and war-making are closely allied. War-making is an integral feature of human society. It long predates the modern state system. Because it *is* such an integral factor, it is deeply implicated in state-making too.

The modern formula for the state was born at Westphalia in 1648 of the exhaustion of war. It did not preclude war, however, which continued to feature as particular state-makers continued to try to extend their realms.

What does it actually mean to take part in a realist world, however? Here, as ever, our own experience is important, since so much of our own lives is a realization of realist rhetoric. If we want to go further, there is Mark Twain's short caricature of how the cruel heart feels that beats within the (extremist) realist breast. I quote in its entirety his "War Prayer" ([1923] 1963, 682):

> O Lord our Father, our young patriots, idols of our hearts, go forth to battle—be Thou near them! With them—in spirit—we also go forth from the sweet peace of our beloved firesides to smite the foe. O Lord our God, help us to tear their soldiers to bloody shreds with our shells; help us to cover their smiling fields with the pale forms of their patriot dead; help us to drown the thunder of the guns with the cries of the wounded, writhing in pain; help us to lay waste their humble homes with a hurricane of fire; help us to wring the hearts of their unoffending widows with unavailing grief; help us to turn them out roofless with their little children to wander unbefriended through the wastes of their desolated land in rags and hunger and thirst, sports of the sun flames of summer and the icy winds of winter, broken in spirit, worn with travail, imploring Thee for the refuge of the grave and denied it—for our sakes, who adore Thee, Lord, blast their hopes, blight their lives, protract their bitter pilgrimage, make heavy their steps, water their way with their tears, stain the white snow with the blood of their wounded feet! We ask it, in the spirit of love, of Him Who is the Source of Love, and Who is the ever faithful refuge and friend of all that are sore beset and seek His aid with humble and contrite hearts. Amen.

Twain's savage satire reminds us how savage human beings themselves can be. It is this propensity for ill will that the classical IR realist cannot ignore. Any reading of history provides evidence aplenty of human perfidy and reason enough not to place oneself at the mercy of one's fellow man. If we are to believe Twain, mercy is not what one is likely to get.

Twain's idea of people is a possible but not a necessary one, however. How likely is such behavior, we might ask, and under what circumstances might it be avoided? There is no definitive answer, though hope springs eternal, as indeed it must.

The experience of inhumanity is awful and immense. This is why realists see reason in diplomatico-military prudence. Twain's story is not the whole story, however, since people can be merciful, and people can be reasonable (not just rational), and people can be much else that is morally affirmative besides. This is scant comfort to those who have suffered cruelly at the hands of others, but it is why a world of interstate competition is arguably not the best of all possible worlds, nor the best of all those that we might construct in its stead.

## *Mercantilism*

Mercantilism, in terms of world affairs, denotes state-making by wealth-making means. It is to IPE what realism is to IR (and nationalism is to IPS). To mercantilists, state power is an end in itself, subsuming the domestic economy and the rights of individuals in the single-minded pursuit of national self-reliance. War is always imminent and the mercantilist motto is the same as the Boy Scouts,' namely, "be prepared."

To economic historians, mercantilism has a wide range of specialized meanings. Indeed, it has such a wide range that as a singular concept it does not mean much to them anymore. It is used, for example, as a historical category, to refer to two centuries of European state-making (the "mercantilist era"). It is used to refer to the way state-makers can intervene to build the material basis for a strong state (the "mercantilist state"). It is also used to refer to the particular strategies that state-makers choose in pursuit of state autonomy ("mercantilist policies").

To students of IPE, however, mercantilism is useful because of its breadth of reference. It is a convenient and historically evocative way of referring to all the wealth-making in world affairs that has the modern state as its central concern. This wealth-making might be reckoned in terms of a favorable balance of trade, or foreign exchange surpluses, or state-centered international production chains, or in more general terms that highlight how state-makers intervene to create the conditions that augment national wealth.

Mercantilist policies are those policies, in other words, that enhance state autonomy and national self-sufficiency. Mercantilist descriptions and explanations of world affairs are meant to clarify why such policies are preferred, and a mercantilist understanding of world affairs will be one where the meaning of a political economy of this kind is apparent to all.

Since mercantilist policies are the politico-economic counterpart to Hobbesian/realism, like that politico-strategic language they tend to be predicated on the assumption that human beings are at best competitive and at worst downright bad. Given no world government so far, state-making is seen in zero-sum terms. State-makers are required to help their own state before all others, in materialistic as well as diplomatico-military terms. Who will fight world market forces on behalf of a state's citizens and in defense of their productive power, the mercantilist might say, if not those who lead them?

The formula for the modern state and state system, first devised at Westphalia in 1648, was a highly creative one, but it did not stop European state-makers from power politicking. The Treaty of Westphalia allowed for defined borders, contiguous territories, sovereign and central governmental institutions, formal equality, and nonintervention. By implication, it allowed for mutual recognition, too (Treaty of Westphalia 1648, Articles 67, 64, 65, 81, 92). Unbeknown to themselves, the princes of Western Europe were bequeathing a model that would work for the entire globe, though a good deal of conflict lay in realizing this bequest.

Mercantilists are heirs to this tradition. They make the "unity and strength" of the modern state their paramount concern. They are economic nationalists, in other words, and their economic nationalism determines their choice of politico-economic policy (Earle 1986, 219).

Historically, unity and strength have meant fostering a monopoly of the means of force "at home" and fostering imperial ambitions abroad. It has meant, at one time or another, "exports and imports . . . rigidly controlled; stocks of precious metals . . . built up and conserved; military and naval stores . . . produced and imported under a system of premiums and bounties; shipping and . . . fisheries . . . fostered as a source of naval power; [and] colonies . . . settled and protected (as well as strictly regulated) as a complement to the wealth and self-sufficiency of the mother country" (Earle 1986, 219).

Today, the means of mercantilist self-help may be quite different. The modern state continues to supply international political economists with a distinctive analytic language, however. In a state-made world, in other words, there is the continuing sense that "'nations matter' (or at least should matter)" and that nationalist sentiments can and should inspire state policies, "not only in regard to national security issues, but also in regard to the welfare of the nation's citizens." In such a world we can safely assume the primacy of mercantilist politico-economic affairs (Levi-Faur 1997, 360, 370).

### Extreme Mercantilism

Contemporary mercantilist strategies include relatively extreme attempts to turn inwards, cutting a state off from the world political economy (autarky). This process of "looking inwards" can be voluntary (as with Myanmar, for example) or it can be an involuntary one (the result of sanctions, for example, as with Cuba). Inward-looking strategies minimize state dependence on others through the active exclusion of the world "outside." They are relatively benign in interstate terms, though autarky imposed by sanctions is clearly exceptional. Either way, said strategies encyst. They promote absolute state autonomy, for good or ill.

Mercantilist strategies include relatively extreme attempts to look outwards as well, making other states dependent on the mercantilistic one (imperialism). This outward-looking approach can feature territorial land-grabs of the kind Iraq made for Kuwait (a bid, in part, to repudiate Iraq's national debt to Kuwait). It is more of a politico-strategic ploy when it takes this form. Or it can feature "economic imperialism" (neoimperialism), which secures a state's material independence by rendering other states materially subordinate.

Extreme mercantilism of this outward-looking kind can be difficult to differentiate, in practice, from more moderate attempts to maximize market shares or to vertically integrate enterprise chains. Strategies like these allow wealth-makers to engage the "outside" world while consciously maximizing state independence at the same time. Such strategies dichotomize the state's inside and outside realms, making what is outside the state part of what is inside it. At the very least, they make what is outside the state less capable of compromising what is inside.

### Moderate Mercantilism

Mercantilist strategies also include attempts to maximize state autonomy in ways that are clearly more moderate. In these cases, the ongoing engagement with the world market and with international capitalists is less aggressive and more defensive. Legislation governing joint ventures or controlled capital imports provides examples of this kind. So do financial measures that regulate banks and banking services and fix currency rates. So do trade tariffs (taxes on imports), quotas (limits on the quantity of imports or on their value), export subsidies (depreciation allowances, cash grants, and tax holidays), and currency controls (that limit the availability of foreign currency for the purchase of foreign goods). So do administrative regulations on imports (bureaucratic procedures, systems of advance payment, minimum domestic product content rules, special marketing standards, and special safety and health provisions). So too do "voluntary" restrictions on imports.

Mercantilist strategies can even include interstate cooperation. Some would see an organization like the European Union, for example, as mercantilism on a regional scale. In their own self-interest, European state-makers have come together to erect common tariff walls against the rest of the world and create their own currency. In so doing, they have furthered their economic nationalism as a group, rather than as single states. Though the collective character of this project seems directly to contradict the mercantilist ethos (which is state-centric, not regional), the protection such a project provides does seem to further national interests. This is evidence, perhaps, of how mercantilism continues to evolve, to meet the demands of the modern day.

Less popular, but still a viable mercantilist option for states with high debts, is default. Twice, for example, since the middle of the last century, Peruvian state-makers have incurred a large public external debt and then defaulted (Thorp and Bertram 1978, 339). They are not alone. Rather than try to trade their way out of trouble or visit blame upon exploitative foreigners in some other way, other state-makers too have found a declaration of national bankruptcy an attractive policy option. Large currency devaluations can have a similar effect, as can debt rollover and forgiveness strategies.

A whole country cannot be repossessed the way a domestic property can. In the nineteenth century, however, the British and the French did physically repossess Egypt. Such a policy is only feasible by indirect means today, via the International Monetary Fund, for example. Declaring default, installing a new state-making regime, blaming the previous one for the old debt, and then waiting until new creditors present for new projects remains a credible mercantilist strategy in a self-help world, however, and one that liberals rightly fear.

### Does Mercantilism Work?

Does mercantilism achieve its putative purpose? Does it promote or does it compromise a state's material autonomy? Moderate mercantilists may advocate trade barriers (tariff or nontariff) that protect local industries, but these can invoke retaliation in kind. Tariffs can make trading more difficult in turn, buying greater state autonomy but at considerable cost to state income. How much this compromises state autonomy will then depend on how bad the situation gets. Extreme forms of mercantilism, autarky for example, can end up undermining state self-sufficiency completely. So it is no idle question: does mercantilism work?

### The Experience of Mercantilism

How do mercantilists respond to their critics? Rather than speak on their behalf, I shall cite instead someone who uses this analytic language because of his personal commitment to the cause it serves, namely, Friedrich List. His work, *The National System of Political Economy* (first written in 1837 but not translated into English until 1885) is the best-known response to the liberalism that sought to supplant mercantilism.

List was "first, last, and above all a German" (Earle 1986, 245). The Germany of his day was radically disunited, however. The separate German states were a regional model of contemporary global affairs (Earle 1986, 246). All trade between them was inhibited by local tariffs and duties (Prussia alone had three thousand dutiable items and a thousand-mile border along which such customs could be collected). "Germany" had no collective face to present to the world. List wanted one, because he wanted a Germany that was nationally united and internationally respected.

List died before Bismarck realized this dream, though he would not have approved of what the Germans did in their quest for "unity and strength" because he was a political liberal as well as an economic nationalist. He would not have approved of what some of his other disciples ultimately made of him either—the Meiji Japanese, for example, who used his ideas to help catch up with the West.

I shall take up List's argument at the point where he confronts Kant's concept of the possibility of a cosmopolitan solution to interstate rivalry; that is, the possibility of a world government and "perpetual peace" ([1885] 1966, 122–127, 131–132, 167–172):

> If . . . we assume a universal union or confederation of all nations as the guarantee for an everlasting peace, the principle of international free trade seems to be perfectly justified. The less every individual is restrained in pursuing his own individual prosperity, the greater the number and wealth of those with whom he has free intercourse, the greater the area over which his individual activity can exercise itself, the easier it will be for him to utilise for the increase of his prosperity the properties given him by nature, the knowledge and talents which he has acquired, and the forces of nature placed at his disposal. As with separate individuals, so is it also the case with individual communities, provinces, and countries . . .
>
> . . . All examples which history can show [however] are those in which the political union has led the way, and the commercial union has followed . . . [U]nder the existing conditions of the world, the result of general free trade would not be a universal republic, but, on the contrary, a universal subjection of the less advanced nations to the supremacy of the predominant manufacturing, commercial, and naval power . . . The system of protection, inasmuch as it forms the only means of placing those nations which are far behind in civilisation on equal terms with the one predominating nation . . . appears to be the most efficient means of furthering the final union of nations and hence also of promoting true freedom of trade. And national economy appears from this point of view to be that science which, correctly appreciating the existing interests and the individual circumstances of nations, teaches how every separate nation can be raised to that stage of industrial development in which union with other nations equally well developed, and consequently freedom of trade, can become possible and useful to it . . .
>
> For similar reasons, the State is not merely justified in imposing, but bound

to impose, certain regulations and restrictions . . . It does not thereby do something which its individual citizens could understand better and do better than it; on the contrary, it does something which the individuals, even if they understood, would not be able to do for themselves . . .

. . .[C]an it possibly be wiser on our part, and more to the advantage of those who nationally belong to us, for us to allow our private industry to be regulated by a foreign national Legislature, in accordance with foreign national interests, rather than regulate it by means of our own Legislature and in accordance with our own interests? . . .

. . . As individual liberty is in general a good thing so long only as it does not run counter to the interests of society, so it is reasonable to hold that private industry can only lay claim to unrestricted action so long as the latter consists with the well-being of the nation . . .

. . . [And] so long as other nations subordinate the interests of the human race as a whole to their national interests, it is folly to speak of free competition among the individuals of various nations . . .

What is it like to take part in a nationalistic project of the sort List recommends? A graphic case in point is that of New Zealand.

Before 1984, when the country began to be privatized and deregulated, its economy was heavily regulated and highly protected, and local anecdotes still abound of the heights to which protectionism was taken. It was not possible, for example, to take out a subscription to the *New York Review of Books* (or any other overseas magazine) without permission from the nation's Reserve Bank. Overseas travel was heavily restricted because of the same limits on foreign currency exchange. An apple grower could only sell two cases of apples at the orchard gate. The rest had to be resold through the Apple and Pear Marketing Board. Margarine was only available on prescription from a registered medical practitioner to protect the Diary Board's sales of locally produced butter.

There were domestic monopolies everywhere. Two kinds of washing machine were available, though both were made by the same company. One shipment of strawberry jam was allowed in from overseas every year, but only from the "mother country," that is, Britain. This jam was highly prized, and local grocery stores would book a case, allowing local households one jar each. When the annual bounty did arrive, individual families would open their jar and eat its contents in ritual, festive fashion, savoring the flavor (so redolent of "home") and extolling its superior virtues.

Special provision had to be made to allow Australia and New Zealand to trade seawater without restriction (Easton 1981, 49). As I said, local anecdotes abound.

The interesting thing is that all of this protectionism was largely taken for granted at the time. To quote Brian Easton, writing before 1984 in a weekly magazine of social comment called the *New Zealand Listener* (later republished in his book, *Economics for New Zealand Social Democrats*, 47–49):

> Despite the public controversy about it, most economists agree that some New Zealand industries should be provided with some protection against foreign competition. The issue in dispute is the level and method of protection.
>
> A firm can be protected in a variety of ways: by a tariff (or tax) on imports, by direct government assistance, by subsidies, by purchasing preference rules, by tax concessions, or by import quotas. If the level of protection is too low, then foreign competitors will swamp the New Zealand market. Industries vital to our development will be destroyed and unemployment will result. If it is too high, industries will use resources inefficiently, growth will be inhibited, and unemployment will again result.
>
> ... Protection, and the government intervention it implies, is a fact of our economic life [however]. The choice, as in so many economic areas, is whether it becomes part of rational economic management or remains based upon half-baked theories, historical accidents and political discretion.

Easton was writing in a politico-economic world very far from the one that came to prevail five years later. What to Easton in 1979 was a self-evident "fact of economic life" became very quickly "history." What he took for granted when he wrote his comments very rapidly ceased to obtain. What he saw as radical change, that is, mere tinkering with protectionism, became after 1984 a very different kind of radical change, that is, wholesale destruction of the entire protectionist edifice.

### Internationalism and Liberalism

Having captured the concept of "realism" as their own, IR realists are able to depict all other accounts of politico-strategic affairs as "nonrealist" and, therefore, as unrealistic. A cunning ploy, for who would want unrealistic people running the world?

This conceptual coup casts every alternative approach into the "idealist" camp. And yet, closer scrutiny of the realist perspective shows realists to be idealists too (Palan and Blair 1993). Realists posit power politicking as an inescapable fact. This fact is not value-free, however, since it amounts to an argument for world affairs staying the way they are, that is, for the modernist state and state system. Particular realists deny this, since they see no reason why the state system should not in due course become some other kind of system. By positing the sheer capacity to prevail as the primary fact of a state-made world, however, realists do endorse the pursuit of national interests and the rightness implicit in securing them. This amounts in practice to an endorsement of national interest as a normative ideal. It is an argument, despite what realists may say, for states and the state system as they currently stand.

### Internationalism

Not only are realists idealists, but idealists are realists too (though not "realists" in the sense used here). It is quite realistic to expect people to cooperate for higher ends than those served by the state, and not just to compete and conflict. This, after all, is what people actually do.

Interstate cooperation takes place for selfish reasons only and, as such, is self-centered and ultimately compatible with a realist point of view. When cooperation takes place for altruistic reasons, it transcends the realist ethos.

State-makers cooperate for both realist and nonrealist reasons. The realist reasons will be tit-for-tat ones that serve self-regarding ends. The nonrealist reasons will not be reducible to self-regarding ends.

Though the politico-strategic bottom line is always state survival, this does not preclude attempts to do more than realism allows. Negotiations for nuclear nonproliferation or for bans on chemical weapons might be seen in this light. They clearly serve the cause of self-help and survival. They also serve a more altruistic (and internationalist) purpose.

### International Organization

Interstate organizations provide a good example of interstate cooperation. Whether universal or regional, multiple or one task, short term or repeated, politico-strategic or politico-economic, functional or strategic, interstate organizations provide plenty of evidence of the pursuit of national self-interest to altruistic and internationalist effect. In contrast to statistics about wars and other measures of interstate competition, therefore, we can cite the existence of 23,888 world-spanning organizations (Union of International Associations 1997/1998, xii). All these organizations facilitate cooperation across state borders. As such they not only facilitate the pursuit of state interest in realist terms. They also help to consolidate a sense of international interest, an interest that is more than the mere sum of its self-centered parts.

The most eminent of these organizations is the United Nations. Set up after World War II, the UN still shows no signs of becoming a protoglobal government. It is one of those organizations that would have to be invented if it did not exist, however. State-makers need somewhere to go to talk about and coordinate general issues of common concern, and the UN provides that common ground.

Other organizations serve internationalist ends, however. Some issues, particularly environmental ones, cannot be dealt with in any other than an internationalist way. Global fish stocks and the quality of the atmosphere have to be conserved by large groups of states if they are to be conserved at all. Realists highlight the amount of free-riding that state-makers do and the amount of self-interest that such cooperation involves. Internationalists highlight instead the amount of goodwill that goes into securing these global public goods and into devising rules for the use of common global property.

*International Arrangements ("Regimes")*

Some international issues are less general and get dealt with by interstate arrangements that are less formally structured than international organizations. Arrangements like these, like the ones made to deal with ozone depletion or intellectual property, are typically defined in terms of the shared principles they stand for or the shared interests they further. The result is the chance they provide participants to promote mutual interests in very specific areas of common concern. These *regimes*, as they are also called, may take in due course the concrete form of an interstate organization, though they may remain no more than an ensemble of rules. This will depend, in part, on the nature of the need. In providing very specific places for state-makers to go and talk about very specific issues, however, they also foster a cooperative rather than a competitive milieu.

Particularly in the United States, internationalists (neoliberalists, neoinstitutionalists) use the idea of international regimes as an antidote to neorealist notions of self-help. There is copious evidence of international arrangements, of state-makers and others working rationally together to realize particular reciprocal benefits, which haas been offered as an alternative to the ideology that realism represents. As such it has been used to make for a more optimistic version of world affairs and, in self-affirming fashion, a more cooperative version as well.

*International Interdependence and Integration*

It is a short conceptual step from issue-based arrangements like these to more comprehensive forms of interstate interdependence and even of interstate integration (Keohane and Nye 1972). The U.S. experience of having a long border with two now friendly countries, Canada and Mexico, has been highly instructive in this regard. Military force is not currently considered a realistic option in either relationship. Many issues between the United States and these two countries, and not just politico-strategic issues either, are dealt with successfully on a regular basis. Why, it then gets asked, should this not be a model for what might be done more broadly?

Is it too much to expect interdependence worldwide? The European Union (EU) is an example on a regional scale. It can also be seen characterizing relations between members of organizations like the OECD (the Organization for Economic Cooperation and Development—the organization of the world's main industrialized states), NAFTA (the North American Free Trade Association), and ASEAN (the Association of Southeast Asian Nations). It is not hard to extrapolate to world affairs built around European, American, and Asian blocs and from there to a global government made out of all three.

Interdependence of the politico-cconomic kind, cascading into the politico-strategic domain, is not inconceivable either. Just the conceiving of it is one facilitating factor. Internationalists, in particular, see such interdependence as entirely possible, and the more extreme they are the more likely they are to believe that this might be a basis for interstate integration.

It is not difficult to extrapolate from the many examples of functional cooperation we find in world affairs to forms of global governance too. The making of global governance by functional, overtly nonstrategic, means stands in marked contrast to concepts of global governance imposed by imperial and overtly strategic means. Could a grand coalition of the kinds of organizations that make it possible to exchange letters and parcels on a global scale succeed in integrating world affairs, where the great powers of this century and the last did not? The idea is appealing. It is an example at the same time, it is often said, of modernity's rationalizing propensities.

*International Democratization*

Another way to foster international interdependence might be to complete the liberal democratic project, with all the world's states becoming democracies (Doyle 1986; Russett 1993; Owen 1994). Stable democracies do not seem to fight each other, a fact that has been seemingly reinforced by globalizing trends in production, finance, communications, and transport. This has given the liberal internationalist agenda of self-determination, free trade, and human rights greater credibility in turn.

In the last fifty years, however, the first step toward interstate interdependence has been simple independence. Many peoples have had to free themselves from imperial rule first, though this has often meant consigning many of them to a human rights hell, rather than a democratic heaven. Getting a world of meaningful democracies has not proved a simple task.

**International Society**

Sovereign states do form a system of states. There is no state without a system of them. In realist terms, this system is a competitive, self-help one, analogous to that of the medieval village of San Gimignano in Tuscany, whose inhabitants lived in seventy stone towers in a perpetual state of war with each other, within a single village. (Similar villages existed in Svanetia in the western Caucasus). Such systems are protosocieties. Their members abide by general rules that are not, however, policed by any superordinate power. Nor do these rules receive enough respect to allow cooperative endeavors that might achieve more than mere survival.

What would make a more cohesive and cooperative system/society possible? Bull prescribes here a common culture or civilization, a common language, a common epistemology, a common religion, a common ethical code, and a common aesthetic or artistic tradition (Bull 1977, 16). And while the modernist project can be seen in this light, it is not yet sufficiently pervasive to result in a world society.

Is such a world society a reasonable expectation? What does the historical record suggest in this regard?

The early European traders and conquistadores had no intentions of this kind at all. They were seeking precious metals and valued commodities and religious converts. While they did initiate diplomatico-military and commercial relations with rulers they did not subdue, and while the influence of their non-European experiences was often profound, the early modernist Europeans were not thinking in terms of establishing an interstate society. They were building empires.

The early modernist state-makers, though, did enter into agreements with their extra-European counterparts. They had no intention of constructing cooperative systems involving the regular exchange of representatives (diplomats), or of observing any of the rule-based practices they were just getting used to among themselves. They never did think consciously in these terms. Like so much else, they stumbled into doing so, legitimizing the practice after the fact.

The non-European rulers that the early modernist state-makers encountered had no intention or desire to build a coherent global society either. These rulers—these Incas and emperors and divers suzereins—did not think of themselves in terms of modernist state-making. Their politico-strategic view of the world had themselves and not Europeans at the top of the global hierarchy. They saw themselves as the definitive human beings. It was the Europeans who were on the outside, who were the interlopers, the barbarians, the infidels, and it was they who had the most to learn. The effects of European power were decisive, however, and the descendants of the non-Europeans, like the Europeans themselves, have been state-making and alliance-building ever since.

## International Law

The best evidence of global mutuality more powerful than that of statist self-interest is international law. International law, whether customary or treaty-made, exists only by interstate agreement. Though not administered by a superordinate global authority, it is law-like in its effects, and it is expressive of idealist as well as realist propensities.

Human rights conventions are often considered the most telling in terms of mutuality and cooperation. They are modernist. They do not get much nonmodernist support. This said, they do attempt to reach a policy-conscious consensus on humane standards that might apply to all people on earth. They are no realist ploy.

In trying to build the common ground upon which to construct human rights conventions, liberals use a number of (highly rationalistic) mind experiments. For example, they invite us to imagine what it might be like to join a new society not knowing in advance whether we will be male or female, old or young, rich or poor, disabled, devoted, or a member of a permanent ethnic minority when we get there. What rules would we be likely to make for such a society, before we left to join it (Rawls 1971)?

While cultural predispositioning will clearly affect the results of any such thought experiment—people raised as individualistic moderns coming to different conclusions from those raised as communalistic premoderns, for example—liberals hope that documents like the Universal Declaration of Human Rights, drawn up by the victors after World War II, will eventually receive universal acceptance in principle. The fact that this hope is contested is indicative of how this universality must be made as well as found.

## The Experience of Internationalism

As the modern state system has come to fruition, realist ideas about human selfishness and competition have burgeoned with it. So too, however, have ideas about humanity's cooperative and altruistic potential.

In constructing a heritage for themselves, internationalists look back over the historical record to find Hugo Grotius. A Dutch jurist, Grotius argued in *The Law of War and Peace* (published in 1625) in favor of the capacity for human cooperation. He wrote before the advent of the modern state, but because he argued from basic assumptions about the social character of human beings, his ideas are felt to apply to the world that came after him (11–16):

> Man is, to be sure, an animal, but an animal of a superior kind, much farther removed from all other animals than the different kinds of animals are

from one another; evidence on this point may be found in the many traits peculiar to the human species . . . [A]mong the traits characteristic of man is an impelling desire for society, that is, for social life—not of any and every sort, but peaceful, and organized according to the measure of his intelligence, with those who are of his own kind; this trend the Stoics called "sociableness." Stated as a universal truth, therefore, the assertion that every animal is impelled by nature to seek only its own good cannot be conceded . . .

. . . This maintenance of the social order . . . which is consonant with human intelligence, is the source of law properly so called. To this sphere of law belong the abstaining from that which is another's, the restoration to another of anything of his which we may have, together with any gain which we may have received from it; the obligation to fulfill promises, the making good of a loss incurred through our fault, and the inflicting of penalties upon men according to their deserts . . .

. . . From this signification of the word law there has flowed another and more extended meaning. Since over other animals man has the advantage of possessing not only a strong bent toward social life . . . but also a power of discrimination which enables him to decide what things are agreeable or harmful . . . in such things it is meant for the nature of man . . . to follow the direction of a well-tempered judgment . . . What is clearly at variance with such judgment is understood to be contrary also to the law of nature, that is, to the nature of man.

. . . [S]ince, by his own admission, the national who in his own country obeys its laws is not foolish, even though, out of regard for that law, he may be obliged to forgo certain things advantageous for himself, so that nation is not foolish which does not press its own advantage to the point of disregarding the laws common to nations. The reason in either case is the same. For just as the national, who violates the law of his country in order to obtain an immediate advantage, breaks down that by which the advantages of himself and his posterity are for all future time assured, so the state which transgresses the laws of nature and of nations cuts away also the bulwarks which safeguard its own future peace. Even if no advantage were to be contemplated from the keeping of the law, it would be a mark of wisdom, not of folly, to allow ourselves to be drawn toward that to which we feel that our nature leads.

To Grotius, "man" is by nature social and rational. Because he is social, he is a law-maker. He makes pacts and he abides by them. Because he is rational, he can work out what is good or bad for himself, and what leads to either end. He can make his pacts accordingly, and this making of pacts, not expediency, is the source of law. It is a secular truth as well, which does not need the sanction of divine authority.

Grotius is a modernist, albeit a very early one, who is still firmly in the grip of premodernist ideas. He wants to prioritize the human capacity for reason as an end in itself, which is why modernist scholars are pleased to appeal to him as someone who understands contemporary world affairs.

Grotius wants to privilege the human capacity for society as well. This capacity makes cooperation ("mutual consent") possible. In a state-made world, it is what makes interstate laws possible too. It is why proponents of politico-strategic internationalism quote Grotius as a key precursor, as a voice, however alien, that speaks from the past about what they mean in the present.

What is it like to take part in the cooperative process, though, not indirectly, as one of the spectators in a state-made world, but more directly, more actively? What is it like to experience interstate internationalism?

Let us return to first principles. The politico-cultural logic of the modernist project is rationalist. As such it not only objectifies, it individuates as well. The politico-social logic of the modernist project exacerbates individuation to give us individualism. When applied to the politico-strategic process of state-making, individualism gives us a liberal result. This result is more radical the more liberal it becomes, since radical liberalism, in politico-strategic terms, does not imply one state for one people. It implies one state for one person. It exalts not the sovereign state but the sovereign individual. And sovereign individuals are not only god-killers. They are king-killers too.

Some (like Leonard Casey of the Hutt River Province in Western Australia) have taken the modernist logic of individualist state-making as a licence to set up their own individualistic "state." Individualists like these, who declare their sovereign selves sovereign states, are usually seen as a joke, or as entrepreneurs. There have been serious attempts to carry this logic to its theoretical conclusion, however, and those who want a country of their own actively welcome a world ungoverned to this degree (Strauss 1984, 98–101).

The attempt to establish an individualistic state means challenging the sovereignty of a "real" state. While individualists who challenge the sovereignty of well-established countries would seem to be making claims to self-determination against huge odds, such challenges (like that of Paddy Roy Bates, who established "Sealand" off the British coast) have sometimes met with a surprising measure of success. The success has come, however, only where the challenged state is in disarray or where it is a liberal one prepared to entertain such claims in its courts of law (Strauss 1984, 132–138).

To attempt such a high degree of self-determination is to experience, personally, the opportunities for conflict and cooperation that state-making entails. Very few people have done so, though, and their experiences are too singular to document here.

While ordinary people rarely experience state sovereignty as such, they can and do experience the state-system as manifest in its diplomatic exchanges. James Basil-Hart, for example, is one who engages in "part-time diplomacy, for fun, profit and prestige," though, as he rightly points out (1992, 1–3):

Part-time diplomacy is not for everyone. It requires patience to set yourself up in a diplomatic position. It could take weeks or it could take years. There are relationships to cultivate, books to study, and a seemingly endless flow of paperwork (the hallmark of diplomacy). But it can be rewarding.

Over the last year, I have become a Trade Representative for one of the republics that broke away from the Soviet Union. I became an Economic Consultant for another breakaway republic. I am also an Honorary Consul for a large Asian country. I have done all this without leaving my London flat, and without even speaking the native tongue of the countries I represent.

. . . I've always been fascinated by diplomacy and we Britons are known for our fondness for titles. Then I read a book about acquiring diplomatic immunity. Unfortunately, it required spending several thousand pounds—a sum well beyond my means. But it did give me the courage to take pen in hand and inquire with foreign governments about representing their interests.

A year later, I hold many titles and represent several foreign countries. I am not paid directly for my official duties, which require only a few hours a week. But I have become very popular on the diplomatic circuit. I am entertained in some of the most respected homes in the country. I am courted by politicians and businessmen who value my connections. I am introduced to the sort of celebrities a common labourer never gets to meet.

. . . [Admittedly b]ecoming a diplomat is not for everyone. The paperwork and delays may be frustrating to some. However, most people will enjoy the work and will find diplomacy to be a terrific hobby. If you enjoy working with foreigners and attending formal occasions, yet you would prefer not to leave the comforts of the civilized world, then part-time diplomacy might be right for you . . .

Since the two hundred countries in the world do not have relationships with every one of the other two hundred countries in the world, or with all the major cities within those other countries, there is always a supply of unfilled, part-time diplomatic appointments for sale or for free. Getting set up as a consul, honorary consul, ministry representative, or the bearer of a "lettre de chancellerie" is entirely feasible, therefore, and part-time diplomacy is a tangible way for ordinary people to get direct access to the interstate world of mutual service. It is also a useful reminder of how the machinery of interstate cooperation is at work all around us, all the time.

### *Liberalism*

Liberalism, as the word suggests, is about freedom, about liberty. It has long-standing politico-strategic and politico-social connotations, but the word is used here to characterize liberalist politico-economy. Given the significance of international political economy in general and of liberalist political economy in particular, it is extremely apt that liberalism stands in the center of the matrix of all the analytical languages discussed here.

Unlike mercantilists, who close wealth-making down around the singular concerns of state sovereignty and state self-reliance, politico-economic liberals free up the global political economy and remove statist constraints. This, they say, gives those who wealth-make the maximum chance to produce, trade, invest, consume, and work. More freedom allows people to make more of their world in marketeering terms, to make more goods and to provide more services. It allows them to put their capital where they like and to sell their labor anywhere they can, stimulating and rewarding entrepreneurial initiative. Liberals believe all this to have beneficial effects for the global economy and for any component of it, including those components organized as states.

Unfettered people not only produce more, liberals believe, but they produce more efficiently as well. Prices are said to see to that, going up when supplies are low or demand is high, stimulating productivity, and making up for the shortfall in supply. The converse happens when demand falls off or there is otherwise too much supply.

The same principle, in liberalist parlance, applies worldwide. Getting statemakers out of the way to let goods and money and people move freely makes for greater wealth not only within states and within regions, but globally as well. There is an added bonus, too, in that people who are better off are said to prefer being able to wealth-make to anything else. They ostensibly prefer the stability that makes wealth-making possible, so that a more liberal world, liberals argue, is a world of less war as well.

Liberalist policies are the politico-economic counterpart to politico-strategic internationalism and politico-social individualism and, like the proponents of both these analytic languages, depict human beings as (rationalistic) individualists. Liberals make much of rationalism. To them, people are learning, evolving beings, who are able to discern and define their personal interests and pursue them, given the chance, with calculating ferocity. Despite the resultant competition, people also, liberals argue, cooperate. Where the pursuit of their separate self-concerns requires it, they are prepared to acknowledge the power of promises and of the cooperation that promises make possible. Without the capacity to make abstract promises, there would be no contracts in their formal, modernist sense (and no doctrine of human rights and no functional global organizations either). The ultimate goal is self-aggrandizement, however, and liberalism is profoundly antistate in this regard. It only countenances state constraints where they clearly facilitate individualistic freedoms.

Politico-economic liberals believe that, given free rein, entrepreneurs combine finance capital, labor, goods, technology, resources, and land to the very best effect, resulting not only in growing profits, but also in a rising tide of material prosperity that lifts everyone at once. Some are lifted more than others, but the disparities in wealth that result from natural or inherited inequalities in individual endowment matter much less in liberal terms than the absolute gains that free enterprise makes for all.

This is *laissez-faire* (leave-it-alone). It is a doctrine designed to punish the commercially inept, reward the innovative and "efficient," and allow the maximum possible freedom to produce and exchange.

The benefits are supposed to be quantifiable as well. It was Sir William Petty who first explored the possibility that market behavior might be described with mathematical precision. He was also, incidentally, the first person to use the term "political economy." He spoke of an "algebra of individual choice," arguing that we should seek terms of "Number, Weight, or Measure" instead of "words and intellectual Arguments," and in a study he made of labor and land he sought a value-free metalanguage that would allow him to equate what these two were worth (Petty [1671] 1899, 3).

Petty wanted what he called political arithmetic, or what we would now call statistics. As a seventeenth-century rationalist he sought "only such Causes, as have visible foundations in Nature." All other arguments depended, he said, upon the "mutable Minds, Opinions, Appetites, and Passions of particular Men." To settle arguments like these, you were just as well off throwing dice (Petty [1671] 1899, 244).

Many contemporary analysts would use both arithmetic and algebra to map market behavior for the same reasons. By describing subjective preferences in numerical terms, they deem these descriptions apt because of their definitive form. This, of course, encourages the conceit that they actually know what they seek to know, when they may have little more than a concise account of it (Hull 1899, lxviii). It is a powerful conceit, though, underpinning, as it does, the entire discipline of econometrics.

In promoting entrepreneurial freedom, liberals are not all of one mind. They tend in practice to be of one of two minds. The first, the more extreme, has been called the liberalism of privilege. The other, the more moderate, has been called the liberalism of the losers (Richardson 1996, 20, 22).

### Extreme Liberalism

The more extreme liberals argue hardest for free enterprise, that is, for the freedom to pursue entrepreneurial initiatives in a commercial environment as unconstrained as possible. They see the market as a place for all to profit from, and they believe that state-makers and state-making can only inhibit the pursuit of personal and, by extension, corporate gain. This is the "official" liberalism of the "international establishment" and of the international business civilization. Its highest priority is marketeering growth, and while it does sanction support for human rights and democratic political institutions, reconciling these with marketeering practice is a "point of tension" within establishment liberalism that is not readily resolved (Richardson 1996, 20).

The more extreme liberals contend that we have little choice in any of this. Modern communications and information technology now allow finance capital to flow freely around the world. We cannot control this flow. We can only cope. The countries who cope the best are the ones the market rewards the most. Those who do not cope get penalized. Their economies do not grow and their peoples suffer accordingly.

Coping in practice means increasing production, in part by containing costs. This means work-force numbers as low as possible. It also means locating production where it can be sustained at low wage rates. And it means high incentives for those managers whom firms believe can cope to most profitable effect.

Coping in practice means getting the state out of the way. This means putting as many public services as possible in private hands, where they are part of the market and can be run most "efficiently," that is, in terms of supply and demand, of profit, not need. Extreme liberals believe that the market will always provide better most of what states provide now. Marketeers will charge for doing so, of course, and those unable to pay their price may not get serviced. The result may be acute personal deprivation. It also presents opportunities, however, and extreme liberals view market services as such.

Getting the state out of the way means minimal legal constraints on owners and managers, and lower taxes so that people have more to spend. A truncated state requires less in the way of public funds, too, the spiral being a virtuous one, with a smaller public sector acting less as a drain on market resources and more as a facilitator and helpmate.

### Moderate Liberalism

The more moderate liberals consider unconstrained free enterprise unsustainable, for the simple reason that those who come into the market already advantaged are likely to prevail over those who do not. They believe state-makers should hold the ring, like sporting umpires or referees do. They see states as necessary to prevent the advantaged from reducing the market to monopolies and oligopolies. And they envisage state-makers providing the externalities and the public goods that entrepreneurs are apt to neglect in their drive to survive and to maximize their gains.

This is the liberalism of those who think we now have the capacity to provide for everyone on the planet and that, where marketeering does not adequately meet people's basic needs, these should be met by state-making means. Where do such seemingly illiberal sentiments come from? In the first place, most liberals have a residual sense of social concern. They grew up in societies, after all. In the second place, liberals know that in a contingent world, it is possible that they might end up needing such assistance themselves. A rational regard for risk would recommend setting in place some governmental safety nets at least, though not, in liberal parlance, at cost to competition.

Much of the argument in political economy, for the last century at least, has been within the liberalist camp over precisely this point: getting the state out or bringing it back in. Note that an argument like this assumes a dichotomy between the market and the state. Achieving this dichotomy was the great triumph of nineteenth-century liberalism. It allowed liberals to create a clear distinction between economics and politics and, having done that, to create a much clearer hierarchy between the two, so that "economics" could be given precedence over "politics" and the market given precedence over the state.

### The Miracle of the Market

The world market is marvelous, representing a veritable "miracle of collective organization." Harris observes that "When it works well, the needs of millions of people are met on a daily basis" (Harris 1983, 9), which is, indeed, an extraordinary achievement.

What primary school child has not been invited to document the source of the everyday goods with which he or she is surrounded? Adam Smith, the founding father of the liberal faith, marveled likewise—using the same rhetorical ploy at the beginning of *The Wealth of Nations* to highlight the same process of unplanned, cooperative supply.

Smith talks of the humble woolen coat of the day laborer. He wonders at the different kinds of work that make such a garment possible. He asks the reader to imagine the "shepherd, the sorter . . . [the] carder, the dyer, the scribbler, the spinner, the weaver, the fuller, [and] the dresser" who made the materials for the coat itself. He envisages the merchants and carriers who brought these materials together; the "ship-builders, sailors, sail-makers, [and] rope-makers" who brought the dyes for it from all over the globe; and the miners, furnace-makers, timber-fellers, charcoal-burners, brick-makers, brick-layers, furnace-workers, mill-wrights, forgers, and smiths, all of whom helped make the shepherd's shears. He thinks of all those who provide the laborer's household effects—his bread and beer, the glass windows in his home—and he concludes by observing how "without the assistance and cooperation of many thousands, the meanest person in a civilized country could not be provided" (Smith [1776] 1892, 9–10).

Smith called his book the wealth of *nations*, and this is what he meant. He envisaged state-makers using politico-economic policies to politico-strategic effect. He was an analytic hybrid, a transitional figure, casting forward to a new kind of world from the context of his own. Wanting a strong Britain, he saw states using wealth-making power in legitimate pursuit of their strategic ends. But he saw this power in terms of free marketeering, not unfree mercantilism, and he celebrated market production and supply for its own sake.

What makes the liberal market work? What makes such cornucopic outcomes possible? In answer to this question, Smith highlighted one happy fact and two important practices. To understand such largesse we must look, he said, at the coincidence of personal and social interest, at the complexity of divisions of labor, and at natural advantage.

### Personal Interest as a Social Good

The coincidence of personal and social interest is the cornerstone of the liberalist creed. "Every individual," Smith said, "is continually exerting himself to find out the most advantageous employment for whatever capital he can command. It is his own advantage . . . which he has in view. But the study of his own advantage, *naturally*, or rather *necessarily* leads him to prefer that employment which is most advantageous to the society" (Smith [1776] 1892, 343; my emphasis).

The widespread acceptance of this singular assertion was the great triumph of eighteenth-century liberalism. A people persuaded that their own self-interest "naturally" or "necessarily" is that of the commonweal have in their heads a most powerful ideological tool. As one contemporary formulation of this ideology has it: greed = good. This neat moral equation takes all the opprobrium out of being self-concerned, and as an equation it is arguably of greater significance for world affairs than anything players can provide.

The natural and necessary coincidence of personal and social interests provides a clear example also of the equilibrium that Smith saw managing markets to the best effect. Without a "hidden hand" to balance all of our competing interests, chaos results. The fact that chaos does not result is evidence in itself, liberals say, of the benevolent basis of market behavior, of the hidden hand at work.

### The Division of Labor

The largesse of the market also derives from the division of labor. As a specific example, Smith cites pin-making. While one worker might make one pin a day, ten men, he reckons, if they divide the eighteen parts of the pin-making process between them, can make 48,000 pins a day (Smith [1776] 1892, 4). Dividing up the manufacturing process into its component parts makes, in other words, for much more efficient production.

## Natural Advantage

The largesse of the market can also be attributed to natural advantage. By this Smith means "the . . . advantage which one country has over another in producing particular commodities." As an example he cites the fact that "[b]y means of glasses, hotbeds, and hot-walls, very good grapes can be raised in Scotland, and very good wine, too, can be made of them at about thirty times the expense for which at least equally good can be brought from foreign countries." He then asks: "Would it be a *reasonable* law to prohibit [as mercantilists might] the importation of all foreign wines merely to encourage the making of claret and burgundy in Scotland?" (Smith [1776] 1892, 347; my emphasis). Note the appeal to reason, the hallmark of modernist liberal thought. Note the assumption also of the individual's desire to consume things and to exercise preferences in this regard. It is this subjective preference, liberals believe, that drives all markets. It is why they thrive. Note also the constructed nature of what is putatively a "natural advantage" and the fact that no advantage is ever simply "natural." All are significant only in context. In this case, the context is that of a wine-imbibing public. In a non-wine-imbibing part of the world, like an Islamic one, such an advantage would have little significance.

In the mind of the nineteenth-century political economist David Ricardo, the concept of natural advantage became the concept of comparative advantage. There it was used to argue that trade is always advantageous, even for countries that have more than anyone else and do everything better than everyone else as well (Ricardo [1817] 1971).

## Acquired Advantage

Advantages are not only "natural," however. They can also be acquired. A natural advantage would be Saudi Arabia's oil reserves (always assuming that the Saudis know they are there, know how to get at them, and know how to market them). An example of an acquired advantage would be the Japanese car industry.

The concept of acquired advantage suggests a role for state-makers as something more than mere ring-holders. It suggests that they might profitably intervene in marketeering practices to supply basic infrastructural goods and services, like transport and communications. It suggests that they might also mediate in market disputes, or facilitate trade, or foster new technologies and investment, or provide for social welfare needs, or regulate interest rates and the money supply, or prevent market behavior that skews market advantage. It suggests that governments might act to preempt civic disorder and the "slow riot" of crime.

## *Market Intervention*

Those who believe that markets become inefficient if marketeers are left to themselves take the moderate liberal approach. Moderate liberals prefer to find a level of governmental intervention that is optimal, rather than minimal, in making markets work. For example, John Stuart Mill argued the case for state intervention in a free market ([1848] 1852). Though it was impossible to say in principle how far the state should be brought back in, in practice it could be highly desirable to use state power to liberal ends. John Maynard Keynes, likewise a marketeer, had no problem with the notion of state intervention either. In the first place, he did not think individuals should be treated as if their market freedom was unlimited and beyond control. Nor did he think personal and communal concerns were always the same. Nor did people, in his view, necessarily act as rational beings, if only because they could not know what the future would bring and how, as a consequence, their self-interest might best be served. Even when their self-interest was evident to them, in his opinion they were not always capable of realizing it. Indeed, Keynes thought that, without working together, most people would never get what they wanted, and that markets worked this way too. He believed therefore that it was important to know that people acting together could be just as effective as people acting apart (Keynes 1926).

## *Hegemonic Stability Theory*

After World War II, the global market was reconstructed around an agreement (made at Bretton Woods) brokered by U.S. state-makers. Keynes took part in the agreement negotiations and the moderate nature of the world liberalism that ensued was due in no small part to him. By this time (1944), however, the United States was the dominant democratic power on earth. It had the most productive economy and the *de facto* world currency. Its state-makers were imbued with liberal beliefs and uniquely qualified to make freer marketeering into a global fact. They were also prepared to "hold the ring" to keep it that way.

The postwar U.S. experience eventually prompted moderate liberals to posit a "hegemonic stability theory" with which to explain and, in turn, to extol the benefits that a world market sponsor can confer, even when that sponsor is blatantly self-interested (Gilpin 1987). According to this theory, a free world market cannot flourish without a power both willing and able to protect the integrity of the system as a whole.

To a mercantilist, such hegemonic behavior is best seen in state-centric, not marketeering terms. The language of liberalism serves only to obscure superpower preponderance and sovereign self-concern. The General Agreement on Tariffs and Trade (GATT), for example, and its successor, the World Trade Organization (WTO), are both means by which the United States has been able to reduce international tariffs and get access to new markets.

To a mercantilist, the monetary system that the Bretton Woods agreements built was also an example of U.S. interests at work. More particularly, the postwar system of fixed exchange rates helped the United States live beyond its means. The United States was always able to cope by printing money and exporting inflation, a privilege it enjoyed because of the power of the U.S. dollar and its own economic productiveness. When other countries lived beyond their means, the International Monetary Fund (IMF) was there to offer loans to make up the current account deficits and to solve the balance of payments crises, but the IMF was dominated by the United States, and IMF loans were always made contingent upon "structural adjustments." These adjustments not only furthered liberalism, they also furthered market access in general and U.S. interests in particular. When less developed countries applied to the World Bank for low interest funds with which to foster development (another Bretton Woods institution, also largely under U.S. control), mercantilists noted that funds were given under the same liberalist conditions, with the same beneficial effects for the United States.

### The Return of Extreme Liberalism

As the postwar world economy changed, more drastic action became necessary to protect U.S. interests. The productive power of the United States was beginning to be matched by that of global competitors. To the west was Japan, whose resurgence under the U.S. security umbrella provided tangible evidence that social capitalism could achieve all that liberal capitalism could promise, and more. To the east was Europe, whose diverse members, under a similar U.S. security umbrella, were uniting to radical regional effect.

Under these circumstances, extreme liberals began to argue for more unfettered marketeering. They sought to dichotomize the state and the market more clearly and to foster, in principle, freer trade and investment flows. They sought to stage a return to what they saw as the first principles of the liberal faith.

## The Miracle of the Market Again

Liberals, whether moderate or extreme, are primarily interested in marketeering, which they deem a natural human practice. They are pleased that a periodic part of human life, which took place only occasionally and in particular places (the village square on Sundays, for example), should have become a universal practice, occurring all the time and everywhere at once (Polanyi [1944] 1957).

In markets, people ostensibly decide what to do in terms of their own personal, rational, wealth-making concerns. The social sum of all these decisions sets prices and regulates the supply and demand of services and goods. The market does this, liberals say, in the most free and efficient manner possible.

Marketeering may mean making calculation king, though the outcome, if liberals are to be believed, enhances the welfare not only of the individual but also of the society as a whole. This includes the world society as well as more local ones.

## On the Margins of the Market

Clearly there are many men and women who want to compete in markets, motivated by the chance of material gain. However, others question whether the "rational economic man" who gets valorized in the process does anything more than promote certain essentialized notions of "hegemonic masculinity." They do not associate this "man" with all of humankind (Tickner 1992, 72). They do not see competition and greed as definitive species traits. They do not see the human propensity to truck and barter as taking precedence over all other human concerns. To these people, highlighting the desire for material gain and granting it primary global status is to deny the significance of what most women (and some men) do when they rear children, make homes, and perform a whole range of tasks that lie outside the marketeering realm.

Women are highly disadvantaged in markets, relative, that is, to men. They find themselves, even in liberal contexts where gender should not be relevant, consigned in disproportionate numbers to occupations deemed appropriate for them in gender-role terms, where they earn less money for the same work. Indeed, the more liberal the world political economy becomes, the worse that many (though not all) women seem to be able to do (*World Survey on the Role of Women in Development* 1989).

Liberals consider the feminization of poverty a short-term phenomenon, though many feminists find it reason enough to be skeptical of the claim that liberalism represents utopia now (Fukuyama 1992). The liberalist claim that the "end of history" is nigh and that material circumstances today are as good as it gets, is not self-evident to many who must live with the effects of these circumstances. Liberals continue to hold out the promise of "trickle down," but for those who wait to see these promises kept, talk of "flooding up" often seems more apt, the tide liberals see lifting all our boats, lifting only the rich boats, not the poor ones.

### The Experience of Liberalism

Friedrich Hayek is the extreme twentieth-century liberal par excellence. In *The Fatal Conceit: The Errors of Socialism*, he not only dismisses socialism out of hand, he also dismisses Keynes' idea that state intervention can be used to maximize market efficiency and performance. It is analytic speech, but his rhetorical purpose is readily apparent. His voice is that of liberalism in its most excessive form (1991, 83, 88):

How What Cannot Be Known Cannot Be Planned

At least before the obvious economic failure of Eastern European socialism it was widely thought . . . that a centrally planned economy would deliver not only "social justice" . . . but also a more efficient use of economic resources. This notion appears eminently sensible at first glance. But . . . the totality of resources that one could employ in such a plan is simply not knowable to anybody, and therefore can hardly be centrally controlled . . . The point is not that whatever economists determine to be efficient is therefore "right," but that economic analysis can elucidate the usefulness of practices heretofore thought to be right . . . It is a betrayal of concern for others, then, to theorise about the "just society" without carefully considering the economic consequences of implementing such a view . . .

The order of the extended economy is, and can be, formed only . . . from an evolved method of communication that makes it possible to transmit, not an infinite multiplicity of reports about particular facts, but merely certain abstract properties of several particular conditions, such as competitive prices, which must be brought into mutual correspondence to achieve overall order . . . Surprising as it may be that such a process exists at all, let alone that it came into being . . . without being deliberately designed, I know of no efforts to refute this contention or discredit the process itself—unless one regards simple declarations that all such facts can, somehow, be known to some central planning authority . . .

More moderate liberals make more direct efforts to reconcile their marketeering predilections with their belief in universal human rights. They are not as quick to consign a close regard for human needs to the dustbin of history as some kind of vestigial quality, self-evidently redundant. Their concept of freedom walks forward on two legs as it were, an individualist and collectivist one, because moderate liberals believe that extreme liberalism is socially destructive and that all the talk about abstract price signals cannot hide the negative effects of marketeering without a human face.

To document what extreme liberals can do in this regard, I return to one of their most notable contemporary laboratories—New Zealand. What follows comes verbatim from a television documentary by Marcia Russell and John Carlaw called, aptly enough, *Revolution* (1996, videocassette). This series of programs details the changes that were made in the country after 1984. The extreme liberal revolution that ensued took New Zealand from a closed, mercantilist, egalitarian society to an open, liberal, inegalitarian one—in less than a decade. The effects were notable, and often unhappy:

*Rt. Hon. David Lange* (Prime Minister 1984–1989):
It was a revolution . . . And because it all happened so quickly you got a lot of bewilderment . . .

*Alan Gibbs* (company director):
. . . [W]e were having to do in a short period what most other countries had done much more gradually . . . [T]here was no alternative, there was no other way.

*Henry Lang* (Treasury Secretary 1968–1976):
Oh yes, well, that's a nonsense . . . There are always alternative policies. Lots of them. And what government is about is to choose the best one . . .

*Presenter:*
. . . [S]huddering reforms to the economy had a price. The egalitarian dream . . . was eroded, as the poverty gap widened . . .

*Rosslyn Noonan* (Royal Commission on Social Policy 1986–1988):
. . . [Indeed] 10 percent of the population was massively enriched. Most of the population . . . stood still in material terms . . . [while] the bottom 20 percent lost ground . . .

*Presenter:*
. . . Did the revolution mean a better future for just some? Was it benign or malign?

*Rt. Hon. David Lange:*
Oh no, the revolution wasn't malign. It certainly wasn't intended to be malign. And there are some people who have done very well out of it. People who don't want the government in their lives can get on with it. For this it has been a bonanza. For people who are disabled, limited, resourceless, uneducated, it has been a tragedy . . .

*Jim Davis* (farmer):
I don't know what we'll do. We go back and we'll fight the bastards to the end. They'll carry me out dead out of that house, before I move. That's me and my kids and my bloody grandkids and everybody. They can get stuffed . . . They've sucked us, they've sucked us dry, they've sucked the whole community dry with their bloody interest rates and now they're going to send their bastard people down here to live on our farms. Well, I'll tell you what, someone will die before we're finished. Bugger them.

What can we say about this poor farmer's plight, standing back to look once again? Studies confirm the picture of growing income inequality he represents. From 1984 to 1996 the richest 5 percent of the population in New Zealand increased their share of the nation's wealth by 25 percent. The next 15 percent of the population stayed the same. The bottom 80 percent saw their share decrease. The farther down we look, in fact, the worse the picture becomes, and it gets worse at a rate that is faster than almost anywhere else in the "developed" world. The picture has an important ethnic dimension too, since it is the indigenous Maori minority who bear the disproportionate brunt of this process of dispossession and despair (Campbell 1998, 18–21).

Disparities in wealth, extreme New Zealand liberals say, should not be allowed to occlude the evidence that, overall, everyone is doing better. It is disposable income that matters, not relative wealth. And while some are doing a lot better than others, this is no more than the reward they get for their higher qualifications, skills, experience, and willingness to work. The incentive for such attributes has to be there, extreme liberals argue, if the market is not to become inefficient again. Inequalities in income are not the cause of social injustice, in this light. They are the preferred alternative to what egalitarianism costs. They are the price that marketeering exacts for a system that is cost-effective and that values those with merit, drive, and entrepreneurial flair.

More moderate liberals argue that even the evidence showing that everyone has more income at their disposal still has to be seen in the context of increased costs of living, increased sales taxes, and economic downturn. More radical critics say that evidence like this also has to be seen in the context of a politico-cultural system that fetishizes personal need and commodifies work.

There are, potentially, ways of constructing the world differently—conservationist ways, for example, that value dynamic equilibrium, not growth, and sustainability, not ecological abuse. These ways are very different from liberalist ones (Trainer 1988). They are less secular or, at least, less materialistic. Like the Buddhist, or the Muslim, or the more Christian kinds of economics, for example, they are more likely to foster "noble virtues" than "ignoble vices" (Schumacher 1973).

Conservationist or spiritual alternatives might seem naive in the context of contemporary world affairs, where large numbers of people (not least, Buddhist, Muslim, and Christian ones) spend much of their time trying to acquire the consumer durables that adorn modernist lives. They are not naive alternatives to those struggling merely to survive, however, to those close to the material limits that liberal markets set.

Material concerns may also be only part of the problem, anyway. There are emotional and spiritual limits to liberal markets as well. The kind of economy that commodifies work, for example, may not only end up with a permanent periphery, inhabited by those who cannot find a job, it may alienate many of those who actually do have a job.

It is no accident, therefore, that alienation is a key starting point for some of liberalism's most trenchant critics. Karl Marx, for example, the most famous critic of them all, certainly knew where to look for the politico-social heart of his politico-economic concerns (Marx and Engels [1846] 1977).

## Globalism and Marxism

Globalists believe that we ought to live in ways that unite people worldwide. They are proponents of globalism, ostensibly the most idealistic of the analytic languages of IR. Spegele distinguishes between "soft" and "hard" globalism, soft globalists seeing globalized living simply as good for us, and hard globalists seeing globalized living as "reasonable, non-utopian and practical" as well (Spegele 1993, 2). Most globalists give practical reasons for advocating something they believe good, making Spegele's distinction one without much of a difference. The distinction does help highlight, however, the way globalism serves a descriptive and explanatory purpose, and not just a prescriptive one.

### Globalism

As an analytic language, globalism describes and explains globalizing trends. In general terms, globalization erases every difference between the local and the global. A globalized world affairs will be one manifest in every corner of the globe, and where every corner of the globe will be manifest in world affairs (Mlinar 1992, 22). In more specific terms, globalization ostensibly results in a world government, a world society (marked by a cosmopolitan sense of self), and a world market (marked by the global movement of finance capital, worldwide production chains, and universal consumerism). While none of this is yet complete, it is arguably in train, and globalists look at how it might be taken further.

## World Government Through World Empire

To those who see world affairs primarily in terms of conflict and competition, world government is likely only as a result of world conquest. To IR realists, for example, a global government could be built only by imperialistic means.

The advent of nuclear weapons has made this scenario unlikely. It is not impossible, however, since an all-out nuclear war is still feasible, and one result of such a war could conceivably be world rule by one of those left. Weapons like these give their holders the capacity to inflict unacceptable damage on any potential adversary, however. They provide the capacity, that is, to threaten nuclear winter and species suicide or, at the very least, nuclear autumn and the loss of many—perhaps most—of the lives of the erstwhile imperialists.

Chemical and biological weapons are considerably cheaper, but they also make it possible to threaten a would-be colonizing power with unacceptable damage.

To IR realists, this is just as well, since the prospect of one-world affairs is distinctly unattractive. Spegele, for example, taking a leaf from the postmodernist book, calls globalism "elitist." "The ideal of a universal humanity which effectively denies nation-state difference," he says, "allows privileged groups within national states to ignore their own group's specificity." These groups, he argues, want everyone in the world to be like them. They want universal humanity to be their own particular version of humanity writ large, and Spegele, for one, sees such an ideal as culturally imperialistic, with us strategically placed individuals passing off self-serving ideals as disinterested and global, and willing away the nation-state from an analytic vantage point that looks impartial, but is not, preventing non-Western peoples from expressing their own experiences in sovereign, statist form (Spegele 1993, 47).

## World Government Through World Law

The same critique applies to those who see world government coming about through the global acceptance of international law (Clark and Sohn 1958, xvi, 346–348). World law would presumably make possible universal disarmament, global nonaggression, world peace, and the mitigation of international material disparities. These could become stepping-stones toward world government. Globalists do not consider it beyond the wit of humankind to realize such a result, though it could well be at the cost of human difference or, at least, the state-centric expression of human difference.

*World Government Through (Con)Federation*

Can we imagine world government built by nonimperial means, from below, perhaps, in the form of a federation or a confederation? Any such government worthy of its transnational name would have to have the authority to deal with the global equivalent of "civil wars." The world's police would have to be able to keep global order. The world's bureaucrats would have to be able to manage a global administration. And the world's courts would have to be able to dispense global justice.

Can we conceive of a state-made system allowing such institutions to subsume their sovereignty? We can if regional organizations formed first. If these organizations included most of the world's states, and if these regional organizations were then made into a coalition-of-coalitions, global in scope, we could get a world confederation, where the component states kept much of their power, but there was a world government. The contemporary appeal of state sovereignty would seem to preclude this for the moment, though a confederation would survive Spegele's critique better than something more solidarist.

### The "Spirit of Commerce"

The sovereignty of states may not be as important as it seems, however. Though Kant's voice is only one of many in this regard, he is notable nonetheless for having posited the spread of the "spirit of commerce" as one way to preclude war and build a global confederation. He also thought that the spread of interstate interrelationships so extensive that a "violation of right in one place" would be felt "throughout the world" might also do the trick. Such a feeling presupposes cosmopolitan sentiments of a very widespread kind, however, plus a universal "moral disposition" capable of sustaining such sentiments (Kant [1795] 1963, 114, 105, 99). Neither state of mind is a small presupposition.

In terms of the "spirit of commerce," it is worth noting the range of institutional practices that regulate—some would say, govern—world affairs already. The Bank of International Settlements (the "bankers' bank"), the International Monetary Fund, the World Bank, and the World Trade Organization play important roles in this regard. So do global insurance and accountancy firms, and the rating agencies too.

The existence of these institutions has helped resuscitate traditions of thought that have long seen them as sources of transnational solidarity (Haas 1958). Analysts have been casting forward in these terms for some time.

## The Spirit of the Times

Since globalism casts forward to a world to come, it prompts questions more than answers. Will Spegele's concerns prove unfounded and the diffusion of modernist ideas of world unity give way to a postmodernist respect for a plurality of cultures and civilizations (Strassoldo 1992, 39)? Will neomedievalism ensue, with sovereign states replaced by the secular equivalent of Western Christendom in the Middle Ages, that is, by a global organization where authorities overlap and loyalties are "multiple" (Bull 1977, 254)? Is there a viable ideal-politik alternative to realpolitik? Globalists remain optimistic. The making of a peaceful world order is not beyond us in principle, nor in practice, either.

## The Experience of Globalism

When we stand close to listen, many globalist voices clamor to be heard. That of Immanuel Kant stands out, however. His suggestions for a "Perpetual Peace" still speak to those who seek a cosmopolitan solution to state-made conflicts and wars ([1795] 1963), 98, 100–101, 111, 114):

The Law of Nations Shall Be Founded on a Federation of Free States

For states in their relation to each other, there cannot be any reasonable way out of the lawless condition which entails only war except that they, like individual men, should give up their savage (lawless) freedom, adjust themselves to the constraints of public law, and thus establish a continuously growing state consisting of various nations . . . which will ultimately include all the nations of the world . . .

. . . What has nature done with regard to this end which man's own reason makes his duty? That is, what has nature done to favor man's moral purpose, and how has she guaranteed (by compulsion but without prejudice to his freedom) that he shall do that which he ought to but does not do under the laws of freedom? . . .

Just as nature wisely separates nations, which the will of every state, sanctioned by the principles of international law, would gladly unite by artifice or force, nations that could not have secured themselves against violence and war by means of the law of world citizenship unite because of mutual interest. The spirit of commerce, which is incompatible with war, sooner or later gains the upper hand in every state. As the power of money is perhaps the most dependable of all the powers (means) included under the state power, states see themselves forced, without any moral urge, to promote honorable peace and by mediation to prevent war wherever it threatens to break out. They do so exactly as if they stood in perpetual alliances, for great offensive alliances are in the nature of the case rare and even less often successful.

In this manner nature guarantees perpetual peace by the mechanism of human passions. Certainly she does not do so with sufficient certainty for us to predict the future in any theoretical sense, but adequately from a practical point of view, making it our duty to work toward this end, which is not just a chimerical one.

We have no experience yet of global government of a politico-strategic kind. There are speculative works that discuss the possibility, and there are historic accounts of what it was like to live in a large empire, but that, so far, is as close as we come.

We do have experience of world governance of a politico-economic kind, however. Perhaps the foundations for Kant's "spirit of commerce" have already been laid. For a graphic description of these foundations, and how they feel, I turn to Walter Wriston's *The Twilight of Sovereignty* (1992, 57–61, 66–67):

> Until recently, what we call money, whether a piece of paper, a bookkeeping entry, or a physical object . . . [was] linked to a physical commodity . . .
> . . . The old discipline of physical commodities has now been replaced by a new kind of commodity: information . . .
> We sit at home and watch a live broadcast of riots in a country on the other side of the earth, and a currency falls, in minutes. We hear by satellite that a leadership crisis has been resolved, and a currency rises. Ten minutes after the news of the disaster at Chernobyl was received, market data showed that stocks of agricultural companies began to move up in all world markets. For the first time in history, countless investors, merchants, and ordinary citizens can know almost instantly of breaking events all over the earth. And depending on how they interpret these events, their desire to hold more or less of a given currency will be inescapably translated into a rise or fall in its exchange value . . .
> The new world financial market is not a geographic location to be found on a map but, rather, more than two hundred thousand electronic monitors in trading rooms all over the world that are linked together. With the new technology no one is in control. Rather, everyone is in control through collective valuations.
> Technology has made us a "global" community in the literal sense of the world. Whether we are ready or not, mankind now has a completely integrated, international financial and information marketplace capable of moving money and ideas to any place on this planet in minutes . . .
> In the seventeenth century the Amsterdam bankers made themselves unpopular in the royal chambers by weighing coins and announcing their true metallic value. Instead of weighing coins and publishing their intrinsic worth, the global market weighs the fiscal and monetary policies of each government that issues currency and places a value on it that is instantly seen by traders in Hong Kong, London, Zurich, and New York . . . Minutes after any official announcement, the Reuters screens light up in the trading rooms of the world. Scores of traders make their judgments about the effects of the new policies on the value of a currency, and then they buy or sell. These buy and sell orders drive the price up or down in minutes. The entire process does not take much more time than it took the Dutch bankers to adjust their scales . . .

The integrated market-system that Wriston describes is highly decentralized. As such it may be a clue as to what kind of global governance we will ultimately get. The unregulated behavior of the brokers he describes already drives not only markets but state-making practices too. This is Kant's "spirit of commerce" at work, and if we listen to Wriston, we might well think we are on the brink of a brave new world. If we look at what this kind of global governance does, however, we might not be so optimistic.

The great transnational firms, 300 of which together command one-quarter of the world's productive assets, represent another part of the "spirit of commerce" and its ostensibly globalizing imperatives. Some analysts claim that the transnational and international activities of these firms have already resulted in a "degree of global integration never before achieved by any world empire or nation-state" (Barnet and Cavanagh 1994, 15). They move through the world like leviathans—huge, hard to control, and bringing great global prosperity (according to liberals), or huge, hard to control, and causing major global exploitation (according to mercantilists and Marxists).

The extent to which the "spirit of commerce" already provides the basis for global governance should not be allowed, either, to obscure how all such globalizing trends have been keenly contested the whole four hundred years since. Many peoples for whom modernist statism and internationalism have meant, in practice, imperialism, exploitation, and even genocide contest Western notions about what is good for the world in this regard. They also contest the kind of people we have to become to have such a world. From their own bitter experience, they fear that a Westernized world means more of what has already been for them an unmitigated disaster. Environmentalists, for example, raise critical questions about the sustainability of Western globalism. Women, too, wonder how they are supposed to figure in a world where they do most of the work and still get only a fraction of the income. Religious believers reject the secularizing aspects of the "spirit of commerce," and postcolonial and indigenous peoples draw attention to the ongoing asymmetries that characterize a globalizing world.

It is worth noting in this regard the ethnocentricity of the current trends, as well. The bias in these trends is clearly highlighted by scholars and leaders from what is still referred to—though it is a Western label and, as such, "laden with negative values"—as the "Eastern" part of the world (Ogura 1993, 37). Asian leaders and scholars envisage an Asian globalism or, more accurately, Asian globalisms, that carry on the world-making practices of the West in their own ways. They promote these as preferred global forms in turn, and if the next century, or the one after that, is dominated by Asian civilizations the way Western civilization has dominated the nineteenth and twentieth centuries, then what Asian critics are saying now may seem highly prescient then.

The notion of the "West" learning from the "East" rather than the other way around is not new in history. It is new in recent Western history, however—hence the difficulty many Euro-Americans have with the idea even in principle, let alone in practice.

To the Chinese, for example, the world made more sense for millennia not as states and nations but as a Middle Kingdom, centered on themselves, with zones of influence extending as far out as tribute could reliably be exacted. The traditions of the West replaced these traditions, but, as in the West itself, the older habits of global governance remain a meaningful diplomatico-strategic alternative. They may well be reasserted in time, though not likely any time soon. It is difficult to imagine the contemporary state system becoming irrelevant in the next few generations, since too many people have too much invested in a statist world order. It is not difficult, however, to imagine many state-makers failing, where they have not failed already, to protect their citizens from harm. Sustained and prominent failure of this sort could well lead to the resurrection of older ideologies and identities or, at least, to their restoration in forms more suited to contemporary times. The Chinese model of powerful core jurisdictions, encircled by regions that are progressively less powerful and more remote, is one such ideology.

A stumbling state system could also see the reemergence of another time-honored alternative to the nation-state—the city-state. Two conspicuous examples exist in Asia—Hong Kong and Singapore—and though Hong Kong has been reabsorbed into China, the example these two models set, not only for China itself but for other countries struggling to hold themselves together, is compelling. A world governed by a stratified network of interlinked cities has historical precedents in both Asia and the West. And intercity relations, already notable in contemporary Asia, are one possible basis for global governance as a whole.

### Marxism

Karl Marx was a self-conscious globalist. He told the story of contemporary affairs in terms of the expansion of capitalism and class war worldwide. To Marx, capitalism was a stage of history through which all of earth's people had to pass. Only then, he believed, would they realize the full potential of the industrial revolution and begin to provide for the species as a whole.

### Radical Universalism

Marx saw individuals as species-beings. People ought to be able to act, he thought, as part of universal humankind. Then, and only then, would they be free. He was well aware of the social significance of states, nations, tribes, faiths, and families, but these were all secondary categories. Marx's concept of the nature of human nature was much more comprehensive. Indeed, as Berki says, "the Marxian vision of man as a species-being is so advanced and so radical that in comparison even such modern ideals as 'internationalism' and 'cosmopolitanism' appear timid and inadequate" (Berki 1984, 232). Marx's primary category was humanity as a whole.

At the moment people are lesser versions of what they might be. They are alienated, psychologically homeless, and estranged (Berki 1984, 229; Marx and Engels [1844] 1959). It cannot be emphasized enough, in fact, that to Marx people's "true home," their "true world," was the whole of humankind. He saw anything short of this as "fragmented, broken up, crumbled, lost" (Berki 1984, 222).

It was capitalism that had this reductionist result, negating what people might become. This was why Marx wanted so much to see capitalism transcended, and why his idea of utopia was the negation of any and every such negation. His concept of communism was not just a collectivist retreat from the rigors of modernist individuation and liberal individualism. It was the realization and affirmation of a sense of self and a way of living that was social, fully human, and therefore finally complete.

Such a radical end would suggest a singularly radical means. This Marx imagined in vivid detail.

## Commodification

With his collaborator Friedrich Engels, Marx saw capitalism as an extraordinarily productive system that all state-makers, "on pain of extinction," would be obliged to adopt. He saw it as needing a "constantly expanding" market. This need, he argued, chased capitalists all over the globe. They "nestle everywhere, settle everywhere, establish connections everywhere," giving a "cosmopolitan" character to production and consumption in every country of the world and destroying "old-established industries" in the process. The new industries draw their raw materials from the "remotest zones," and their products are consumed, not only at home, but in "every quarter of the globe" (Marx and Engels [1848] 195, 37).

Marx saw cheap commodities (the new "heavy artillery") compelling the recalcitrant to accept the new methods of production and the new form of civilization. In the process, whole continents would be cleared for cultivation, entire populations "conjured out of the ground." Who could have known, he declared, that one day there might be "too much civilization, too much means of subsistence, too much industry, too much commerce," and that the appropriation by the ruling class of the value of what that "too much" made possible would cause the whole system's demise (Marx and Engels [1848] 1975, 38–39, 40).

The ultimate collapse of capitalism, like that of all previous modes of production (feudalism, for example), would come about, Marx believed, because of the way it engendered antagonistic social relations. In capitalism's case, this antagonism was between the global bourgeoisie, the owners and managers of the means of production (the factories and their sources of finance), and the global proletariat, who sell their work as a commodity for a wage.

### Wage-Work

Marx's account of capitalism is the key. He characterized capitalism not only in terms of the private ownership of the means of production (the liberal definition of the term), but in terms of wage-work and the labor theory of value as well. By paying wages, employers can keep whatever workers produce. The surplus that accrues over and above the wages-bill, in other words, the capitalist can consume or invest. This, Marx said, is how under capitalism exploitation works.

### Class War

Marx tried to prove in some detail that, over time, capitalists would find their rates of profit falling, their capacity to produce outstripping people's capacity to consume, and their need to amalgamate compelling. In turn, they would not be able to sustain a system whose workers were satisfied. As a consequence, the opposing interests of the two key classes would become clearer and their differences progressively more acute. The end result would be revolution. The workers would overthrow the owners and managers, dismantle the state-making edifices that are capitalism's political face (the socialist phase), and institute a new, more equitable, and therefore more liberal civilization (the communist utopia).

Behind Adam Smith's "invisible hand" of liberal harmony, in other words, Marx saw class disharmony instead. He saw the market not as liberals do, as a set of voluntary exchange relations, but as a compulsory and compulsive place, where people are driven either by the need to accumulate capital or the need to earn money by selling their work. Note: driven, not coerced. Unlike slaves or serfs, legally free workers enter into contracts with capitalists to whom they sell their work-power. These are contracts that either party can rescind. The exploitation this makes possible is indirect, and as a consequence so are the dominance/subordinance relations that result from them. In Marxist parlance this does not make these contracts less exploitative. It merely makes them harder to see.

Marx saw this system becoming worldwide, which raises the question whether the revolution he predicted could take place only once the capitalist globalization process was complete. Did world revolution have to await the advent of world capitalism? In Marx's terms, this was very definitely the case. It was left to his followers to explain why the process was taking so long.

It fell to Marx's followers, for example, to marry the politico-economic thrust of his perspective with the ongoing politico-strategic significance of the state. This was no easy task since, to Marx himself, "the suggestion of mutual accommodation of two sets of irreconcilable principles, namely those on which the states-system rests and those that the international communist movement was to adopt, would have seemed little short of madness" (Kubalkova and Cruickshank 1985, 4).

Marx's followers faced the fact of a sovereign state system that was far too entrenched to be readily denied. It is no accident that the communist governments that came to power in Marx's name were statist, therefore. They may have adhered rhetorically to international proletarianism, but they were obliged by their sovereign status to account for what was unaccountable in Marx's terms.

### Extreme Marxism

To the more extreme, more revolutionary Marxists, who see capitalist globalization still resulting in global class conflict, the hour of the last instance (when capitalism gets demolished) has merely been deferred. There are few such die-hards left, though there are still lessons to be learned from thinking of capitalists as committed, because of the core principles of their ideology, to a relentless expansionism that, like a running man flailing forward, has to crash some day. Surplus capital, and particularly free-flowing short-term speculative capital, currently swamps the world market, profoundly affecting global production and patterns of wage-labor. Capitalists continue to seek new markets. Profits can never be taken for granted and the formation of global monopolies proceeds apace. Imperialism in its nonterritorial, trade- and investment-based forms still abounds. And while the contradictions are not acute enough to result in worldwide, working-class revolution, maybe we should wait.

### Moderate Marxism

To the more moderate, less revolutionary Marxists, who see global class conflict as having gone into reverse, class differences have become blurred.

In the highly industrialized parts of the global political economy, where class conflict should be getting worse, large-scale share issues have allowed workers to become owners too. Members of the proletariat invest in property and become *rentiers*, and work provides them with a sense of meaning as well as alienation. Also, many of the world's bourgeoisie sell their labor for wages, making the line between the bourgeoisie and the proletariat harder to draw.

To those more moderate Marxists, who see global class conflict as distorted rather than reversed, class differences have been compromised by countervailing practices. As far as these Marxists are concerned, while the injustice of world capitalism is still patently obvious and the need to mitigate its worst effects still acute, world capitalism has not come to pass the way Marx imagined. While we may still see world capitalism in Marxist terms, that is, we cannot see it anymore in Marx's terms.

## Technological Change

One form of this thesis highlights technological change. For example, more mechanized factories and farms have less need for wage-labor, particularly unskilled wage-labor. At the same time, new communications and transport technologies have allowed capitalists to locate production in poorer parts of the world, where many people are keen to become wage earners. The result distorts global class conflict and inhibits global class struggle. It makes for integrated managements, a more unified global bourgeoisie, disaggregated work-forces, and a less unified global proletariat.

Technological change has also made for a world political economy in two parts, one capitalist and one extracapitalist. In the capitalist part there is global class conflict, albeit in muffled forms. In the noncapitalist part the marginalized subsist in ways parasitic upon the capitalist world or completely independent of it. They are "superfluous" to the global production process (Cox 1995, 40–41).

## Dependency

The concept of two worlds features in other accounts of how global class conflict has been skewed, though here the worlds are depicted, in core/periphery terms, as two parts of one political economy. A large literature on "dependency," for example, was once devoted to analyzing this process. It documented the way in which politico-economic change made poorer countries subservient to richer ones, with the connivance of local elites. The richer global North was seen, very briefly, as requiring a poorer global South, the overdevelopment of the former being contingent upon the underdevelopment of the latter (Frank 1966).

This literature is dated now, especially in the light of Asian and Latin American growth patterns. The relationship between development and dependency, most of the original analysts now admit, is more complex than dependency theory allows, which is why particular state-makers, like those of Singapore, have been able to play the system to their developmental advantage. They have demonstrated in the process that there is no global inevitability to the poverty trap. Dependency still helps to explain, however, how the surpluses of poor states get transferred abroad (Schwartz 1989). It also helps explain why global hierarchies of politico-economic dominance and subordinance still persist.

## World Systems Theory

Another Cold War literature of this sort talks of capitalism as having been a world system since the sixteenth century, with one international division of labor shaping every national part (Wallerstein 1979). The notion of uneven development between a global core and periphery, with a semiperiphery in between, is still used to discuss how countries like the United States move into tertiary, knowledge-intensive industries (the core) while countries like China become sites for secondary manufacturing (the semiperiphery). Overly deterministic as an account of general patterns of practice, and overly convinced of its empirical usefulness, world systems theory still reminds us that world affairs can and do work in unfamiliar ways.

## Neo-Gramscianism

Among those who tried to explain why class conflict did not result in revolution was the Italian communist Antonio Gramsci (1972). His ideas on hegemony now feature in a range of analyses that highlight how transnational capitalists use politico-economic power to control state-making elites. These analyses highlight the influence of liberalist ideology over the global ruling class, which includes by now a transnational managerial class. They endorse in the process the larger significance of rationalist modernity (Cox 1987, 359–360; Gill 1993).

## The Feminist Critique

To feminists, no change in the mode of production will change male dominance. Marxist-inspired feminists remain hopeful that a socialist revolution will liberate women as well as men. Only a meaningful socialism, they say, will provide women with meaningful equality of opportunity. Only this kind of socialism will stop the way "housewifization" is used to divide labor and to consign women to the army of reserve workers and to reproduction in the home. Non-Marxist feminists are not so reassured. They do not find the experience of socialist countries convincing. They do not see a mere change in the capitalist mode of production eliminating patriarchy. Moreover, they see Marxist class analysis obscuring the significance of work not done for a wage. The last point is particularly serious since much of this work is done by people who are women, in the home and in the subsistence sectors of the world political economy. Much of this work is essential to the continued accumulation of global capital (Tickner 1992, 85–90).

### The Experience of Marxism

Marx saw capitalism being dismantled by the proletariat and by revolution—not by anyone else or in any other way. Extreme Marxists still concur. More moderate Marxists do not.

Exploitation is the key. While capitalist commodities may be mute, in other words, every Marxist will heed the sounds commodities make. With every step that Marxists take, for example, they hear their shoes exclaim. The exclamation is that of the Fourth World worker who sewed the soles. With each cup of tea that Marxists drink, they hear it cry out. The cry is that of the malnourished Tamil worker who plucked the leaves (Harris 1983, 9–10).

This is one way to get close and listen to what Marxists believe to be important. Another way is to listen to Marx himself, as in *The German Ideology* ([1846] 1977, 54–56):

> In history up to the present it is . . . an empirical fact that separate individuals have, with the broadening of their activity into world-historical activity, become more and more enslaved under a power alien to them . . . a power which has become more and more enormous and, in the last instance, turns out to be the *world market* . . . But it is just as empirically established that, by the overthrow of the existing state of society by the communist revolution . . . and the abolition of private property which is identical with it, this power . . . will be dissolved; and that then the liberation of each single individual will be accomplished in the measure in which history becomes transformed into world history . . . Only then will the separate individuals be liberated from the various national and local barriers, be brought into practical connection with the material and intellectual production of the whole world and be put in a position to acquire the capacity to enjoy this all-sided production of the whole earth . . .

Marx believed that if we continue to produce as atomized individuals, persistent crises will prevail. He thought that once we are aware of our species status, however, we will produce accordingly and will want to provide for all.

As far as he and Engels were concerned, the alternative to global marketeering is equally global. Since capitalism today is still globalizing, the alternative to it is not yet manifest. We must wait a while yet, to find out what this is, though the hope is there. Utopia is nigh.

Meanwhile, marketeering continues to replace precapitalist production systems with capitalist ones, and all the contemporary talk of social movements and global civil society should be heard with this fact in mind. Though written in 1980, Paul Harrison's description of precapitalist production is still relevant in this regard. The following extract from his book, *The Third World Tomorrow*, reminds us what this transition to capitalism can mean as lived by those taking part. No analytic account of class-consciousness, social organization, or civil dissent can tell us as much (130–132):

> When I visited Bagh Nanak Chand, he and his two teenage sons and orphaned nephew were handmaking black, wedge-heeled women's sandals. Inside the family, a rudimentary form of division of labour is practised. Chand and his elder son cut out the leather for the uppers and sew them by hand. The nephew fits them to the lasts . . . the younger son squats by a charcoal fire and finishes the surface with a heated iron . . . The shoes are neat and workmanlike . . . [b]ut . . . will sell on the lower, bazaar end of the home market and command low prices . . .
>
> At around 5:30 p.m. Chand collects the day's sandals into a large flat wicker basket . . . and goes to the main road to hail a cycle rickshaw. He gets out at Hing Ki Mandi, Agra's shoe market . . . Chand carries his load down one of the arcades where the middlemen, most of them prosperously dressed, sit crosslegged surrounded by shoeboxes. Chand stops at the premises of a white-haired merchant . . . in Western dress . . . He passes over the sandals, pair by pair . . . [T]he middleman . . . turns them to check from every angle for defects and size. If he finds faults he will correspondingly reduce the price. A short haggle with few words ensues—there's little point arguing with a middleman. Chand reluctantly accepts 12 rupees a pair . . .
>
> . . . Chand is paid—but not in cash. The middleman reaches down a pad of printed promissory notes (*purchas*) and fills it in for 144 rupees—postdated for payment three months later. This means that Chand is giving the dealer three months' credit. As Chand's family lives and works from hand to mouth, he has no choice but to seek out a special dealer in promissory notes, who will cash the *purchas* immediately. But he will deduct a discount of between 2 and 5 per cent for every month he has to wait for full payment from the middleman. For his 144-rupee *purcha*, Chand gets only 127 rupees, losing 12 per cent of the face value. But as labour and profit account for only a quarter of the selling price of the shoes, he is actually losing almost half his family's net income.

This is not an example of capitalist exploitation since Chand is not selling his labor for a wage. Chand is part of a precapitalist political economy that has survived into the present but that capitalism is replacing. Similar sandals, factory-made by globalized production chains, are now no doubt undercutting his prices and, since he has no hope of getting the capital to become an entrepreneur, he is now no doubt forced to seek work from someone else. There is no job for him, however, since the sandal factory is likely to be in China, not India, and any other paid work is extremely scarce where he lives. There is no welfare assistance, either, to tide him over while he looks for what is not there. He and his family are destined to beg and starve, and *that* is capitalism. It may not be what capitalism does to everyone, but it is what capitalism does to Chand and to those he supports and to those he loves.

# Conclusion

# A Constructed World

To most of us, world affairs appear to be unavoidable. They are part of an environment that seems to be predestined. We accept their consequences without much thought, unless something goes wrong. Then we ask: what are these affairs? And were they really meant to be?

Most of us, in other words, do not think much about world affairs most of the time, and when we do, we accept them as largely preordained. If, however, there is widespread violence, or market collapse, or profound alienation, then world affairs impinge with more than ordinary force, and we ask: what can we do? What can we change?

Changing world affairs is not easy or simple, not only because they seem inevitable or predestined, but also because world affairs are the outcome of no overall plan. The closer we look at world affairs, the more obvious it becomes that no one and no group designed the modern state system, or modern market capitalism, or modern world society, or modernity itself. Many had to act to get the relevant concepts widely accepted, but only in retrospect is it possible to see what their actions meant and how the practices that constitute the relevant concepts came to be.

People do try to plan world affairs, and their policies abound. Since what was intended in the past resulted in something so unintended in the present, however, why do they bother? Will not what they intend to do now have unintended consequences in the future, frustrating those intentions and foiling their grand and not-so-grand designs? Perhaps it is wiser to counsel inaction. But even inaction shapes world affairs, allowing particular versions of them to proceed by default and the purposes of those who promote these versions to prevail.

Questions like those above are rhetorical, since people do bother. They clearly do not think their policy attempts are futile, in part because they suffer from delusions of efficacy and also because some people do succeed in realizing their intentions. They do this often enough at least to give hope to others and to make their intentions seem realistic. Unintended consequences do have cumulative outcomes, and if we can figure these out, we can get our policies to work, at least some of the time.

Though the patterns of human practice that currently characterize world affairs were first planned by particular people at particular times to specific ends, these practices became patterns of global significance only afterwards, by accident. Only afterwards did it become clear what innovations were the world-shaping ones. Three hundred years ago, among the advocates of a wide range of specific objectives, particular policy entrepreneurs wanted nonintervention, laissez faire trade, self-approbation, or a more rationalistic way of life. No one anticipated several centuries later two hundred sovereign states in a reciprocating world system, or five hundred huge firms in global market array, or the Universal Declaration of Human Rights, or science and technology. No one thought privileging reason as an end in itself would lead to the industrial revolution, global imperialism on the part of the West, or the world order and disorder that resulted.

Faced with particular problems, people contrived equally particular solutions, couched in terms of how they understood world affairs at the time. Their contrivances made patterns over time—especially to pattern-seeking creatures like ourselves—though these patterns represented no grand concept, grinding its way down through the years. There was no millennial design.

No analytic language is able to account for all historical circumstances. Marxists might claim otherwise for a materialist explanation of human affairs. Or realists might say that power politicking predicts all. The world affairs we inherit are irreducibly contingent, however, and so are the world affairs we bequeath to those who take up where we leave off. No matter how hard we try to anticipate and control them, world affairs are the outcome of purpose *and* chance, fancy *and* the fortuitous, resolution *and* the unforeseen.

When we ask: Who do these world affairs serve? What is their purpose? And why? the answers we can give can only be for now. The course of human history is always changing, and world affairs with it, and though we may feel we can summarize these affairs, for the moment at least, our summary is not definitive. There are many ways to regard the past, and no amount of prescience will ever compensate for the contingencies involved in finding out the future.

Modernists like to think we can do better than this. Their linear conception of time and their Euclidean conception of space allows them, they say, not only to picture the world from one moment to the next, but also to picture its shape in the main. By compressing their sense of reality to a point and removing it from the phenomenal world, the more ambitious of them say they are able to survey all that was and all that will be. They see themselves contemplating all of reality—perhaps not in detail, but at least in general terms (Toynbee 1957; Spengler 1961). They see themselves standing not in the stream of life's events but on its bank or in some far place from which they are able to apprehend the whole world-river as it were, from mountain to mouth, from spring to sea.

Visualize, such a modernist might say of this particular moment, all of earth's people—several billion human beings—connected by "millions of cobwebs" in local, regional, and global networks. These networks represent "trade flows, letters exchanged, tourist movements, aircraft flights, population movements and transactions in ideas, cultures, languages and religions" (Burton 1968, 8).

A compelling picture, perhaps, and a comprehensive one too, but where, despite all the transaction and flow, are the discontinuities that also characterize world affairs? Burton's view of the world highlights how busy it is from one moment to the next, but it downplays in the process the boundaries and borders, the disjunctures and the disconnections that also describe the way human relationships look. What seems an objective picture illuminates one important aspect of world affairs, but only by putting another in its shade. And while we can always decide to turn our mental attention to the neglected aspect—the one cast in the shade—that means to stop seeing so clearly the webs of transaction and transgression that we began with.

Standing back mentally to observe can make for greater clarity, in other words, but the clarity always comes at a cost. This cost is the lack of clarity about what is not being observed. Objectifying limits as it looks, confounding our understanding at the same time as it clarifies it. It promises testable knowledge, but always either about limited aspects of the world, or breadth, not depth.

The cost is higher than mere aspect-dependence, or superficiality, since the rationalist mind-gaze assumes that the world is encompassed by what rationalism can do. In choosing to look at the world analytically, the detached observer casts it in terms amenable to the use of reason as an explanatory tool. In the example given above, for instance, the world was first imagined as made up of separate human beings. Only then was it imagined as linked in networks as well. The networks, that is, while seemingly of primary concern, were actually secondary. The primary focus was on individuals-in-the-world. Only a rationalist/modernist would see the world so, thus misrepresenting life's meaning for most of earth's people. Most people are profoundly embedded in their societies. Most people would not agree that the world is made up of discrete individuals who are then networked or interconnected. For most people in the world, their obligations are intrinsic, not added on, because most people in the world are sociated, not individuated. They are related intrinsically, not extrinsically. To any observer prepared to get close to listen to people or to take part in what they do, this is self-evident. It is common sense. A view of the world, like the rationalist one, that constructs another account of it in order to be able to explain and understand it is no account of the world at all. It is a view of something else. It is a view of what rationalism requires in order for rationalism to make common sense.

The modernist propensity for using reason to objectify with provides us with a powerful mental tool. There is no doubt about that. But it is not as reliable a tool as modernists make it out to be. It is not good, for example, at analyzing a wide range of variables at the same time, especially since it must have tractable material to work on. And as reality is always emerging, the rationalistic scrutiny of any part or parts of it can provide no more than an indistinct version of the whole. Making reality knowable by rational means requires us to impose upon it key features it does not possess or possesses only in part. So: how then does reality look when undistorted by the rationalist mind-gaze? What is this powerful tool *not* showing us? What does it *not* have to say? How do world affairs seem in other, less incomplete, less distorted ways?

Questions like these take on even greater meaning when we realize that rationalism limits not only what people see, but also what they do. Rationalism is an invitation to become more self-referential, and though reflection is a form of action, since thinking is doing too, the more we reflect, the more we are likely to appreciate the complexities and the contingencies of world affairs and the less we are likely to see any point in making changes. Even where we believe change is warranted, once aware of the range and power of the social forces at work in the world, we may feel that even to attempt reform is pointless (Satris 1986). As we move mentally away from the world, the immediacy of life's moment is taken from us, and we find ourselves watching more and acting less. While we may appreciate acutely the need for new initiatives, our growing mental grasp may preclude the sense that it is worthwhile taking any initiative at all.

Not doing anything would be well warranted if this were the best of all possible worlds but this is not the best of all possible worlds. The accounts that rationalistic moderns provide of world affairs are not accounts of the best world affairs there might be. The violence and destruction and wholesale human misery that characterize so much of world affairs is devastating testimony to that fact, and the inaction that rationalism can predispose us to is not warranted if this is the best we can do. The status quo, in other words, requires change.

How can we change an entire world? And what should we change it to? These are not easy questions to answer. World affairs are not readily conceived in their entirety, nor is it easy to institute a new order of things, particularly on such a large scale. Since outcomes are always uncertain; since there are many alternatives to these particular world affairs, each of which articulates its own version of what should be preferred; since our moral awareness is limited at best, it is hard to say for certain what a better world would be. The promotion of a preferred cause could just as well frustrate that cause further, too. We have no guarantee—the complexities of the subject being what they are—that we shall be able to expedite what we decide we want to do.

As argued at the beginning, these are perennial dilemmas. If we do not see ourselves as living in the best of all possible worlds and we try as a consequence to envisage a better world, we soon realize that, though we make our own history, we do not do so as we please (Marx and Engels [1852] 1962, 247). This does not stop us trying to bring about the changes we consider desirable, while at the same time trying to find out, as objectively as we can, what might inhibit these changes and what might promote them. It is likely to make us more humble, however, about what we think we can achieve, and more selective, perhaps, about who we choose to achieve it with.

If we do reject inaction, if we seek not only to philosophize about the world, but also to make what we believe to be a more advanced version of it (Marx and Engels [1846] 1977, 123), we do compromise our cognitive authority. We do lose, to some extent, the status we acquire in a rationalistic world by being seemingly nonpartisan.

This would suggest that *not* being partisan is therefore a source of cognitive authority, but this is not so. Those whose passion is dispassion, those who prefer reason as an end in itself and who are prepared to allow their reasoning to lead where it will—they, too, are compromised. They, too, are not trustworthy, believable, or necessarily "sound." The passion for dispassion is a passion, too, however self-muting it may seem. Our linguistic predispositions, the basic categories of our thought, craft our consciousness before we even begin to turn our minds to describing and explaining world affairs. We can be honest about all this and work with it, as most social scientists try to do. Or we can pretend to a detachment that presumes moral innocence but amounts, in practice, to a particular kind of hypocrisy.

This is ultimately an argument for keeping our options open. How open, however? Since our notions of what is appropriate in this regard will depend upon the analytic language we speak and the ideological perspective it provides, this issue can get quickly mired in relativities. If we think we already know what is most worth doing, is this only because we have decided in advance what human beings are like today and will be like in the future and what can be done with them or to them as a consequence? This does not leave us with much in the way of alternatives. Perhaps dichotomizing the problem into the convinced and the uncertain, the decisive and the unsure, is not a very fruitful way to proceed. Perhaps we should try a more multidimensional approach.

The multidimensionality of world affairs is not a feature of the contemporary study of IR/IPE. Indeed, as we have seen above, the whole discipline is deeply imbued with a partial account of how world affairs work and what they mean.

If we accept this conclusion and choose a more multidimensional approach, however, what would this look like? What might we do better in this regard?

The first step, I would argue, is to include in the core of the discipline not only IR and IPE, but also IPS and WPC. This step would require analysts to consider politico-social and politico-cultural concerns as well as politico-strategic and politico-economic ones.

The second step would be to augment rationalism with other ways of knowing. This would mean subjectifying as well as objectifying. It would require the consistent pursuit of experientially proximal as well as distal research.

Let us look again at IR/IPE/IPS and WPC. The whole sequence was represented at the beginning of this book as a series of maps, one behind the other. Behind the map of states, it was said, lies a map of firms and capital flows, while behind this map lies a map of nations, individualists, and collectives. All three maps were read in the context of another map too, a global map that documents the march of modernity and the plight of the main nonmodernist alternatives to it.

This sequence is a typically modernistic one. It assumes, for example, a linear array. As such it does not do justice to the extent to which the main analytic languages that are used to make world affairs are entangled with each other. A more accurate image, therefore, might be a globe depicting all of the world's states, which, twisted open like a Russian doll, reveals another globe that displays all the world's firms, which, twisted open, reveals another globe of individuals. This last globe, twisted open, reveals Rodin's statue of a thinker.

The metaphor of globes depicts these different dimensions enclosing one another, rather than hanging apart like maps. The sequence is still linear, however. The globes are still discrete. They are not entangled.

The metaphor of globes does not allow for the fact that the thinker, for example, is not a solitary entity, but a person engaged in a social act made possible only by the language he thinks in. He is part of an ongoing process, part of a culture and a society, and can only be put apart from these constitutive contexts notionally or analytically. Globes in sequence, in other words, do no more justice to the way the main analytic languages make the world, and the integrally entangled nature of that world, than maps in sequence do.

Analytic entanglement is a basic feature of world affairs. No analytic language exists in isolation from the others, despite what its proponents may say or do.

Consider the state. This is a key unit of analysis in contemporary world affairs and much discussed as a consequence. States are territorial, sovereign entities, built upon the belief in nonintervention and mutual recognition held by the state-makers who craft them.

Moving away from the practices that politico-strategic analyses emphasize (domestic ordering, boundary maintenance, interstate relating), we find other practices to account for. These are more politico-economic in character. Here state-makers can be found furthering the idea of state self-reliance, furthering or frustrating market efficiency, or serving the interests of a global, capital-owning, technomanagerial ruling class.

As participants in markets, both white and black, and including the global one, state-makers help to maintain the structures of law and order that make individual and corporate marketeering possible. State-makers spend a lot of their time, that is, creating the conditions they think best augment the material well-being of themselves and (some, at least) of their citizens.

Moving away even more, we find yet other practices to account for that are politico-social in character. Here state-makers further the idea of the nation-state, for example. Since nearly all state-makers subscribe to the global ethos of nationalism, any account of the state will need to include an account of nation-making too. Here state-makers further or frustrate the social autonomy of individuals, competing for influence and power with nonstate collectives and social movements as well.

At this point we find the contemporary discipline petering out. Analysts of world affairs do not treat politico-social practices with the same regard as they do those of governance or sustenance. They do not see matters of identity and social coherence as significant as diplomatico-military or material ones. And this neglect is damaging not only for the discipline itself, which remains as a consequence a partial and truncated version of what it might be. This neglect also has a negative effect on world affairs themselves, since ordinary people get stuffed into pigeon-holes they do not inhabit or that do not do justice to what they think, how they behave, and what they might become. Pigeon holing people like this not only distorts world affairs but also distorts what world affairs might become.

All of these practices also marginalize large numbers of earth's people, who may live within states in territorial terms, but receive few of their services. Then again, the services they receive may be only those of the state's coercive arms (the military or the police). If these people are part of the modernist project, they may, as a consequence, see "the state" as promoting masculinism, or rights abuse, or conflict, or planetary destruction. If they are not part of this project, then they are not likely to see the state in such abstract terms, and state-making will take place despite them, and over them, but still to their cost.

Telling the story of state-making as an analytically entangled one shows that the state is not just a set of diplomatico-military concerns. It shows that it is also a matter of wealth-making, self-making, and, ultimately, mind-making too. Telling this story not only in terms of the three main dimensions modernists make of world affairs, but also in terms of all the analytic languages that characterize these dimensions, shows how wide the range of languages happens to be. It also shows how hard it is to keep them conceptually apart.

While detailing the way entanglement works provides a more meaningful image of world affairs than maps and Russian dolls, does it ultimately capture the extent to which the various dimensions of modernist world affairs constitute each other? Does it really account for the politico-cultural context in which modernist world affairs are made? And if not, how can we capture the quality of entanglement best?

There is a problem, right at the start, with choosing to separate the subject into different dimensions, then trying to connect them and contextualize them. It is the problem all rationalist objectivizing presents. To clarify, we categorize. To analyze, we conceptualize.

Conceptual clarity comes at a price, however, as already noted above. Here it is paid in terms of the failure to appreciate the uncategorized character of what it is we want to explain and understand.

Once we conceptualize world affairs, this is how we know world affairs. These categories are how we make out world affairs to be, and how we come to know world affairs.

What we come to know may not be world affairs, however. World affairs may be "best" or at least "better" described in other terms entirely, or in noncategorical or extracategorical terms that do not fragment and distort the subject in quite the same way.

If we ask, for example, what the "best" description and explanation of "the state" might be, our answer will usually be couched in one of a number of different analytic languages. There is no neutral language we can use without fear of contradiction, but we still have to answer the question somehow. So we do so in terms of our assumptions about human nature. Our analytic language will be built upon them, and our notion of what is "best" will articulate them.

It is possible to establish the descriptive and explanatory supremacy of one preferred language by decree, though decreed accounts have only the force of the form of power they require for their dissemination. This power is not their own. It comes from somewhere else.

If we do not use decree, if we do not impose a preferred analytic language by outright force, then we are faced with the task of making it prevail by persuasive means alone. Having decided to speak the language of IR/realism, for example, or feminist/Marxism, we must then confront those who speak IPE/liberalism, or spiritual/premodernism, and argue our case, seeking to prevail by convincing them that we are right.

The limits this process sets are apparent at once, since who is to say that the analytic language we choose adequately accounts for "the state"? Perhaps the state is "best" or "better" described in a holistic language none of us speaks. Perhaps one of these languages *is* the "best," only its antagonists will not admit it. And how, without revelation or force, are we—or they—to know? Persuasion never seems to do it. Argument alone never seems enough.

Let us review entanglement more systematically. Since this book describes the three dimensions of world affairs that modernists make (high, low, and even lower), let us consider entanglement as the way these three dimensions constitute each other.

State-making can be realist, internationalist, and globalist. Market-making can be mercantilist, liberal, and Marxist. And the connections between the two are diverse and complex.

Classical mercantilists, for example, who are the political economists most interested in state autonomy, see market-making ("low politics") as state-making ("high politics") by other means. They take the interrelationship between these two for granted. To them, consolidating or augmenting a state's wealth or productive capacity means consolidating or augmenting a state's strategic power. If it seems necessary to use diplomatico-military force to close borders and enforce authority or to project the capacity to protect national interests, then so be it. If, on the other hand, it is possible to generate the wealth necessary for strategic might—might that can in turn make for more mercantilism—then that is good too.

Extreme liberals, on the other hand, are most interested in personal or corporate wealth, seeing state-making ("high politics") as an impediment to market-making ("low politics"). They argue for as little governmental presence as possible. They are not interested in what market-making can do to foster politico-strategic capacities, since a prosperous world, in their view, is a peaceful one anyway. While prosperity promotes peace, peace is necessary to allow for the marketeering that makes for prosperity. This is why the less radical liberals see reason in state intervention—the use of state power to secure an ordered environment for trade and investment, at home and abroad.

State-making as a market-making ploy (the state nurturing the market) can have paradoxical consequences. In the case of a poorer state like "Mexico," for example, the state-makers want, among other things, to provide a stable domestic environment that attracts foreign investors and fosters domestic market activity. Not only do many state-makers earn a lot of money themselves this way, but a productive economy provides the tax base that pays for the police and the army. These act in turn to keep order and make the market "stable."

The repression required to monopolize the domestic use of force can do considerable damage to the individual rights that liberals consider politically desirable, however. Fostering liberal economics can end up, in other words, directly subverting the prospects for liberal politics. This is especially so where state-makers deny basic moral entitlements and basic human rights in their bid to nurture the market and get the money they need with which to play this role.

The key contradiction that liberals are always trying to resolve—the contradiction between their conception of "economics" and their conception of "politics"—would not mean much to a Marxist, however. In Marxist parlance, categories like "capital" and "labor" matter more than "economics" and "politics." To a Marxist, economics and politics are not linked since linkage assumes that politics and economics are separate domains; instead, they are related dialectically with reference to the contemporary mode of production, capitalism. To a Marxist, there is no such thing as liberal economics compromising liberal politics. There are power and production instead, with politics germane to *both* the public sphere of power ("politics" proper, in liberal parlance) *and* the private sphere of production ("economics," in liberalist terms).

The situation that faced U.S. state-makers in Europe after World War II is just one revealing example in this regard. The finances forthcoming at this time, through the International Bank for Reconstruction and Development and the International Monetary Fund, were not enough to resuscitate Europe's productive capacity. Meanwhile, U.S. producers were flooding the world with their manufactured goods. European countries were paying in what to them was foreign currency, namely, U.S. dollars, and since they had little such currency left, the situation quickly became critical. A Europe unable to buy U.S. products would have driven the United States into recession (Moffitt 1984, 26–27). Indeed, it was this very prospect, and not just fear of Soviet Communism, that made it possible for President Truman to win congressional support for the Marshall Plan that funded Europe's eventual recovery.

Marxists see the kind of dilemma Europeans feared after World War II in the context of twentieth-century capitalism. They highlight the existence of a transnational class of owners and managers who carry state passports, but who are able to trade, finance, and buy labor-power and resources around the globe. Because of its common interest in owning and managing, this class shares more with each other than with fellow "nationals" not of their class. Those not of this class are mostly wage-laborers, and though they potentially constitute a transnational class, too, wage-workers remain much more state-bound. In Marxist terms, the global "head" is kept separate from its "hands," and each hand in turn is kept separate from the other by nationalistic means (Hymer 1972, 103–105). In Marxist terms, in other words, state-making is used to further the interests of the ruling class—both capital-owning and technomanagerial. As far as Marxists are concerned, it is *these* entangled interests that most feature in world affairs (Cox 1987). Statism is part of capitalism.

Liberals, by contrast, put all the aspects of a case like this European one in a marketeering context. They highlight the interplay between economics and politics as the one competes with the other. To them, Euro-American state-makers and Euro-American capitalists are separate groups, the state-makers setting up representative democracies, free markets, and feelings of individualism, and the capitalists seeking profits. The more extreme liberals see profiteering as a universal panacea, requiring only the most minimal involvement by the state. The more moderate liberals see the need for much more active state support and a much more entangled set of regional affairs. To both extreme and moderate liberals, however, statism and capitalism are independent, albeit related, processes. State-making sets the conditions under which individuals can be realized, and market-making is the way an individual's interests are actually met.

Mercantilists, by the way, see all the aspects of this European example in statist terms. They see the United States and the European state-makers as doing whatever was required to sustain state integrity. They see state-makers using capitalism to further the interests of the state. Thus the Cold War made it possible for the United States to project its power into Europe long after World War II was over. The United States was obliged in due course to accept economic nationalism in Europe too, but in a way that secured continuing American access and influence. To a mercantilist, statists will always use capitalism this way, furthering the interests of "the state," pulling people together into territorial domains and emphasizing their common interests, while pushing them apart in terms of their national identities.

The relationships between "low" politics and "even lower" politics are also entangled. Market-making can be mercantilist, liberal, and Marxist, while self-making can be nationalist, individualist, and collectivist in character. The connections between the two are diverse and complex as well.

Mercantilists are economic nationalists. Their protectionist policies are presented not only in politico-economic terms, however. As just noted, they exploit politico-social sentiments of nationalist exceptionalism as well.

Liberals are also apt to look beyond the politico-economic dimension for ideological support. Politico-social individualism in particular is the basis for liberalist marketeering, though liberals can get support from collectivists too. It was Solidarity, for example—the collectivist movement in Poland— that led the social revolution there that resulted in marketeering reforms.

Classical as well as moderate Marxists see the primary agenda of the capitalist mode of production as being not only politico-economic but politico-social too. Materialistic individualists are both the cause and consequence of capitalism, though in Marxist terms individualists form class collectives and the proletariat ones are destined to reorganize the whole mode of production, whereupon a new kind of society is supposed to become possible. (Less patient Marxists try to expedite the revolutionary process by acting as "vanguards" of postcapitalism, though Marx himself was not a Marxist in this regard).

The nature of the relationships between politico-social (even lower politics) and politico-strategic affairs (high politics) is similarly entangled. State-making can be realist, internationalist, and globalist, while self-making can be nationalist, individualist, and collectivist. Like the connections described above, the ones here are diverse and complex too.

State-makers of every sort, for example, whether realist, internationalist, or globalist, tend to depict world affairs in terms of the rules, procedures, and signaling practices of the world's strategic and diplomatic elites. Their commitment to their statism is manifest in a wide range of now-conventional practices, from border policing to war. State-makers and state-breakers both reify the state, drawing boundaries not only on the ground but also in people's heads. This is nationalism and it entails the creation of a national domain that has an "inside" peopled by loyal, solidarist citizens and an "outside" peopled by dissident, nonsolidarist noncitizens (such as terrorists, exiles, pirates, and refugees).

A wide range of social movements has arisen, in fact, to articulate beliefs about world affairs other than those that state-makers hold. These movements may be relatively powerless in conventional politico-strategic terms. However, they have the capacity to explore other ways of prevailing, ways without arms or wealth, which obtain their power from belief itself and from the solidarity that shared belief engenders. This makes social movements a direct threat to the monopoly that state-makers of every sort assert over what people believe about the organization and practice of world affairs. The human imagination is a powerful force, particularly so when individuals use it to organize socially around coherent and meaningful alternatives to current world affairs.

Entanglements ramify throughout the entire matrix. Indeed, given the notional nature of the categories used to highlight various aspects of modernist world affairs, they are the matrix.

They ramify beyond it, as well, since the whole project, the entire attempt to construct these particular world affairs, creates peripheries. The nine narratives, the nine analytic languages that characterize the modernist accounts of the discipline, are not the only ones. Others, equally authoritative, lay equal claim to core status and strive to get heard. There are the feminist narratives, for example, that are within but on the margins of the modernist project (like liberal or Marxist feminism). And there are the feminist narratives outside of the modernist project that are on the margins of the whole process (like premodernist or postmodernist feminism).

Confining our awareness to parts of the matrix only limits our account to less than the whole. Limits like these make it easier for global proponents of particular parts of the discipline to have their version of world affairs pass as the only version possible. But at what cost?

## For Whom?

Any comprehensive account of the world affairs of our day and age must highlight the making of modernity. Western modernism has made itself felt most profoundly in the form of two ongoing revolutions, a scientific and an industrial one. These revolutions are the basis of the West's military and material, social and cultural power, and they are the reason that Western modernists benefit disproportionately from the exercise of power these revolutions put at their disposal.

The nonmodernist alternatives to the modernist project, both premodernist and postmodernist, must contend as a consequence with the global reach of rationalism. There is no escaping the significance of this ideology. There is no escaping its politico-strategic, politico-economic, and politico-social concomitants either.

This is a very broad-brush conclusion. By the same token, it is easy to forget that we are still in the middle of these scientific and industrial revolutions, which are arguably the most significant revolutions in written human history. The requisite mind-moves began to be made only three hundred years ago, and it is only in the last one hundred—the span of a single long life—that humankind has begun to feel the full brunt of what modernist rationalism makes possible.

Modernist rationalism makes for statism, capitalism and individualism on a global scale. These analytic languages and the ideologies they generate work together to synergistic effect. The heart of the matter is the priority given the use of reason, however, and the way this makes possible a radical form of mental distance and a highly individuated sense of self.

If we move from the politico-cultural context of modernism to modernist world affairs themselves, we find that world affairs like these—of the kind we have at the moment—are first of all for state-makers. This is where the study of world affairs is at its conventional best, documenting the complexities of contemporary state-making and the contemporary state system.

Rationalistic individualism has made state-making notably more democratic, though in principle, therefore, the citizens of a state are also its beneficiaries. In practice, state-makers may have few resources at their command. They may have little to offer "their" people, except more or less radical abuses of power.

As well as the civic benefits that membership in the state is supposed to confer, there are supposed now to be a whole raft of human rights, held up beside what state-makers do as a kind of moral measure. Those state-makers who comply are deemed humane. Those who do not are found wanting for not providing the basic entitlements that are anyone's due.

Like the implementation of human rights, democratization is also a key modernist process. Popular control of the state by all those designated citizens is far from being a universal experience, however, and even where citizens have long been able to hire and fire their state-makers, the process is always ongoing. It is never finally complete.

Rationalistic individualism has also made wealth-making notably more capitalistic. In principle, the members of a free market are all its beneficiaries. In practice, these members rely on wealth trickling down—a much contested concept. In liberal parlance, we are all winners where markets are free. And while some win more than others, if all the factors of production move freely, we are all supposed to win something. In mercantilist and Marxist parlance, however, this win-win outcome is far less clear.

Radical individualism is not a category that stands out when we ask who world affairs are for. As modernist rationalism spreads, however, and as more people objectify and acquire a "punctual" sense of themselves, they begin to explore the freedom that being socially detached and disembedded provides. They become politicians, entrepreneurs, and members of social movements, for example, crafting world affairs in their own image and trying to define who world affairs are for in the process.

To those on the margins of modernist world affairs, the question of who benefits can have a very different answer, however. They highlight other categories, too, that describe in their own terms whom world affairs are for. Thus feminists highlight the extent to which modernist world affairs are for men. Conservationists note the extent to which modernist world affairs are for those who pollute the environment and deplete its nonrenewable resources, thus jeopardizing the lives of those who will live after us. Indigenous peoples know modernist world affairs as benefiting those to whom they lost their lands. Peace-makers, who see state-makers as war-makers too, see world affairs benefiting statist, military, and diplomatic leaders and the protection rackets they run (Tilly 1985). Religious people—Christians, Buddhists, Muslims, Hindu—see modernist world affairs as the domain (and I am generalizing more than a little gratuitously here) of the sinful, the desirous, the pagan, and those not devout. Unemployed and poor people know that modernist world affairs are for those with work and for the well-to-do. Non-Westerners know these world affairs as Western ones. Neo-Nazis say Zionists and non-Aryans benefit most. And so on.

There are many such groups and movements who provide revealing perspectives on world affairs. It is possible to see in them all the seedbeds of potential world affairs. They are a fertile source of alternative perspectives and a rewarding place to look for ways in which world affairs might be redescribed, re-explained, and understood anew. What kind of crop they portend is another matter again, but it is from the peripheries that we get some of the most challenging accounts of world affairs. It is on the margins that some of the most ambitious arguments are put, arguments that can also be controversial, unsettling, and prophetic too.

How much of this complex picture is provided by IR/IPE? Chapter 4 provides the answer. The rest of this book articulates the question.

## To Do What?

The matrix that frames the discussion above allows a systematic answer to the question: who does what? In politico-strategic terms, modernist world affairs either protect state sovereignty by realpolitik means (realism), or promote international organizations and the global rule of law (internationalism), or promote greater global governance (globalism). In politico-economic terms, modernist world affairs either protect state sovereignty by material means (mercantilism), or maximize market profits (liberalism), or lay the foundations for postcapitalist socialism and communism (Marxism). In politico-social terms, modernist world affairs either legitimize states in essentialist terms (nationalism), or valorize the self (individualism), or create compensatory groups and movements (collectivism).

In the politico-cultural context in which all the above are set, modernist world affairs further the use of reason as an end in itself. All of the analytic languages are part of this project, part, that is, of a massive attempt to promote the acceptance of rationalism worldwide.

All of this discussion exaggerates the coherence of the modernist project. If we listened only to what was said above, we would think that there was a global organization of rationalists going house-to-house, village-to-village, and town-to-town, trying to recruit people to the modernist cause. There is no such organization, however. There is no such recruitment drive.

The modernist project does not have to be a conscious plan. All it has to do is set a luminous example. The example includes scientific knowledge, medical expertise, mass industrial production, and modern consumer goods. It includes transport and communications systems able to span the globe, world media, profound assumptions about what currently constitutes an appropriate school curriculum, the need for universities, preferred notions about standards of living, and preferred ways of living at these standards. These are the "heavy artillery" with which modernists assail nonmodernist societies. Their "demonstration effects" induce radical changes in premodernist peoples. And they set the universalizing and homogenizing trends that postmodernists contest and seek to transcend.

## Why?

Why have world affairs? What can we say they are for?

A premodernist community would cast its answer to questions like these in terms of what the community as a whole needs if it is to flourish or even survive. Good world affairs are seen by premodernists, in the modernist context at any rate, as those that protect and promote the interests of their community. Bad world affairs are those that jeopardize the viability of the community and threaten its well-being. Since the ultimate value is attached to the group, the worth of modernist world affairs is assessed accordingly.

In modernist terms it is possible to offer world affairs itself in answer to the question: For what? World affairs are these world affairs. "World affairs" is the name we give to what states, firms, and individuals currently do on a global scale. This is the "why" of world affairs. We do not have to justify them. They are simply what has emerged historically in the perennial human struggle to make do and get by, and they warrant no further consideration in terms of reason or purpose or worth.

Few would want to leave it at that, however. Few would want to judge the reason, purpose, and worth of modernist world affairs only by such criteria as their capacity to prevail or "succeed."

Modernist world affairs, it is true, are able to sustain a huge planetary population, much bigger than was ever deemed possible before. Providing for this population is a continuing challenge, however. The worth of modernist world affairs is questionable, in other words, when judged on such instrumental grounds as whether people are fed and housed, clad and kept well, taught and justly treated, and allowed to develop a personalized sense of meaning and significance. A modernist might say that any alternative is bound to be worse. The most ardent modernists tend to come from the rich, Western parts of the world, however. They tend to be male. It is an argument that those not rich, Western, and male tend to find less convincing. The worth of modernist world affairs is also questionable when we consider their unintended consequences. Though many of these are highly commendable, modernity's very success creates problems that certainly tax and could ultimately overwhelm its best efforts to solve them. Modernity accelerates the play between our intentions and the unintended consequences of our (in this case, rationalistic) actions, and the everyday experience of ordinary people confirms the scale and pitch of the result.

Postmodernists tend to see modernist world affairs as radically reductionist. They see a limited range of rationalistic world affairs offered as universally valid and eternally desirable. Postmodernity makes it hard to argue for any other kind of world affairs, however, since postmodernists discern no firm ground on which to stand and say: "these are better world affairs than those."

Lack of such ground would seem to leave it to the mighty to define what is right in the world, which the mighty are perennially pleased to do. The issue of right remains unresolved, however.

What is right? The argument over this question never ends, since any absolute answer to it is obliged to assume only one kind of human being, and, in practice, there are different kinds of human being. Everyone embodies the different aspects of human nature to varying degrees. Choosing any one aspect would seem somewhat arbitrary, therefore, which is why modernist pluralism and postmodernist relativism both try to eschew any such choice. Given who we are (complex), pluralism and relativism are clearly preferable to modernist absolutism.

Given a whole world of deep differences, the argument for tolerating diverse moral purposes has its merits. It is not an argument that an absolutist would accept, and even the most tolerant of all find some moral purposes abhorrent and would reject them (though the grounds for doing so assume a hierarchy of values of the sort that pluralism and relativism actively eschew). As I said, the argument never ends.

Postmodernists also seek to prevent analysts of world affairs closing the discipline down around particular analytic languages. Deploring any attempt to do so, they seek instead to keep open the possibility of alternative points of view.

After World War II, for example, students of world affairs were preoccupied with diplomatico-military power. Realism was the dominant narrative of the day. Much was said about the attempt to reconcile the seemingly obvious "fact" of competitive state power with the "value" of cooperation.

Relatively little was said, however, about the mounting struggle for self-determination going on throughout the great European empires. There was little discussion in the classic works of IR realism, for example, of the claims to independence that were soon to radically reshape world affairs, quadrupling the number of states in the system and putting such issues as "economic development," rapid social change, and cultural imperialism on the global agenda. There was no discussion at all of the masculinist spin to world affairs, or of environmental issues, or of the hazards of extreme individuation.

While the most prominent analysts of world affairs did ultimately allow discussion of cooperative international strategies and of international political economy, liberalism supplied the preferred terms in which such issues were discussed. Little was said about the social dimension of the subject. The core commitment to scientific methodology was decreed nonnegotiable. And the voices of the marginalized remained unheard.

These terms are what postmodernists mean by closure. They warn against it and they deplore it, much to mainstream chagrin. Yet again it is worth recalling the role played here by the proponents of IR/IPE. They offer their partial descriptions of world affairs and their partial explanations of them in lieu of more holistic ones. They distort what they study to make it amenable to rationalist analysis. Their results help sustain a form of world affairs constructed of sovereign states and capitalist markets. It helps reinforce our sense of such constructs as tangible and inevitable. But it does so only by concealing the significance of IPS, WPC, and the margins modernity makes.

This is not an innocent role. It is justified in terms of the good that states do and the benefits that capitalist accumulation confers. Not everyone experiences states as good, however, or capitalist accumulation as beneficial. Indeed, the common sense of ordinary people can be more telling than the uncommon sense of analysts in this regard.

Similar comments can be made about IPS and WPC too. A priority placed upon the self is not universally meritorious. Nor is a high priority placed upon using reason. Many ordinary people do not, for example, want to be rationalistic and individuated, materialistic and secular. Many prefer to be intuitive and communal, idealistic and divine.

### The Experience of World Affairs

If we accept, as this book argues that we should, that there are limits to how we currently seek to know these world affairs, then what is to be done? Acknowledging the importance of analytic entanglement and of commonsense insight is not enough. We need to look at analysis and insight themselves. We need to look at the way the light of the mind not only illuminates but also blinds, how we might transcend the limits this light sets, and by nonanalytic means.

The alternative we seek, I would argue, is the conscious attempt to complement rationalistic enquiry with nonrationalistic enquiry or what, compared to analytic outlook, might be called nonanalytic "in-feel." It is to engage in participant research, personal narrative, direct experience, and any other form of understanding that is more closely involved. It is to take an extrarationalistic turn that allows us not only to objectify, but to subjectify as well.

Most rationalists are likely to see any such attempt as a return to emotive obscurantism. They are likely to see nonrationalism as far too akin to irrationalism for comfort. And they will not condone it for fear that their hard-won mental distance will be jeopardized by ways of knowing of little or no relevance to telling the truth.

They will continue, however, to fail to anticipate, even as one of a range of scenarios, future events of the same order of magnitude as the collapse of the Soviet Union. And they will continue to assist in skewing the study of world affairs in modernist ways.

World affairs studies that are basically skewed are world affairs studies that leave much unsaid. What is unsaid, however, may well be what we want to know. We may need to look where the key is lost, as the old story goes, and not where the light shines brightest. That is why, to quote Foucault, "[w]e must try to determine the different ways of not saying . . . things, how those who can and those who cannot speak . . . are distributed, which type of discourse is authorised . . . [and] which form of discretion is required" (Foucault 1990, 27). While rationalists would say that the "discretion" Foucault recommends is best gained by authorizing rationalism only, by standing back, that is, to look at world affairs as objectively as possible, what if standing back like this means knowing some things and not others? We cannot know if what we learn by rationalistic means is all that we can or should learn. Rationalism is part-knowing, after all. We cannot assume that we will be able to tell this way who is not able to speak and what they might say. Rationalism does not provide a comprehensive account of world affairs. Arguably it does not offer an accurate account of world affairs either.

Hence the case made here for complementing how we see from a distance, despite how natural or normal this may currently appear, with what we hear and experience standing close to listen and taking part. Other social studies—sociology and anthropology, for example—garner knowledge this way. We should do so too. We should supplement and complement our more systematic analyses of world affairs in a similar fashion. We should take what is no more or less than a constructivist turn. How else can we find out, not only the various facts of world affairs, but the feel of those facts as well?

# References

Addelson, Kathryn. 1994. *Moral Passages: Toward a Collectivist Moral Theory.* New York: Routledge.

Adler, Emanuel. 1997. "Seizing the Middle Ground: Constructivism in World Politics." *European Journal of International Relations* 3: 319 363.

Amaturo, Winifred. 1995. "Literature and International Relations: The Question of Culture in the Production of International Power." *Millennium: Journal of International Studies* 24: 1–25.

Anderson, Benedict. 1991. *Imagined Communities: Reflections on the Origin and Spread of Nationalism.* London: Verso.

Aristotle. 1946 (384–322BC). "De Poetica" in *The Works of Aristotle*, vol. 11, ch. 22. Oxford: Clarendon Press.

Ashley, Richard. 1984. "The Poverty of Neorealism." *International Organization* 38: 225–286.

————. 1988. "Untying the Sovereign State: A Double Reading of the Anarchy Problematique." *Millennium: Journal of International Studies* 17: 227–262.

Augustine. [1467] 1972. *Concerning the City of God against the Pagans.* Harmondsworth: Penguin.

Banks, Michael. 1966. "Two Meanings of Theory in the Study of International Relations." *Yearbook of World Affairs.* London: Stevens and Sons.

Barnet, Richard, and John Cavanagh. 1994. *Global Dreams: Imperial Corporations in the New World Order.* New York: Simon and Schuster.

Barrington-Moore, J.B. 1967. *The Social Origins of Dictatorship and Democracy.* London: Allen Lane.

Basil-Hart, James. 1992. *Part-Time Diplomacy for Fun, Profit and Prestige.* Port Townsend, WA: Loompanics Unlimited.

Beer, Francis, and Robert Hariman, eds. 1996. *Post-Realism: The Rhetorical Turn in International Relations.* East Lansing: Michigan State University Press.

Berger, Peter, and Thomas Luckmann. 1966. *The Social Construction of Reality.* Harmondsworth: Penguin.

Berki, R.N. 1984. "On Marxian Thought and the Problem of International Relations." In *Culture, Ideology and World Order*, ed. R.B.J. Walker. Boulder: Westview Press.

Berman, Marshall. 1980. *The Politics of Authenticity: Radical Individualism and the Emergence of Modern Society.* New York: Atheneum.

————. 1982. *All That Is Solid Melts into Air: The Experience of Modernity.* New York: Simon and Schuster.

Bernstein, Richard. 1983. *Beyond Objectivism and Relativism: Science, Hermeneutics and Praxis.* Oxford: Basil Blackwell.

Bleiker, Roland. 1998. "Retracing and Redrawing the Boundaries of Events: Postmodern Interferences with International Theory." *Alternatives* 23: 471–497.

Boas, Franz. 1938. *The Mind of Primitive Man.* New York: The Macmillan Company.

Bull, Hedley. 1966. "International Theory: The Case for a Classical Approach." *World Politics* 18: 361–377.

————. 1977. *The Anarchical Society: A Study of Order in World Politics.* London: Macmillan.

————. 1984. "The Emergence of Universal International Society." In *The Expansion of International Society,* ed. Hedley Bull and Adam Watson. Oxford: Clarendon.

Bull, Hedley, and Adam Watson, eds.1984. *The Expansion of International Society.* Oxford: Clarendon.

Burton, John. 1968. *Systems, States, Diplomacy and Rules.* Cambridge: Cambridge University Press.

Butalia, Urvashi. 1997. "Blood." *Granta* 57: 13–22.

Calhoun, Craig. 1997. *Nationalism.* Buckingham, UK: Open University Press.

Campbell, Gordon. 1998. "For Richer or Poorer." *New Zealand Listener* 164, no. 3039 (August 8–14): 18–21.

Carr, E.H. [1939] 1991. *The Twenty Years' Crisis, 1919–1939: An Introduction to the Study of International Relations.* London: Macmillan.

————. 1945. *Nationalism and After.* London: Macmillan.

Carroll, Berenice. 1972. "Peace Research: The Cult of Power." *Journal of Conflict Resolution* 16: 585–616.

Carse, James. 1986. *Finite and Infinite Games.* Harmondsworth: Penguin.

Checkel, Jeffrey. 1998. "The Constructivist Turn in International Relations Theory." *World Politics* 50: 324–348.

Clark, Grenville, and Louis Sohn. 1958. *World Peace through World Law: Two Alternative Plans.* 3d ed. Cambridge: Harvard University Press.

Clifford, James, and George Marcus, eds. 1986. *Writing Culture: The Poetics and Politics of Ethnography.* Berkeley: University of California Press.

Cohn, Carol. 1987. "Sex and Death in the Rational World of Defense Intellectuals." *Signs* 12: 687–718.

Comte, Auguste. 1875. *The Positive Philosophy.* 2d ed. London: Trubner.

Confucius. 1989. *Analects.* Trans. Arthur Waley. New York: Vintage.

Cottingham, John. 1984. *Rationalism.* London: Paladin.

Cox, Robert. 1987. *Production, Power and World Order: Social Forces in the Making of History.* New York: Columbia University Press.

————. 1995. "Critical Political Economy." In *International Political Economy: Understanding Global Disorder,* ed. Bjorn Hettne. London: Zed Books.

Descartes, René. [1637] 1912. *A Discourse on Method.* London: J.M. Dent.

Deudney, Daniel. 1996. "Ground Identity: Nature, Place, and Space in Nationalism." In *The Return of Culture and Identity in IR Theory,* ed. Yosef Lapid and Friedrich Kratochwil. Boulder: Lynne Rienner Publishers.

Deutsch, Karl. 1953. *Nationalism and Social Communication: An Enquiry into the Foundations of Nationality.* New York: John Wiley.

————. 1963. *The Nerves of Government.* New York: Free Press.

Devetak, Richard. 1995. "The Project of Modernity and International Relations Theory." *Millennium: Journal of International Studies* 24: 27–51.

Doyle, Michael. 1986. "Liberalism and World Politics." *American Political Science Review* 80: 1151–161.

Duara, Prasenjit. 1996. "Historicizing National Identity, or Who Imagines What and When." In *Becoming National*, ed. Geoff Eley and Ronald Suny. Oxford: Oxford University Press.

Earle, Edward Mead. 1986. "Adam Smith, Alexander Hamilton, Friedrich List: The Economic Foundations of Military Power." In *Makers of Modern Strategy from Machiavelli to the Nuclear Age*, ed. Peter Paret, Princeton: Princeton University Press.

Easton, Brian.1981. *Economics for New Zealand Social Democrats*. Dunedin, New Zealand: John McIndoe.

Elias, Norbert. 1991. *The Society of Individuals*. Oxford: Basil Blackwell.

Fairbanks, Charles. 1993. "The Nature of the Beast." *The National Interest* 31: 46–56.

Fingarette, Herbert. 1972. *Confucius: The Secular as Sacred*. New York: Harper Torchbooks.

Fiske, John. 1987. *Television Culture*. London: Methuen.

Flax, Jane. 1990. *Thinking Fragments: Psychoanalysis, Feminism, and Postmodernism in the Contemporary West*. Berkeley: University of California Press.

Foucault, Michel. 1984. "What Is Enlightenment?" In *The Foucault Reader*, ed. Paul Rabinow. New York: Pantheon.

———. 1990. *The History of Sexuality: An Introduction*. Harmondsworth: Penguin.

Frank, Andre. 1966. "The Development of Underdevelopment." *Monthly Review* 8: 17–31.

Frederick, Howard. 1993. *Global Communication and International Relations*. Belmont, CA: Wadsworth Publishing.

Frost, Mervyn. 1996. *Ethics in International Relations: A Constitutive Theory*. Cambridge: Cambridge University Press.

Fukuyama, Francis. 1992. *The End of History and the Last Man*. Harmondsworth: Penguin.

Gaddis, John. 1992/1993. "International Relations and the End of the Cold War." *International Security* 17: 5–58.

Gardner, Katy, and David Lewis. 1996. *Anthropology, Development and the Post-Modern Challenge*. London: Pluto Press.

Geertz, Clifford. 1987. "'From the Native's Point of View': On the Nature of Anthropological Understanding." In *Interpreting Politics*, ed. Michael Gibbons. Oxford: Basil Blackwell.

Gellner, Ernest. 1983. *Nations and Nationalisms*. Oxford: Basil Blackwell.

———. 1992. *Reason and Culture*. Oxford: Basil Blackwell.

———. 1994. *Encounters with Nationalism*. Oxford: Basil Blackwell.

George, Jim. 1994. *Discourses of Global Politics*. Boulder: Lynne Rienner Publishers.

Giddens, Anthony. 1990. *The Consequences of Modernity*. Stanford: Stanford University Press.

———. 1991. *Modernity and Self-Identity: Self and Society in the Late Modern Age*. Stanford: Stanford University Press.

Gill, Stephan, ed. 1993. *Gramsci, Historical Materialism and International Relations*. Cambridge: Cambridge University Press.

Gilpin, Robert. 1984. "The Richness of the Tradition of Political Realism." *International Organization* 38: 287–304.

———. 1987. *The Political Economy of International Relations*. Princeton: Princeton University Press.

Goodman, Paul. 1956. *Growing Up Absurd*. New York: Vintage.

Goody, Jack. 1996. *The East in the West.* Cambridge: Cambridge University Press.

Gramsci, Antonio. 1972. *Selections from the Prison Notebooks of Antonio Gramsci.* New York: International Publishers.

Gregory, Bruce. 1990. *Inventing Reality: Physics as Language.* New York: John Wiley.

Grotius, Hugo. [1625] 1925. *De Jure Belli Ac Pacis Libri Tres* ("The Law of War and Peace"). Trans. F. Kelsey. Oxford: Clarendon.

Guibernau, Montserrat. 1996. *Nationalisms: The Nation-state and Nationalism in the Twentieth Century.* Cambridge: Polity Press.

Haas, Ernst. 1958. *The Uniting of Europe.* Stanford: Stanford University Press.

Habermas, Jurgen. 1979. *Communication and the Evolution of Society.* London: Heinemann.

Harding, Sandra. 1986. *The Science Question in Feminism.* Ithaca: Cornell University Press.

Harre, Rom. 1979. *Social Being: A Theory for Social Psychology.* Oxford: Basil Blackwell.

Harris, Nigel. 1983. *Of Bread and Guns.* Harmondsworth: Penguin.

Harrison, Paul. 1980. *The Third World Tomorrow: A Report from the Battlefront in the War against Poverty.* Harmondsworth: Penguin.

Harvey, Elizabeth, and Kathleen Okruhlik, eds. 1992. *Women and Reason.* Ann Arbor: University of Michigan Press.

Hawkes, Terence. 1972. *Metaphor.* London: Methuen.

Hayek, Friedrich. 1991. "The Fatal Conceit: The Errors of Socialism." In *The Collected Works of F.A.Hayek,* ed. William Bartley III. Chicago: University of Chicago Press, 1991.

Heidegger, Martin. 1977. *The Question Concerning Technology, and Other Essays.* New York: Harper Torchbooks.

Hobbes, Thomas. [1651] 1957. *Leviathan.* London: J.M.Dent.

Hollis, Martin, ed. 1973. *The Light of Reason: Rationalist Philosophers of the 17th Century.* London: Fontana.

Hollis, Martin, and Steve Smith. 1990. *Explaining and Understanding International Relations.* Oxford: Clarendon.

Hoogvelt, Ankie. 1982. *The Third World in Global Development.* London: Macmillan.

Hopf, Ted. 1998. "The Promise of Constructivism in International Relations Theory." *International Security* 23: 171–200.

Huisken, Ron. 1989. "Nuclear Weapons: Making Do with (Much) Less." *Peace and Disarmament News.* Department of Foreign Affairs and Trade, Canberra, July.

Hull, Charles, ed. 1899. *The Economic Writings of Sir Wm Petty.* Cambridge: Cambridge at the University Press.

Huntington, Samuel. 1996. "The West Unique, Not Universal." *Foreign Affairs* 75: 28–46.

Hymer, Stephen. 1972. "The Internationalization of Capital." *Journal of Economic Issues* 6: 91–111.

Kahler, Miles. 1998. "Rationality in International Relations." *International Organization* 52: 919–941.

Kant, Immanuel. [1784] 1963. "What Is Enlightenment?" In *Kant on History,* ed. Lewis Beck. Indianapolis: Bobbs-Merrill.

———. [1795] 1963. "Perpetual Peace." In *Kant on History,* ed. Lewis Beck. Indianapolis: Bobbs-Merrill.

———. [1785] 1991. *The Metaphysics of Morals.* Cambridge. Cambridge University Press.

Kaplan, Morton. 1966. "The New Great Debate: Traditionalism vs. Science in International Relations." *World Politics* 19: 1–20.

Katzenstein, Peter, ed. 1996. *The Culture of National Security: Norms and Identity in World Politics.* New York: Columbia University Press.

Katzenstein, Peter, Robert Keohane, and Stephen Krasner. 1998. "International Organization and the Study of World Politics." *International Organization* 52: 645–685.

Keller, Evelyn. 1985. *Reflections on Gender and Science*. New Haven: Yale University Press.

Keohane, Robert, and Joseph Nye, eds. 1972. *Transnational Relations and World Politics*. Cambridge: Harvard University Press.

Keynes, John Maynard. 1926. *The End of Laissez-Faire*. London: Hogarth Press.

Kubalkova, Vendulka, and Albert Cruickshank. 1985. *Marxism and International Relations*. Oxford: Clarendon.

Kuhn, Thomas. 1970. *The Structure of Scientific Revolutions*. Chicago: University of Chicago Press.

Lakoff, George, and Mark Johnson. 1980. *Metaphors We Live By*. Chicago: University of Chicago Press.

Lapid, Yosef, and Friedrich Kratochwil, eds. 1996. *The Return of Culture and Identity in IR Theory*. Boulder: Lynne Rienner Publishers.

Latour, Bruno, and Steve Woolgar. 1979. *Laboratory Life: The Social Construction of Scientific Facts*. Beverly Hills: Sage Publications.

Lenin, Vladimir. [1916] 1985. *Imperialism, the Highest Stage of Capitalism*. Peking: Foreign Languages Press.

Lerner, Gerda. 1986. *The Creation of Patriarchy*. Oxford: Oxford University Press.

Levi-Faur, David. 1997. "Economic Nationalism: From Friedrich List to Robert Reich." *Review of International Studies* 23: 359–370.

Lindholm, Charles. 1997. "Does the Sociocentric Self Exist? Reflections on Markus and Kitayama's 'Culture and the Self.'" *Journal of Anthropological Research* 53: 405–422.

Linklater, Andrew. 1996. "The Achievements of Critical Theory." In *International Theory: Positivism and Beyond*, ed. Steve Smith et al. Cambridge: Cambridge University Press.

List, Friedrich. [trans. 1885] 1966. *The National System of Political Economy*. New York: Augustus M. Kelley.

Lloyd, Genevieve. 1984. *The Man of Reason: "Male" and "Female" in Western Philosophy*. Minneapolis: University of Minnesota Press.

Locke, John. [1690] 1894. *An Essay Concerning Human Understanding*. Vol. 2. Oxford: Clarendon.

Lodziak, Conrad. 1986. *The Power of Television: A Critical Appraisal*. London: Pinter.

Lukes, Steven. 1973. *Individualism*. New York: Harper and Row.

Mabbott, J.D. 1958. *The State and the Citizen*. London: Arrow Books.

Machiavelli, Niccolò. [1513] 1961. *The Prince*. Harmondsworth: Penguin.

Manning, Charles. 1962. *The Nature of International Society*. London: G. Bell.

Marcus, George, and Michael Fischer. 1986. *Anthropology as Cultural Critique: An Experimental Moment in the Human Sciences*. Chicago: University of Chicago Press.

Markus, Hazel, and Shinobu Kitayama. 1991. "Culture and the Self: Implications for Cognition, Emotion and Motivation." *Psychological Review* 98: 224–253.

Marx, Karl, and Friedrich Engels. [1844] 1959. *Economic and Philosophic Manuscripts of 1844*. Moscow: Foreign Languages Publishing House.

———. [1846] 1977. *The German Ideology*. London: Lawrence and Wishart.

———. [1848] 1975. *Manifesto of the Communist Party*. Peking: Foreign Languages Press.

———. [1852] 1962. "The Eighteenth Brumaire of Louis Bonaparte." In *Selected Works, Karl Marx and Friedrich Engels*, Vol. 1. Moscow: Foreign Languages Publishing House.

Mayall, James. 1990. *Nationalism and International Society.* Cambridge: Cambridge University Press.

Mazzini, Giuseppe. 1979. *Mazzini's Letters.* Westport, CT: Hyperion Press.

McCloskey, Donald. 1986. *The Rhetoric of Economics.* Brighton, UK: Wheatsheaf.

Merchant, Carolyn. 1980. *The Death of Nature: Women, Ecology, and the Scientific Revolution.* San Francisco: Harper and Row.

Mies, Maria, et al. 1988. *Women: The Last Colony.* London: Zed Books.

Mill, John Stuart. [1848] 1852. *Principles of Political Economy with Some of Their Applications to Social Philosophy.* 3d. ed. London: John W. Parker.

Miner, Horace. 1956. "Body Ritual among the Nacirema." *American Anthropologist* 58: 503–507.

Mlinar, Zdravko. 1992. "Individuation and Globalization: The Transformation of Territorial Social Organization." In *Globalization and Territorial Identities,* ed. Zdravko Mlinar. Aldershot, UK: Avebury.

Moffitt, M. 1984. *The World's Money: International Banking from Bretton Woods to the Brink of Insolvency.* London: Michael Joseph.

Morgenthau, Hans. [1948] 1972. *Politics Among Nations: The Struggle for Power and Peace.* 5th ed. New York: Knopf.

Morris, Brian. 1994. *Anthropology of the Self: The Individual in Cultural Perspective.* London: Pluto Press.

Needham, Joseph. 1954. *Science and Civilisation in China.* Vol.1. Cambridge: Cambridge University Press.

Neufeld, Mark. 1993. "Interpretation and the 'Science' of International Relations." *Review of International Studies* 19: 39–61.

Nozick, Robert. 1989. *The Examined Life: Philosophical Meditations.* New York: Simon and Schuster.

———. 1993. *The Nature of Rationality.* Princeton: Princeton University Press.

Nugent, Stephen, and Cris Shore, eds. 1997. *Anthropology and Cultural Studies.* London: Pluto Press.

Ogura Kazuo. 1993. "A Call for a New Concept of Asia." *Japan Echo* 20: 37–44.

Onuf, Nicholas. 1989. *World of Our Making: Rules and Rule in Social Theory and International Relations.* Columbia: University of South Carolina Press.

———. 1998. "Everyday Ethics in International Relations." *Millennium: Journal of International Studies.* 27: 675–676.

———. 1999. "Worlds of Our Making: The Strange Career of Constructivism in International Relations." In *Visions of International Relations,* ed. Donald Puchala. Forthcoming.

Oommen, T.K. 1997. *Citizenship, Nationality, and Ethnicity: Reconciling Competing Identities.* Cambridge: Polity Press.

Osborne, Peter. 1992. "Modernity Is a Qualitative, Not a Chronological, Category." *New Left Review* 192: 65–84.

Ourossoff, Alexandra. 1993. "Illusions of Reality: False Premisses of the Liberal Tradition." *Man.* 28: 281–298.

Owen, John M. 1994. "How Liberalism Produces Democratic Peace." *International Security* 19: 87–125.

Palan, Ronen, and Brook Blair. 1993. "On the Idealist Origins of the Realist Theory of International Relations." *Review of International Studies* 19: 385–399.

Peterson, V. Spike. 1994. "Gendered Nationalism." *Peace Review* 6: 77–83.

Peterson, V. Spike, and True, Jacqui. 1998. "'New Times' and New Conversations." In *The 'Man' Question in International Relations,* ed. Marysia Zalewski and Jane Parpart. Boulder: Westview Press.

Pettman, Jan Jindy. 1996. *Worlding Women: A Feminist International Politics.* Sydney: Allen and Unwin.

Pettman, Ralph. 1979. *State and Class: A Sociology of International Affairs*. London: Croom Helm.

———. 1997. "Communication and Information Exchange: State Sovereignty Affirmed or Under Siege?" In *State and Sovereignty: Is the State in Retreat?* ed. Gilbert Wood and Louis Leland. Dunedin, New Zealand: University of Otago Press.

Petty, William. [1671] 1899. *The Economic Writings of Sir Wm Petty*. Ed. Charles Hull. Cambridge: Cambridge University Press.

Polanyi, Karl. [1944] 1957. *The Great Transformation*. Boston: Beacon Press.

Postman, Neil. 1985. *Amusing Ourselves to Death: The Public Discourse in the Age of Show Business*. New York: Viking.

Rand, Ayn. 1961. *For the New Intellectual*. New York: Signet.

Randall, Vicky. 1987. *Women and Politics: An International Perspective*. 2d ed. London: Macmillan.

Rawls, John. 1971. *A Theory of Justice*. Cambridge: Harvard University Press.

Rescher, Nicholas. 1988. *Rationality: A Philosophical Inquiry into the Nature and the Rationale of Reason*. Oxford: Clarendon.

Ricardo, David. [1817] 1971. *On the Principles of Political Economy and Taxation*. Harmondsworth: Penguin.

Richardson, James. 1996. "Contending Liberalisms: Past and Present." Paper read at the convention of the International Studies Association and the Japan Association of International Relations, Makuhari, Japan, September.

Rosaldo, Renato. 1989. *Culture and Truth: The Remaking of Social Analysis*. Boston: Beacon.

Rosenberg, Justin. 1990. "What's the Matter with Realism?" *Review of International Studies* 16: 285–303.

Rousseau, Jean-Jacques. [1758] 1960. *Politics and the Arts: Letter to M. D'Alembert on the Theatre*. New York: Cornell University Press.

Ruggie, John. 1998. "What Makes the World Hang Together? Neo-utilitarianism and the Social Constructivist Challenge." *International Organization* 52: 855–885.

Rushkoff, Douglas. 1997. *Children of Chaos*. London: Flamingo.

Russell, Bertrand. 1979. *History of Western Philosophy*. London: Unwin Paperbacks.

Russell, Eric Frank. 1963. *The Great Explosion*. London: Dennis Dobson.

Russell, Marcia, and John Carlaw. 1996. *Revolution*. Auckland: Images Ink Ltd. Videocassette.

Russett, Bruce M. 1993. *Grasping the Democratic Peace: Principles for a Post–Cold War World*. Princeton. Princeton University Press.

Rutland, Peter. 1993. "Sovietology: Notes for a Post-Mortem." *The National Interest* 31: 109–122.

Said, Edward. 1978. *Orientalism*. London: Routledge and Kegan Paul.

———. 1993. *Culture and Imperialism*. London: Vintage.

Sapir, Edward. 1921. *Language: An Introduction to the Study of Speech*. Oxford: Oxford University Press.

Sartre, Jean-Paul. 1965. *Nausea*. Harmondsworth: Penguin.

Satris, Stephen. 1986. "Student Relativism." *Teaching Philosophy* 9: 193–205.

Schumacher, Ernst. 1973. "Buddhist Economics." In *Toward a Steady-State Economy*, ed. Herman Daly. San Francisco: W.H. Freeman.

Schuman, Frederick. 1948. *International Politics: The Western State System and the World Community*. 4th ed. New York: McGraw Hill.

Schwartz, Herman. 1989. *In the Dominions of Debt: Historical Perspectives on Dependent Development*. Ithaca: Cornell Univerity Press.

Shearing, Clifford, and Philip Stenning. 1985. "From the Panopticon to Disney World:

The Development of Discipline." In *Perspectives in Criminal Law*, ed. Anthony Doob and Edward Greenspan. Aurora, Ontario: Canada Law Book.

Shweder, Richard. 1984. "Anthropology's Romantic Rebellion against the Enlightenment, or There's More to Thinking Than Reason and Evidence." In *Culture Theory: Essays on Mind, Self, and Emotion*, eds. Richard Shweder and Robert Le Vine. Cambridge: Cambridge University Press.

Shweder, Richard, and Edmund Bourne. 1984. "Does the Concept of the Person Vary Cross-Culturally." In *Culture Theory: Essays in Mind, Self, and Emotion*, ed. Richard Shweder and Robert Le Vine. Cambridge: Cambridge University Press.

Smith, Adam. [1776] 1892. *An Inquiry into the Nature and Causes of the Wealth of Nations*. London: George Routledge and Sons.

Smith, Anthony. 1991. *National Identity*. Harmondsworth: Penguin.

Spegele, Roger. 1992. "Richard Ashley's Discourse for International Relations." *Millennium: Journal of International Studies* 21: 147–182.

———. 1993. "Deconstructing Globalism in International Relations." Paper read at the annual meeting of the International Studies Association, Acapulco, March. (Later published as "Is Robust Globalism a Mistake?" *Review of International Studies* 23 (1997): 211–239.)

———. 1996. *Political Realism in International Theory*. Cambridge: Cambridge University Press.

Spengler, Oswald. 1961. *The Decline of the West*. New York: Knopf.

Spiro, Melford. 1993. "Is the Western Conception of the Self 'Peculiar' within the Context of the World Cultures?" *Ethos* 21: 107–153.

Strassoldo, Raimondo. 1992. "Globalism and Localism: Theoretical Reflections and Some Evidence." In *Globalization and Territorial Identities*, ed. Zdravko Mlinar. Aldershot, UK: Avebury.

Strauss, Erwin. 1984. *How to Start Your Own Country*. Port Townsend: Lompanics Unlimited.

Swift, Jonathan. [1726] 1946. *Gulliver's Travels and Selected Writings in Prose and Verse*. London: Nonesuch.

Sylvester, Christine. 1994. *Feminist Theory and International Relations in a Postmodern Era*. Cambridge: Cambridge University Press.

Taylor, Charles. 1987. "Interpretation and the Sciences of Man." In *Interpretive Social Science: A Second Look*, ed. Paul Rabinow and William Sullivan. Berkeley: University of California Press.

———. 1989. *Sources of the Self: The Making of the Modern Identity*. Cambridge: Cambridge University Press.

———. 1991. *The Ethics of Authenticity*. Cambridge: Harvard University Press.

———. 1992. "Atomism." In *Communitarianism and Individualism*, ed. Shlomo Avineri and Avner de-Shalit. Oxford: Oxford University Press.

Thorp, Rosemary, and Geoffrey Bertram. 1978. *Peru 1890–1977: Growth and Policy in an Open Economy*. New York: Columbia University Press.

Thucydides. [416BC] 1945. *The History of the Peloponnesian War*. London: J.M. Dent.

Tickner, J. Ann. 1992. *Gender in International Relations: Feminist Perspectives on Achieving Global Security*. New York: Columbia University Press.

———. 1996. "Identity in International Relations Theory: Feminist Perspectives." In *The Return of Culture and Identity in IR Theory*, ed. Yosef Lapid and Friedrich Kratochwil. Boulder: Lynne Rienner Publishers.

Tilly, Charles. 1985. "War Making and State Making as Organized Crime." In *Bringing the State Back In*, ed. Peter Evans et al. Cambridge: Cambridge University Press.

Toennies, Ferdinand. [1887] 1955. *Community and Association*. London: Routledge and Kegan Paul.

Toulmin, Stephen. 1992. *Cosmopolis: The Hidden Agenda of Modernity.* Chicago: University of Chicago Press.

Toynbee, Arnold. 1957. *A Study of History.* Oxford: Oxford University Press.

Trainer, Ted. 1988. *Developed to Death: Rethinking Third World Development.* London: Marshall Pickering.

Treaty of Westphalia. October 24, 1648. <http: //www.tufts.edu/fletcher/multi/ historical.html>.

Triandis, Harry. 1995. *Individualism and Collectivism.* Boulder: Westview Press.

Twain, Mark. [1923] 1963. *The Complete Essays of Mark Twain,* ed. Charles Neider. New York: Doubleday.

UNDP [United Nations Development Program]. 1995. *Human Development Report.* Oxford: Oxford University Press.

Union of International Associations. 1997/1998. *Yearbook of International Organizations.* 34th ed. 4 vols. Munich: K.G. Saur.

Vasquez, John. 1995. "The Post-Positivist Debate: Reconstructing Scientific Enquiry and International Relations Theory After Enlightenment's Fall." In *International Relations Theory Today,* ed. Ken Booth and Steve Smith. Oxford: Polity Press.

Vico, Giambattista. [1744] 1984. *The New Science of Giambattista Vico.* 3d ed. Ithaca: Cornell University Press.

Waever, Ole. 1998. "The Sociology of a Not So International Discipline: American and European Developments in International Relations." *International Organization* 52: 687–727.

Walker, R.B.J. 1987. "Realism, Change, and International Political Theory." *International Studies Quarterly* 31: 65–86.

———. 1988. *One World/Many Worlds: Struggles for a Just World Peace.* Boulder: Lynne Rienner Publishers.

———. 1989. "Notes on the Coming Global Civilization Project." (Unpublished discussion paper.)

———. 1993. *Inside/Outside: International Relations as Political Theory.* Cambridge: Cambridge University Press.

Wallerstein, Immanuel. 1979. *The Capitalist World-Economy.* Cambridge: Cambridge University Press.

Waltz, Kenneth. 1979. *Theory of International Politics.* Reading, MA: Addison-Wesley.

Watts, Alan. 1989. *The Book on the Taboo Against Knowing Who You Are.* New York: Vintage.

Westen, Drew. 1985. *Self and Society: Narcissism, Collectivism, and the Development of Morals.* Cambridge: Cambridge University Press.

Whorf, Benjamin. 1956. *Language, Thought and Reality.* New York: John Wiley.

Wiarda, H. 1981. "The Enthocentrism of the Social Science [sic] Implications for Research and Policy." *Review of Politics* 43: 163–197.

Wight, Martin. 1978. *Power Politics,* ed. Hedley Bull and Carsten Holbraad. Leicester: Leicester University Press.

Williams, Raymond. 1983. *Keywords: A Vocabulary of Culture and Society.* London: Fontana.

Wolf, Eric. 1982. *Europe and the People without History.* Berkeley: University of California Press.

*World Survey on the Role of Women in Development.* 1989. New York: United Nations.

Wriston, Walter. 1992. *The Twilight of Sovereignty: How the Information Revolution Is Transforming Our World.* New York: Charles Scribner's Sons.

Yuval-Davis, Nira. 1997. *Gender and Nation.* London: Sage Publications.

# Index

**Ralph Pettman** holds the foundation Chair of International Relations at the Victoria University of Wellington. A graduate of the University of Adelaide, Dr. Pettman received his Ph.D. at the London School of Economics and Political Science. He subsequently taught and researched international relations theory, international political economy, and Asian Pacific affairs in Australia, the United Kingdom, the United States, and Japan. He is the author and editor of ten books, the most recent of which is entitled *Understanding International Political Economy, with Readings for the Fatigued.*